G. HERBERT'S

POETICAL WORKS.

# THE POETICAL WORKS

OF

# GEORGE HERBERT.

---

### With Life, Critical Dissertation, and Explanatory Notes,

BY THE

REV. GEORGE GILFILLAN.

---

WIPF & STOCK · Eugene, Oregon

Wipf and Stock Publishers
199 W 8th Ave, Suite 3
Eugene, OR 97401

The Poetical Works of George Herbert
With Life, Critical Dissertation, and Explanatory Notes
By Herbert, George and Gilfillan, Goerge
Softcover ISBN-13: 978-1-7252-9894-1
Hardcover ISBN-13: 978-1-7252-9895-8
eBook ISBN-13: 978-1-7252-9896-5
Publication date 1/29/2021
Previously published by James Nichol, 1853

This edition is a scanned facsimile of the original edition published in 1853.

# ON THE LIFE AND POETICAL WORKS OF GEORGE HERBERT.

"LIFE," it has been said, "is a Poem." This is true, probably, of the life of the human race as a whole, if we could see its beginning and end, as well as its middle. But it is not true of all lives. It is only a life here and there, which equals the dignity and aspires to the completeness of a genuine and great Poem. Most lives are fragmentary, even when they are not foul—they disappoint, even when they do not disgust —they are volumes without a preface, an index, or a moral. It is delightful to turn from such apologies for life to the rare but real lives which God-gifted men, like Milton or Herbert, have been enabled to spend even on this dark and melancholy foot-breadth for immortal spirits, called the earth.

We class Milton and Herbert together, for this, among other reasons, that in both, the life and the poems were thoroughly correspondent and commensurate with each other. Milton lived the "Paradise Lost" and the "Paradise Regained," as well as wrote them. Herbert was, as well as built, "The Temple." Not only did the intellectual archetype of its structure exist in his mind, but he had been able, in a great measure, to realise it in life, before expressing it in poetry. His piety was of a more evangelical cast than Milton's—his purity was tenderer and lovelier—he had more of the Christian, and less of the Jew. Milton ranks with the austere and sin-denouncing prophets of ancient Israel—Herbert reminds us of that " disciple whom Jesus loved."

Before, however, proceeding to analyse his character, and criticise his Poem, we have the facts of his life to record. " Holy George Herbert" was born in Montgomery Castle, Shropshire, on the 3d day of April 1593. This castle, afterwards levelled to the ground during the Civil War, was then the seat of an ancient, wealthy, and reputable family. His father was Richard Herbert, surnamed of Blakehall, in Montgomery, who sprang from a long line of knights. His mother was Magdalene Newport, the youngest daughter of Sir Richard Newport, of High Arkall, in the county of Salop. Like most of the mothers of men of genius, she was a remarkable person, distinguished by her wit, her " cheerful gravity," her godliness, her kind-heartedness, and her fond appreciation of her son. She was wont to say that, as the mother of seven sons and three daughters, God had given her Job's *number* and Job's *distribution*. George was the fifth son. The eldest of the family is well known as Lord Herbert of Cherbury—a title which he obtained, on account of his services when ambassador in France, from Charles I. He was a gallant and chivalrous man; but is now chiefly known by his book, *De Veritate prout distinguitur a Revelatione*, an argument against Revealed Religion—or, properly speaking, is remembered mainly for the memorable hallucination he has recorded in his preface.

George spent his childhood under the watchful eye of his mother, in the society of two of his brothers, and under the tuition of a chaplain. When he had reached the age of four, his father died. At twelve, he was transferred to Westminster School, where, under the care of Dr Neale and Mr Ireland, according to honest Izaak Walton, " the beauties of his pretty behaviour and wit shined and became so eminent and lovely in this his innocent age, that he seemed to be marked out for piety, and to become the care of Heaven and of a particular good Angel to guard and guide him." While at this school, he profited much in the learned languages, and especially in Greek. About the age of fifteen, he was elected out of that school for Trinity College, Cambridge, and repaired to that university in the year 1608. His mother, knowing well what nurseries of vice universities are, and deeply anxious that a promise so morally fair as her son's should not be blasted, recommended him to the special charge of Dr Nevil, then Master of the college and Dean of Canterbury, who provided him a tutor, and acted towards him like a second father. His mother had previously to this removed to Oxford, in order to give her eldest son Edward, and some of her younger children, the benefits of a university education. There she became acquainted with the celebrated Dr Donne, and an "amity," to use Walton's language, was begun between them, "made up of a chain of suitable inclinations and virtues,—an amity like that of St Chrysostom to his dear and virtuous Olympias." He was at that time a poor struggling man, with a wife and family, and she supplied him with funds, besides honouring him with her friendship. This admirable woman, after continuing twelve years a widow, was married a second time, to the Earl of Danby; and Dr Donne lived long enough to shed tears at her death, and to pronounce a funeral oration over her grave.

Meanwhile, George was pursuing a calm, pious, and diligent career at Cambridge. His mother's image seemed to hang up like a picture, in his still study-chamber, restraining him from vice, calming down passion, and smiling him on to labour. Even in the "morning of that short day of his life," he seemed to be marked out for virtue and to "become the care of Heaven." He was made Bachelor of Arts in the year 1611; Major Fellow of the college in 1615; and in the same year, when he was only twenty-two years of age, he became Master of Arts. It is notable, that during all his college career his principal diversion was music. This is another of the points in which he resembles Milton. While many of his youthful contemporaries were engaged in riot, or "assembling themselves by troops in the harlots' houses," holy George Herbert sate alone and aloft in his evening chamber, with a musical instrument in his hand, to the piercing call of which his own peaceful thoughts and the solemn stars of night appeared in unison to arise. Thus he "relieved," he said, "his drooping spirits, composed his distracted thoughts, and raised his weary soul so far above the earth, that it gave him an earnest of the joys of heaven before he possest them." The power of music has been felt by brutes and by brute-like men; but how far deeper is its influence upon prepared and holy spirits, on whom it does *not*, as on common mortals, "pour beautiful disdain," but in whom it awakens strange yearnings—dim delightful memories—obscure and mighty joys, which they may hereafter recognise in loftier stages of their existence!

By this habitual practice of the art of music did Herbert shield his young soul, at that period when the passions are strongest and most dangerous. Companions he had few— only Dr Nevil sometimes invaded his studious solitude, and cheered him by his company. He regretted afterwards that he kept himself so shy, and so much aloof, in deportment and in dress, from his inferiors in rank,—a regret in which we cannot share. His pride was, on the whole, a pure, and noble, and defensive pride. It taught him habits of deep self-communion, and enabled him to accumulate those materials whence he was afterwards to pile up the stately fabric of "The Temple."

In the year 1619, he was elected orator for the university. The duties of this office were various. We quote, from one of his letters, his own description of what he had now to do. "The orator's place is the finest place in the university, though not the gainfullest; yet that will be about £30 per annum. But the commodiousness is beyond the revenue, for the orator writes all the university letters, makes all the orations, be it to king, prince, or whatever comes to the university. To requite these pains, he takes place next the doctors, is at all their assemblies and meetings, and sits above the proctors; is regent or non-regent at his pleasure, and such like gaynesses, which will please a young man well." In this situation, highly honourable in itself, and especially to him on account of his youth, he spent eight years, and obtained universal credit for the taste, tact, facility, and felicity with which he discharged its duties. While acting in this capacity, "King Jamie," as he is often familiarly called, sent the university one of his pedantic books, entitled *Basilicon Doron*, and our hero was appointed to acknowledge the gift. He did so, in a Latin letter still extant, with so much elegance, such agreeable flattery, and with a mixture of conceits so suitable to James's capacity and taste, that he was delighted, made particular inquiry about the orator, and declared him to be the jewel of the university. George Buchanan or John Milton would not have told James, " *Liber hic vester summovet oceanum ambientem*, adeo ut qui non subjiciuntur ditioni, *eruditioni vestræ* obtemperent; *per hunc imperas orbi universo*, victoriæque gloriam absque crudelitate effusi sanguinis, delibas." But George Herbert, with all his excellencies, was, partly by temperament and partly by position, very much of a courtier, and held lofty notions of prerogative, alike in church and state. Hence, when the brave and witty Andrew Melville assailed the liturgy, ceremonies, and government of the Church, in divers bitter versicles, Herbert strained his genius and Latinity to reply, in the " Angli Musæ Responsariæ," to be found in some editions of his poems. He lavished not a little flattery, too, upon Prince Charles, and on Lord Bacon, the latter of whom became intimate with, and dedicated his translation of some of David's Psalms to, his " very good friend, Mr George Herbert." He included, also, among his warm friends, Dr Andrews, Bishop of Winchester, Sir Henry Wotton, and Dr Donne, who left him, at his death, a precious seal, bearing the figure of Christ crucified upon an anchor, with the inscription—*Crux mihi anchora*. During the first years of his oratorship, Herbert was far from idle. He studied Italian, Spanish, and French, very carefully, the more that he entertained the ambition of being made Secretary of State. Latterly, in the prosecution of this aim, and from love of the court life, he was seldom to be found in Cambridge, except when the king was there, and when panegyrics, eloquent and overdone as laureates' odes, were always forthcoming. His delight was in London. The king had given him a handsome sinecure of £120 a-year, which had once belonged to Sir Philip Sydney; and with this, and the annuity he had from his family, and the proceeds of his college and his oratorship, he, according to

Walton, enjoyed his genteel humour for clothes, and for court-like company, leaving one Herbert Thorndike to be his substitute at the university. It is curious to think of the author of "The Temple" as a fop, learned in varieties of velvet doublets, laden with alderman-like chains of gold, and profound in questions referring to the buckles and hose of the period! But it is as curious, and far more pleasing to notice, that his biographers and friends have never hinted that the purity he had retained at Cambridge in youth was lost in London in manhood. Often as in "The Temple" he accuses himself, his allusions seem rather to point to frivolities and vanities, than to faults or vices.

He was, however, subject to infirmities and illnesses of various sorts—now scorched by severe fever, and now threatened by consumption, and always worn out by the edge of intense study. His wit, he used to say, was like a "pen-knife in too narrow a sheath, too sharp for his body." This bred in him a strong desire to leave the university, to decline all study for a season, and to travel in foreign parts. To this, however, his mother, doubtless for satisfactory reasons, was decidedly opposed; and, with a spirit rare in grown-up children, he cheerfully submitted to her pleasure.

While Herbert, instead of travelling abroad, was dancing attendance at Court, and expecting promotion, two of his principal friends, the Duke of Richmond and the Marquis of Hamilton, died. They were followed to the grave by King James himself, and with him expired all Herbert's ambitious hopes. He retired to the neighbourhood of London, where, for a season, he communed with his own heart and was still. The question was, should he return to "the painted pleasures of a court, or enter into sacred orders"? He soon made up his mind to the latter step, induced partly by his mother's earnest wish, partly perhaps by disappointment and chagrin, but principally by a deep and growing sense of the vanity of earthly things, and of the grandeur and reality of the things above. He had come at last completely within the attraction of heaven, and all the rest of his short life was spent in revolving in narrowing circles around the great orb. No sooner had he formed the resolution than he proceeded to put it in practice. Within a year he was made deacon, and in July 1626 he was appointed Prebendary of Layton Ecclesia in the diocese of Lincoln. The church at this place he found in a ruinous condition, and his first step was to raise a subscription for repairing it. He succeeded, it is said, in making it a very gem.

In the year 1629, being thirty-four years of age, he was seized with a quotidian ague, and in order to remove it by change of air, he went to Woodford in Essex, where some of his friends, and his brother Sir Henry, were residing. There, in the course of a year, by following a strict dietary regimen, he was completely cured of the ague, although, in its place, a consumptive tendency began more decidedly to discover itself. In the sharpest of his fits he would sometimes cry, "Lord, abate my great affliction or increase my patience; but, Lord, I repine not; I am dumb, Lord, before thee, because thou doest it." His next remove was to Dauntsey in Wiltshire, "a noble house in a choice air," owned by Lord Danvers. Here, by spare diet, exercise, and avoiding all study, he became so well and strong, that he determined on two important steps—to marry, and to enter on the order of priest in the English Church. These had long been the two main wishes of his mother's heart, but she was not permitted to see the accomplishment of either, having died in 1627. At her death he had resigned his oratorship.

His marriage was singular and even romantic in its circumstances. He had a friend in Wilts, named Charles Danvers, who had a family of nine daughters, and who had often publicly expressed a desire that Mr Herbert should marry one of them, but especially his daughter Jane, because Jane *was his beloved daughter*. He had often spoken of the subject to Herbert, and often to Jane, so that she fell in love with him before she had ever seen his face, and he, it would seem, was very favourably disposed toward her. Her father, unfortunately, died before they met, but some friends procured an interview, and certainly Love never did his work in a more rapid and masterly style than on this occasion, nor did ever Marriage tread more closely on Love's heels;—in three days they were one, and Herbert might have boasted, *Veni, vidi, vici,* were it not that he had conquered long before he came. This princelike mode of courtship seems to have had a happy issue; Walton says, quaintly and beautifully, " The Eternal Lover of mankind made them happy in each other's mutual and equal affections and compliance, indeed so happy that there never was any opposition betwixt them unless it were a contest which should most incline to a compliance with the other's desires. And though this begot and continued in them such a mutual *love,* and *joy,* and *content,* as was no way defective; yet this mutual *content,* and *love,* and *joy* did receive a daily augmentation, by such daily obligingness to each other, as still added such new affluences to the former fulness of these divine souls, as was only improvable in heaven, where they now enjoy it."

Soon after his marriage, the rectory of Bemerton fell vacant, and, through the influence of the Earl of Pembroke, Herbert was presented with it. After many searchings of heart, he was, at last, on the 26th of April 1630, inducted into the pleasant parsonage of Bemerton, which is about a mile from Salisbury. He was in the thirty-sixth year of his age. At his induction he was, according to a custom then prevalent, shut up in the church alone and left to toll the bell; but as he stayed longer than usual, his friend Mr Woodnot looked in at the window and saw him lying prostrate in prayer on the ground before the altar, pouring out, it was found, passionate prayers for Divine aid, and ejaculating rules for the future management of his life—prayers which were heard, and rules which were rigidly observed. On the night of his induction he told Mr Woodnot that he was " sure to live well, because the virtuous life of a clergyman is the most powerful eloquence to persuade all that see it to reverence and love, and at least to desire to live like him. And this I will do because I know we live in an age that hath more need of good examples than precepts." On the third day after he was made rector, he exchanged his sword and gay clothing for a canonical habit, and returning to Bainton, where his wife's relations resided, he saluted his wife, and reminded her of the new position she now occupied, and of the new duties—particularly increased humility—which were now incumbent on her. Like a meek and brave disciple of Jesus Christ, she accepted, and afterwards fully sustained, the gracious burden her husband thus gave her to bear.

And now began a career of labour, so short, so sweet, and so splendid in its holy lustre, that we can best compare it to an autumnal day in the close of October, when the union of the softest of suns and the meekest of earths is as brief as it is bright and perfect, reminding us of that beautiful strain of the Poet himself—

> "Sweet day, so cool, so calm, so bright,
> The bridal of the earth and sky;
> The dew shall weep thy fall to-night;
> For thou must die."

He commenced his ministerial work, as at Layton, by repairing the church, the chancel, and the parsonage. He began, too, immediately to care for the poor, to visit the sick, and, in the grand, simple, immortal language of Burke, "to *remember the forgotten.*" He next bound himself by a set of written resolutions, which we find now condensed in his little book called the *Country Parson*, to perform his duties in regular system and series. His first text was, "Keep thy heart with all diligence;" and it soon became apparent that he meant it to apply to himself as much as to his parishioners. His first sermon was elaborate, flowered with many of his after "Temple" ornaments, and delivered with much eloquence. But he soon found that a rich feather does not always imply a strong wing, and that the force of a shaft is not always in proportion to the plumage which surrounds it. He became, as all true preachers become at length, much more practical and simple; he tried, too, to get his audience to *realise* the meaning of the English Church service; and, as it was said of Augustus that he found Rome brick and left it marble, so let Herbert have this praise, that he found religion in his parish an empty form, and left it an earnest reality. He gave his people a reason for every ceremony and form of their ritual,—he did something far more than this, he convinced them that *his* soul and heart were thoroughly in the service. He commenced the practice of catechising his flock every Sunday afternoon, and generally secured a full and attentive audience. His love for order and decorum led him to reprove nothing more severely than indecency of behaviour during the time of public worship. Along with his wife, and three nieces of his, and all his family, he went twice every day to church prayers, at the hours of ten and four, and " then and there lifted up pure and charitable hands to God in the midst of the congregation." This could not fail of producing an impression upon the neighbourhood; a great quiet revival of religion was the result. Most of his parishioners, and many gentlemen from the neighbourhood, constantly attended his chapel during week-days. Not a few let their plough rest in mid furrow, when *Mr Herbert's Saints' Bell* rung to prayers, and they are said to have found or fancied that when resumed it moved more briskly to the tune of the good man's blessing.

His main recreation continued to be music, and his joy in it seemed to increase as he neared the glorious region where it is married for ever to perfect holiness and bliss. In his own fine words, he now heard " church bells beyond the stars," and " *the sound of glory ringing in his ears.*" He composed himself many hymns and anthems, and set and sung them to his lute or viol. Not contented with singing these to himself alone in his morning garden, or in his still study, he walked twice every week to Salisbury Cathedral, that on the billows of its organ his soul might find a " nearer way to the celestial gate," and when he came back, would declare that he had found a heaven upon earth there. His life, indeed, at all times, seemed a piece of heaven. His charity was unbounded; his habits were severely simple; his affections flowed out in a perpetual stream of cheerful fulness upon all around him. He gave, through his wife, who was his almoner, a tenth of all his tithes to the poor of the parish. On one occasion, he found a poor man and his horse in great distress, the horse fallen, and the man unable to aid him; he put off his clerical coat, helped, good Samaritan-like, the man, received and returned his blessing, and arrived in Salisbury covered with mire, instead of in his usual clean apparel; but met the wonder of his friends, by telling the occasion, and adding, that the thought of what he had done would prove *music to him at midnight.*

During all this time, he had been at intervals composing the inimitable strains which now form " The Temple." The Temple of Solomon arose amid the sublimest silence; no axe or hammer was heard in its building: the Temple of George Herbert arose to the sound of the lute and the viol, for it would seem that many if not all its harmonious numbers, were sung aloud by the Poet to his instrument. The poem was not published till after his death, but seems for a considerable time before to have been his darling task, and one of the secret solaces which refreshed his spirit amid its manifold labours, and amid the symptoms which began to multiply, and to prove that his constitution was crumbling, and that " he was now ready to be offered, and the time of his departure was at hand." Consumption was the gentle messenger sent to conduct him to his Father's house, resembling a reluctant and lingering executioner, kissing, ere it killed, the heavenly man. He was at length confined to his house, or to the chapel adjoining it, where he continued to read prayers constantly twice every day, although very weak, till, at his wife's request, who observed this practice to be wasting and wearing him out, he resigned it to his friend, Mr Bostock, yet said he would continue " a hearer of them till this mortal shall put on immortality." By and by, he was confined to his couch, where one Mr Duncan, a friend of Herbert's friend Nicholas Ferrar (a man of remarkable piety and learning), found him lying spent to a shadow, but with a mixture of majesty and humility in his countenance and bearing which affected him to awe and tears. The same gentleman, returning after five days, found him still alive, but very much weakened. It was on this occasion that he seems first to have betrayed to any one the existence of his poem. Bowing down upon his bed of death, he handed a little volume to Mr

Duncan, and said, "Sir, I pray you, deliver this little book to my dear brother Ferrar, and tell him, he shall find in it a picture of the many spiritual conflicts that have passed between God and my soul before I could subject mine to the will of Jesus my Master, in whose service I have now found perfect freedom. Desire him to read it, and then, if he can think it may turn to the advantage of any dejected poor soul, let it be made public; if not, let him burn it, for I and it are less than the least of God's mercies." Mr Duncan, with the precious volume in his possession, had now to leave him, but his old friend Mr Woodnot came down from London, and during the three weeks which preceded his death never ceased to wait on him night and day, till he at last closed his eyes. He was, besides, visited and prayed for by all the neighbouring clergy, including the Bishop and Prebendaries of the Cathedral Church at Salisbury; and his wife and his three nieces were unwearied in their attentions. He was, we said, spent to a shadow, but was a shadow soon to *become a substance*, and he felt himself about to put on another house, a tabernacle not of this building. His conversation was calm, elevated, and heavenly. He told his friends, that all the joys he once valued, such as beauty, wit, music, and pleasant conversation, had now all past him like a dream, or as a shadow that never returns; he was now about to *make his bed in the dark*, but praised God that he was prepared. A number of similar expressions, glowing with hope and love, escaped his lips, till the bystanders began to think that his words were a cluster of roses fallen over the wall of heaven upon him ere he was ready to enter in. The Sunday before his death, he rose from his bed, called for one of his instruments, took it up in his hand, proceeded to play and sing—

> "My God, my God,
> My music shall find thee,
> And every string
> Shall have his attribute to sing."

And added a portion of his beautiful hymn, entitled "Sunday." "Thus," says Walton, "he sung on earth such hymns and anthems as the angels and he and Mr Ferrar are now singing in heaven."

On the day of his death, he said to Mr Woodnot, "I am sorry I have nothing to present to God but sin and misery—but the first is pardoned, and a few hours shall put a period to the second." Mr Woodnot reminded him of the good deeds he had done; he answered, "They be good works, if they be sprinkled with the blood of Christ, and not otherwise." After some severe struggles, and having requested his wife and nieces, who were weeping in extreme anguish, to leave the room, he committed his last will to Mr Woodnot's care; and then crying out, "I am now ready to die; Lord, forsake me not, now my strength faileth, but grant me mercy for the merits of my Jesus. And now, Lord, Lord, now receive my soul!" he breathed his last. May not every one take up the language of his biographer, and say, "I wish, if God be so pleased, that I may die like him"? It was the year 1633.

Thus, at Bemerton, for three years lived and laboured one of the most thoroughly Christian gentlemen that ever breathed. His piety had a primitive depth and simplicity, and his holiness was blended with mild and gentle elements. His was that "cheerful godliness" which Wordsworth less happily has ascribed to a greater than he. In person he was tall, straight, and thin; he seemed purged, resolute, and stripped, as one who was soon to join a spiritual company.

His poem, "The Temple," after some vexatious delay (in this also resembling the "Paradise Lost") on account of two lines which the licenser objected to—which were these—

"Religion stands a-tiptoe in our land,
Ready to pass to the American strand"—

was at last published in Cambridge—Mr Ferrar superintending the press—and became instantly popular. It was just an alabaster box of ointment suddenly broken, and its perfume, like ointment poured forth, spread near and far. By the time that Izaak Walton wrote the life of the author, twenty thousand copies of the work had been circulated. Since, the issue has been very large, and its reputation is still on the increase.

We come now to criticise "The Temple," although the term criticism applied to what is a bosom companion rather than a book may seem cold and out of place. We come, then, we shall rather say, to announce our profound love for the work, and to assign certain reasons for that love. We may first, however, allude to the faults with which it has been justly charged. These are, however, venial, and are those not of the author so much as of his day. He is often quaint, and has not a few conceits, which are rather ingenious than tasteful. Anagrams, acrostics, verbal quibbles, and a hundred other formulæ, cold in themselves, although indigenous to the age, and greatly redeemed by the fervour his genius throws into them, abound in "The Temple," and so far suit the theme, that they remind us of the curious figures and devices which add their Arabesque border to the grandeur of old Abbeys and Cathedrals. It was the wild, crude rhythm of the period, and had Herbert not conformed himself to it, he had either been a far less or a far greater poet than he was. Yet, though bound in chains, he became even in durance an alchymist, and turned his chains into gold.

Herbert has, besides, what may be considered more formidable faults than these. He is often obscure, and his allegorising vein is opened too often, and explored too far; so much so, that had we added a commentary or extended notes on "The Temple," it would have necessarily filled another volume nearly as large as the present. This the plan of our publication, of course, entirely forbids. We may merely premise these advices to those who would care to understand as well as read the succeeding poem:—1*st*, Let them regard it as in many portions a piece of picture-writing; 2*dly*, Let them seek the secret of this, partly by a careful study of the book itself, and partly by reading the similar works of Donne, Quarles, Giles Fletcher, and John Bunyan; 3*dly*, Let them believe in Herbert, even when they do not understand him; and, 4*thly*, Let them rejoice that the great proportion of the book is perfectly clear and plain, to Christians by experience, to poets by imaginative sympathy, to all men in general by the power of conscience, the sense of guilt, and that fear of the terrors and that hope of the joys of a future state of being, by which all hearts at times are moved.

Yet, Herbert, although his mind wrought in a superinduced atmosphere of mysticism, and although he is commonly classed with those whom Dr Johnson calls the metaphysical poets, was by no means naturally or generally a mystic. The form of his writing was sometimes dark and involved, but the substance and matter of it were generally clear. His views of religion, at least, seem to us to have been exceedingly explicit and distinct. He belonged neither to Paul (the metaphysical), nor altogether to Cephas (the ceremonial), nor to Apollos (the rhetorical), nor even, although he resembled him much, to John (that lovely flower on the breast of Christ), but to Jesus himself, whom he so often calls his "Master," and whom he loved with a love passing the love of women. Emphatically, he was a worshipper of Jesus Christ; and all his nature, and all his genius, spread out their full riches only to the magnet of the God-Man of Nazareth. His love to him amounted to a personal passion. It is said of Robert Hall, that in prayer he sometimes seemed absolutely to *see* Christ, and so probably it was with Herbert. But it was not the glorified Christ that he saw, so much as the pale sufferer at Calvary crowned with thorns, bleeding, forsaken, with his eyes full of a far look of love and sorrow, as they gazed down on his murderers, and with his lips now uttering the awful question to his Father, "My God, my God, why hast thou forsaken me?" and now asking heaven, earth, and hell, "*Was ever grief like mine?*" The atonement was his favourite doctrine, and how heavily does he lean all the weight of his hope upon the Cross!

Next to the person of Christ, Herbert's passion was the Church of England. Coleridge justly remarks, that fully to appreciate him, the critic must be "an affectionate and dutiful child of the Church, and from habit, conviction, and a constitutional predisposition to ceremoniousness in piety, as in manners, find her forms and ordinances aids of religion, not sources of formality." To these qualifications we cannot pretend. But although "constitutionally predisposed" to despise ceremony, we grant, that all the beauty which does exist in these rites and forms has been extracted by Herbert, and that he has added to them a supplemental interest, and shed on them the gentle glow of his own genius. The "Church," surrounded by its immemorial trees and quiet grave-stones, hung with its simple belfry, and with its spire peacefully pointing up like a finger to the sky, illuminated within by its painted and storied windows, with its altar, its communion elements, its rustling Prayer-books, its kneeling worship, its deep amens and devout ejaculations, its infants entering to be baptized like new stars to be "named of God," the white surplice of the priest, the solemn tones of the clerk, and the voice of the organ arising ever and anon, like an unearthly accompaniment to the devotion which it seems to gather up in folds of melody and to lift to heaven,—all this stands before us in Herbert's verse, as in the light of an autumnal day—a light which can not only beautify the decayed, and make solitary places glad, and withered leaves seem gold, but which can add a deeper beauty to the beautiful, can not only make the earthly spiritual, but the spiritual appear sacred, and the sacred divine. In what a spirit of filial affection does this Poet, looking to the "British Church," say—

> "I joy, dear mother, when I view
> Thy perfect lineaments and hue,
>    Both sweet and bright
> *Beauty* in thee takes up her place,
> And dates her letters from thy face,
>    When she doth write."

So far, unquestionably, he is correct. For if gorgeous but melo-dramatic and meretricious grandeur distinguish the service of the Church of Rome, and if that of the Presbyterian Church be marked by severe simplicity, approaching, in certain circumstances, to the sublime,—that of the Church of England has unquestionably more beauty why it should be desired. May we not conceive of, and shall there not yet be realised, a still better form of worship than any of the three, —better, because combining all their merits without their defects, the simple psalmody and unformal prayers of Scottish devotion, blended or alternated with the rich music and the outward reverence of the English, and relieved and beautified by a few of the pictorial glories which have exerted such power in the Roman Catholic service, and which might be redeemed and devoted to other ends?

"The Temple," looking at it more narrowly, may be viewed in its devotional, in its poetical, and in its philosophical aspects, which we may figure as its altar, its painted window, and its floor and foundation. First, as a piece of devotion it is a Prayer-book in verse. We find in it all the various parts of prayer. Now like a seraph he casts his crown at God's feet, and covers his face with his wings, in awful adoration. Now he looks up in His face, with the happy gratitude of a child, and murmurs out his thanksgiving. Now he seems David the penitent, although fallen from an inferior height, and into pits not nearly so deep and darksome, confessing his sins and shortcomings to his Heavenly Father. And now he asks, and prays, and besieges heaven for mercy, pardon, peace, grace, and joy, as with "groanings that cannot be uttered." We find in it, too, a perpetual undersong of praise. It is a Psalter, no less than a Prayer-book. And how different its bright sparks of worship going up without effort, without noise, by mere necessity of nature, to heaven, from the majority of hymns which have since appeared! No namby-pambyism, no false unction, no nonsensical raptures, are to be found in them; their very faults and mannerisms serve to attest their sincerity, and to shew that the whole man is reflected in them. Even although the poem had possessed far less poetic merit, its mere devotion, in its depth and truth, would have commended it to Christians, as, next to the Psalms, the finest collection of ardent and holy breathings to be found in the world.

But its poetical merit is of a very rare, lofty, and original order. It is full of that subtle perception of analogies which is competent only to high poetical genius. All things, to

Herbert, appear marvellously alike to each other. The differences, small or great, whether they be the interspaces between leaves, or the gulfs between galaxies, shrivel up and disappear. The ALL becomes one vast congeries of mirrors—of similitudes—of duplicates—

> " Star nods to star, each system has its brother,
> And half the universe reflects the other."

This principle, or perception, which is the real spring of all fancy and imagination, was very strong in Herbert's mind, and hence the marvellous richness, freedom, and variety of his images. He hangs upon his " Temple " now flowers and now stars, now blossoms and now full-grown fruit. He gathers glories from all regions of thought—from all gardens of beauty—from all the history, and art, and science then accessible to him,—and he wreathes them in a garland around the bleeding brow of Immanuel. Sometimes his style exhibits a clear massiveness like one of the Temple pillars, sometimes a dim richness like one of the Temple windows; and never is there wanting the Temple music, now wailing melodiously, now moving in brisk, lively, and bird-like measures, and now uttering loud pæans and crashes of victorious sound. It has been truly said of him, that he is "inspired by the Bible, as its vaticinators were inspired by God." It is to him not only the "Book of God, but the God of Books." He has hung and brooded over its pages, like a bird for ever dipping her wing in the sea; he has imbibed its inmost spirit—he has made its divine words " the men of his counsel, and his song in the house of his pilgrimage," till they are in his verse less imitated than reproduced. In this, as in other qualities, such as high imagination, burning zeal, quaint fancy, and deep simplicity of character he resembles that " Child-Angel," John Bunyan, who was proud to be a babe of the Bible, although his genius might have made him without it a gigantic original.

We might have quoted many passages corroborating our impressions of the surpassing artistic merit of George Herbert's poem. But the book, as well as the criticism, is now in the reader's hands, and he is called upon to judge for himself. We may merely recommend to his attention, as especially beautiful and rich, " The Church-Porch," " The Agony," " Redemption," " Easter," " Sin," " Prayer," " Whitsunday," " Affliction," " Humility," " To all Angels and Saints," " Vanity," " Virtue" (which contains the stanza so often quoted, " Sweet Day," &c.), " The British Church," " The Quip," and " Peace." Many more will detain and fascinate him as he goes along,—some by their ingenious oddity, some by their tremulous pathos, some by the peculiar profundity of their devotional spirit; and the rest by the sincerity and truth which burn in every line.

We have spoken of the philosophy of " The Temple." We do not mean by this, that it contains any elaborately constructed, distinctly defined, or logically defended system, but simply that it abounds in glimpses of philosophic thought of a very profound and searching cast. The singular earnestness of Herbert's temperament was connected with—perhaps we should rather say *created* in him—an eye which penetrated below the surface, and looked right into the secrets of things. In his peculiarly happy and blessed constitution, piety and the philosophic genius were united and reconciled; and from those awful depths of man's mysterious nature, which few have more thoroughly, although incidentally, explored than he, he lifts up, not a howl of despair, nor a curse of misanthropy, nor a cry of mere astonishment, but a hymn of worship. We refer especially to those two striking portions of the poem entitled " Man " and " Providence." The first is a fine comment on the Psalmist's words, " I am fearfully and wonderfully made." Herbert first saw, or at least first expressed in poetry, the central position of man to the universe—the fact that all its various lines find a focus in him—that he is a microcosm to the All, and that every part of man is, in its turn, a little microcosm of him. The germ of some of the abstruse theories propounded by Swedenborg, and since enlarged and illustrated by the author of *The Human Body, Considered in its Relation to Man* (a treatise written with a true Elizabethan richness of style and thought, and which often seems to approach, at least, great abysses of discovery), may be found in Herbert's verses. "Man," Herbert says, "is everything and more." He is "a beast, yet is or should be more." He is "all symmetry—full of *proportions, one limb to another, and all to all the world besides.*"

"Head with foot hath private amity,
And both with moons and tides."

"His eyes dismount the highest star
*He is in little all the sphere.*
Herbs gladly cure our flesh, *because that they
Find their acquaintance there.*"

"*Each thing is full of duty.*"

"More servants wait on Man,
Than he'll take notice of. in every path
He treads down that which doth befriend him,
When sickness makes him pale and wan.
Oh, mighty love! Man is *one world*, and hath
Another to attend him"

How strikingly do these words bring before us the thought of Man the Mystery! "What a piece of workmanship" verily he is! He is formed as of a thousand lights and shadows. He is compacted out of all contradictions. While his feet touch the dust, and are of miry clay, his head is of gold, and strikes the Empyrean. He is mysteriously linked on the one side to the beasts that perish, and has an affinity as mysterious, on the other, to the angels of God. Nay, inanimate nature itself claims "acquaintance" with this "quintessence of dust." The periods of his life bear a striking analogy to the seasons; his brain at times moves to the moon; his heart, as well as cheek, is coloured by the sun; his advancement as a species bears a distinct relation to the changes of the earth's surface and to its place in the heavens; he is the representative of the universe, has imbibed at once its glories and its glooms, has snatched from the star its fire and its mystery, and vibrates like the string of a harp to every breath of the great system with which he is indissolubly connected. Made in the image of God, and having notions of and aspirations after absolute perfection, he is, and in some measure knows himself to be, a vile sinner. Lord of earth, sea, air, and all their riches, he is a fretful, discontented, hating, hateful, and, on the whole, so far as his present life goes, miserable wretch. He is in one view a whole, and in another a yawning fragment; and, according to the angle at which you see him, resembles now a full moon, now a crescent, and now a waning orb. Able to " weigh the sun," span the fields of space, acquainted with the times and seasons of the heavenly bodies, full of " thoughts that wander through eternity," he is yet doomed to sicken, to die, and to have his low grave kissed, in scorn or pity, by the orbs whose spots he has numbered and whose eclipses he has foretold. Humboldt speaks of the Andes as including the world in their vast sweep, all climates, and seasons, and productions of earth being found between their base and their summit, between the ocean below and the hoary head of Chimborazo above; thus man rises from his dim embryo up to his grey head in age, touching, as he ascends, all conditions of being, and rising in parallel to all gradations of the universe, and remaining in each and all a mystery, having, indeed, all mysteries compounded and compressed in his one mysterious self. " When I consider the heavens," says David, " what is man?" But may we not with all reverence invert David's statement, although not his spirit, and say, " When we consider man, what (in grandeur, incomprehensibility, and terror) are the heavens?"

"For *us* the winds do blow;
The earth doth rest, heaven move, and fountains flow."

Many of Herbert's modern admirers, while quoting the rest of these verses on " Man," omit its last stanza, although it seems to contain the moral of the wondrous Fable he had told, the solution of the Great Riddle he had propounded. Man is in a great measure a mystery, because he has forsaken his God; he is a wondrous Palace untenanted by the only Being whose presence can fill the crevices, supply the deficiencies, occupy the vast rooms, glorify the gloomy places, explain the mysteriousness, and fulfil the destiny of the fabric; and whenever He shall return to it, Man's contradictions shall be reconciled, his controversies ended, all that is now ambiguous about him shall be explained, and while his microcosmal character shall continue, it shall assume a diviner meaning, and become as pure as it is universal.

> "Since then, my God, thou hast
> So brave a Palace built; O dwell in it,
> That it may dwell with thee at last!
> Till then, afford us so much wit
> That *as the world serves us*, we may *serve thee*,
> And both thy Servants be."

We need not dwell on his minor productions. His Latin poems we have decided to omit, as not calculated to interest the general reader, preferring, rather, to give his collection of " Proverbs," on account of their exceeding richness. We published, indeed, Milton's, but his was an extraordinary case, and *his* Latin poems stand in the very first category. We have, with former editors, annexed " The Synagogue," a poem written in imitation of " The Temple," by Christopher Harvey, which, in piety, if not altogether in poetic genius, forms a proper pendant to Herbert's works, and ranks to it as the " History of Tender Conscience " does to the " Pilgrim's Progress." Herbert has, besides, written a prose work, entitled, *The Priest to the Temple; or, The Country Parson,* full of childlike piety and pithy advice, bordering sometimes, indeed, on the superstitious, and sometimes on the austere. Altogether, there are few places on earth nearer Heaven, filled with a richer and holier light, adorned with chaster and nobler ornaments, or where our souls can worship with a more entire forgetfulness of self, and a more thorough realisation of the things unseen and eternal, than in " The Temple " of George Herbert. You say, as you stand breathless below its solemn arches, " This is none other than the house of God, it is the gate of Heaven. How dreadful, yet how dear is this place!"

# CONTENTS.

## THE TEMPLE.—

| | PAGE | | PAGE |
|---|---|---|---|
| Aaron | 183 | Hope | 124 |
| A Dialogue-Anthem | 178 | Humility | 67 |
| Affliction . . 40, 58, 70, 89, 97 | | Jesu | 113 |
| Anagram | 75 | Jordan | 52, 102 |
| An Offering | 153 | Joseph's Coat | 166 |
| Antiphon | 48, 92 | Judgment | 198 |
| A Parody | 194 | Justice | 95, 146 |
| Artillery | 143 | Lent | 85 |
| Assurance | 162 | Life | 94 |
| A True Hymn | 177 | Longing | 154 |
| Avarice | 74 | Love | 49, 200 |
| A Wreath | 196 | Love-joy | 118 |
| Bitter-sweet | 180 | Love unknown | 132 |
| Business | 114 | Man | 90 |
| Charms and Knots | 96 | Man's Medley | 134 |
| Christmas | 79 | Mary Magdalen | 182 |
| Church Lock and Key | 62 | Matins | 58 |
| Church Monuments | 61 | Misery | 100 |
| Church Music | 62 | Mortification | 98 |
| Church Rents and Schisms | 145 | Nature | 39 |
| Clasping of Hands | 164 | Obedience | 104 |
| Coloss. iii. 3, "Our life is hid with Christ in God" | 83 | Paradise | 136 |
| | | Peace | 127 |
| Complaining | 149 | Perirrhanterium | 3 |
| Confession | 129 | Praise | 57, 152, 165 |
| Conscience | 106 | Prayer | 46, 103 |
| Constancy | 69 | Providence | 118 |
| Content | 65 | Redemption | 34 |
| Death | 196 | Repentance | 43 |
| Decay | 99 | Self-condemnation | 179 |
| Denial | 77 | Sepulchre | 35 |
| Dialogue | 115 | Sighs and Groans | 81 |
| Discipline | 188 | Sin | 40, 59 |
| Divinity | 138 | Sins Round | 124 |
| Doomsday | 197 | Sion | 107 |
| Dotage | 175 | Submission | 94 |
| Dulness | 117 | Sunday | 72 |
| Easter | 36 | Superliminare | 19 |
| Easter-Wings | 37 | The Agony | 31 |
| Employment | 52, 76 | The Altar | 19 |
| Eph. iv. 30, "Grieve not the Holy Spirit," &c. | 139 | The Answer | 177 |
| | | The Bag | 157 |
| Even-song | 60 | The Banquet | 191 |
| Faith | 44 | The British Church | 110 |
| Frailty | 68 | The Bunch of Grapes | 131 |
| Giddiness | 130 | The Call | 163 |
| Good Friday | 33 | The Church | 19 |
| Grace | 56 | The Church-floor | 63 |
| Gratefulness | 126 | The Church-porch | 3 |
| Grief | 172 | The Collar | 159 |
| Heaven | 199 | The Cross | 172 |
| Holy Baptism | 38 | The Dawning | 113 |
| Holy Communion | 46 | The Discharge | 150 |
| Home | 108 | The Elixir | 195 |

xxviii                           CONTENTS.

|  | PAGE |  | PAGE |
|---|---|---|---|
| The Family | 141 | The Sacrifice | 20 |
| The Flower | 174 | The Search | 169 |
| The Foil | 185 | The Size | 142 |
| The Forerunners | 186 | The Sinner | 32 |
| The Glance | 180 | The Son | 176 |
| The Glimpse | 160 | The Star | 71 |
| The Hold-fast | 148 | The Storm | 135 |
| The Holy Scriptures | 53 | The Temper | 50, 51 |
| The Invitation | 190 | The Thanksgiving | 29 |
| The Jews | 159 | The Twenty-third Psalm | 181 |
| The Method | 137 | The Water-Course | 179 |
| The Odour | 184 | The Windows | 64 |
| The Pearl | 87 | The World | 82 |
| The Pilgrimage | 147 | Time | 125 |
| The Posy | 193 | To all Angels and Saints | 75 |
| The Priesthood | 168 | Trinity Sunday | 64 |
| The Pulley | 167 | Ungratefulness | 80 |
| The Quiddity | 66 | Unkindness | 93 |
| The Quip | 111 | Vanity | 84, 112 |
| The Reprisal | 30 | Virtue | 86 |
| The Rose | 187 | Whitsunday | 55 |

THE CHURCH MILITANT . . . . . . . . . . . . . 201
L'Envoy . . . . . . . . . . . . . . . . . . . . 209

MISCELLANEOUS:—

| New Year's Gift to his Mother | 211 | To his Successor at Bemerton | 214 |
| A Paradox, &c. | 212 | On Lord Danvers | 214 |

THE SYNAGOGUE, by the REV. C. HARVEY, M A.—

| A Paradox | 272 | The Church-warden | 243 |
| A Stepping-stone to the Threshold of Mr George Herbert's |  | The Church-yard | 219 |
|  |  | The Circumcision, or New- |  |
| "Church-porch" | 218 | year's Day | 255 |
| Church Festivals | 251 | The Clerk | 240 |
| Church Officers | 238 | The Communion Table | 234 |
| Church Utensils | 224 | The Curb | 277 |
| Comfort in Extremity | 268 | The Deacon | 245 |
| Communion Plate | 236 | The Dedication | 218 |
| Confusion | 270 | The Epiphany, or Twelfth-Day | 257 |
| Engines | 287 | The Font | 225 |
| Inmates | 273 | The Journey | 286 |
| Inundations | 282 | The Loss | 278 |
| Invitation | 267 | The Nativity, or Christmas-Day | 254 |
| Resolution and Assurance | 269 | The Overseer of the Poor | 241 |
| Sin | 284 | The Passion, or Good Friday | 258 |
| Subterluminare | 217 | The Priest | 247 |
| The Annunciation, or Lady-Day | 253 | The Pulpit | 231 |
| The Ascension, or Holy Thursday | 262 | The Reading-pew | 226 |
|  |  | The Resurrection, or Easter Day | 260 |
| The Bible | 229 | The Return | 281 |
| The Bishop | 249 | The Sabbath, or Lord's Day | 252 |
| The Book of Common Prayer | 228 | The Search | 279 |
| The Church | 221 | The Sexton | 239 |
| The Church-gate | 220 | Travels at Home | 285 |
| The Church-porch | 222 | Trinity Sunday | 265 |
| The Church-stile | 219 | Vows Broken and Renewed | 269 |
| The Church-walls | 221 | Whit-Sunday | 263 |

JACULA PRUDENTUM; or, OUTLANDISH PROVERBS, SENTENCES, &c. 291

# THE TEMPLE,

### AND OTHER POEMS.

# THE TEMPLE.

## THE DEDICATION.

Lord, my first fruits present themselves to thee;
Yet not mine neither; for from thee they came,
And must return. Accept of them and me,
And make us strive, who shall sing best thy Name.
   Turn their eyes hither, who shall make a gain:
   Theirs, who shall hurt themselves or me, refrain.

## THE CHURCH PORCH.

### PERIRRHANTERIUM.

Thou, whose sweet youth and early hopes enhance
Thy rate and price, and mark thee for a treasure,
Hearken unto a Verser, who may chance
Rhyme thee to good, and make a bait of pleasure:
   A verse may find him, who a Sermon flies,
   And turn delight into a Sacrifice.

Beware of lust; it doth pollute and foul
Whom God in Baptism wash'd with his own blood:
It blots the lesson written in thy soul;
The holy lines cannot be understood.
   How dare those eyes upon a Bible look,
   Much less towards God, whose lust is all their book!

Wholly abstain, or wed.  Thy bounteous Lord
Allows thee choice of paths : take no by-ways ;
But gladly welcome what he doth afford ;
Not grudging, that thy lust hath bounds and stays.
   Continence hath his joy : weigh both ; and so
   If rottenness have more, let heaven go.

If God had laid all common, certainly
Man would have been th' encloser ; but since now
God hath impaled us, on the contrary
Man breaks the fence, and every ground will plough.
   O what were man, might he himself misplace !
   Sure to be cross he would shift feet and face.

Drink not the third glass, which thou canst not tame,
When once it is within thee ; but before
May'st rule it, as thou list : and pour the shame
Which it would pour on thee, upon the floor.
   It is most just to throw that on the ground,
   Which would throw me there, if I keep the round.

He that is drunken may his mother kill
Big with his sister : he hath lost the reins,
Is outlaw'd by himself : all kind of ill
Did with his liquor slide into his veins.
   The drunkard forfeits Man, and doth divest
   All worldly right, save what he hath by beast.

Shall I, to please another's wine-sprung mind,
Lose all mine own ?  God hath given me a measure
Short of his can, and body ; must I find
A pain in that, wherein he finds a pleasure ?
   Stay at the third glass : if thou lose thy hold,
   Then thou art modest, and the wine grows bold.

## THE CHURCH PORCH.

If reason move not Gallants, quit the room
(All in a shipwreck shift their several way) ;
Let not a common ruin thee entomb :
Be not a beast in courtesy, but stay,
   Stay at the third cup, or forego the place.
   Wine above all things doth God's stamp deface.

Yet, if thou sin in wine or wantonness,
Boast not thereof; nor make thy shame thy glory.
Frailty gets pardon by submissiveness ;
But he that boasts, shuts that out of his story :
   He makes flat war with God, and doth defy,
   With his poor clod of earth the spacious sky.

Take not His name, who made thy mouth, in vain :
It gets thee nothing, and hath no excuse.
Lust and wine plead a pleasure, avarice gain :
But the cheap swearer through his open sluice
   Lets his soul run for nought, as little fearing :
   Were I an *Epicure*, I could bate swearing.

When thou dost tell another's jest, therein
Omit the oaths, which true wit cannot need :
Pick out of tales the mirth, but not the sin.
He pares his apple that will cleanly feed.
   Play not away the virtue of that name,
   Which is thy best stake, when griefs make thee tame.

The cheapest sins most dearly punish'd are ;
Because to shun them also is so cheap :
For we have wit to mark them, and to spare.
O crumble not away thy soul's fair heap.
   If thou wilt die, the gates of hell are broad ·
   Pride and full sins have made the way a road.

Lie not ; but let thy heart be true to God,
Thy mouth to it, thy actions to them both :
Cowards tell lies, and those that fear the rod ;
The stormy working soul spits lies and froth.
    Dare to be true. Nothing can need a lie :
    A fault, which needs it most, grows two thereby.

Fly idleness, which yet thou canst not fly
By dressing, mistressing, and complement.
If those take up thy day, the Sun will cry
Against thee ; for his light was only lent.
    God gave thy soul brave wings ; put not those feathers
    Into a bed, to sleep out all ill weathers.

Art thou a Magistrate? then be severe :
If studious ; copy fair what time hath blurr'd ;
Redeem truth from his jaws : if Soldier,
Chase brave employments with a naked sword
    Throughout the world. Fool not ; for all may have,
    If they dare try, a glorious life, or grave.

O England! full of sin, but most of sloth!
Spit out thy phlegm, and fill thy breast with glory :
Thy Gentry bleats, as if thy native cloth
Transfused a sheepishness into thy story :
    Not that they all are so ; but that the most
    Are gone to grass, and in the pasture lost.

This loss springs chiefly from our education.
Some till their ground, but let weeds choke their son :
Some mark a partridge, never their child's fashion :
Some ship them over, and the thing is done.
    Study this art, make it thy great design ;
    And if God's image move thee not, let thine.

## THE CHURCH PORCH.

Some great estates provide, but do not breed
A mastering mind; so both are lost thereby:
Or else they breed them tender, make them need
All that they leave; this is flat poverty.
   For he, that needs five thousand pound to live,
   Is full as poor as he that needs but five.

The way to make thy son rich, is to fill
His mind with rest, before his trunk with riches:
For wealth without contentment, climbs a hill,
To feel those tempests, which fly over ditches.
   But if thy son can make ten pound his measure,
   Then all thou addest may be call'd his treasure.

When thou dost purpose ought (within thy power),
Be sure to do it, though it be but small:
Constancy knits the bones, and makes us stour,
When wanton pleasures beckon us to thrall.
   Who breaks his own bond, forfeiteth himself:
   What nature made a ship, he makes a shelf.

Do all things like a man, not sneakingly:
Think the king sees thee still; for his King does.
Simpering is but a lay-hypocrisy:
Give it a corner, and the clue undoes.
   Who fears to do ill, sets himself to task:
   Who fears to do well, sure should wear a mask.

Look to thy mouth: diseases enter there.
Thou hast two sconces, if thy stomach call;
Carve, or discourse; do not a famine fear.
Who carves, is kind to two; who talks, to all.
   Look on meat, think it dirt, then eat a bit;
   And say withal, *Earth to earth I commit.*

Slight those who say amidst their sickly healths,
Thou livest by rule. What doth not so but man?
Houses are built by rule, and commonwealths.
Entice the trusty sun, if that you can,
   From his Ecliptic line; beckon the sky.
   Who lives by rule, then, keeps good company.

Who keeps no guard upon himself, is slack,
And rots to nothing at the next great thaw.
Man is a shop of rules, a well-truss'd pack,
Whose every parcel underwrites a law.
   Lose not thyself, nor give thy humours way:
   God gave them to thee under lock and key.

By all means use sometimes to be alone.
Salute thyself: see what thy soul doth wear.
Dare to look in thy chest; for 'tis thine own:
And tumble up and down what thou find'st there.
   Who cannot rest till he good fellows find,
   He breaks up house, turns out of doors his mind.

Be thrifty, but not covetous: therefore give
Thy need, thine honour, and thy friend his due.
Never was scraper brave man. Get to live;
Then live, and use it: else, it is not true
   That thou hast gotten. Surely use alone
   Makes money not a contemptible stone.

Never exceed thy income. Youth may make
Even with the year: but age, if it will hit,
Shoots a bow short, and lessens still his stake,
As the day lessens, and his life with it.
   Thy children, kindred, friends upon thee call;
   Before thy journey fairly part with all.

## THE CHURCH PORCH.

Yet in thy thriving still misdoubt some evil;
Lest gaining gain on thee, and make thee dim
To all things else. Wealth is the conjurer's devil;
Whom when he thinks he hath, the devil hath him.
Gold thou may'st safely touch; but if it stick
Unto thy hands, it woundeth to the quick.

What skills it, if a bag of stones or gold
About thy neck do drown thee? raise thy head;
Take stars for money; stars not to be told
By any art, yet to be purchased.
   None is so wasteful as the scraping dame:
   She loseth three for one; her soul, rest, fame.

By no means run in debt: take thine own measure.
Who cannot live on twenty pound a year,
Cannot on forty: he's a man of pleasure,
A kind of thing that's for itself too dear.
   The curious unthrift makes his clothes too wide,
   And spares himself, but would his tailor chide.

Spend not on hopes. They that by pleading clothes
Do fortunes seek, when worth and service fail,
Would have their tale believed for their oaths,
And are like empty vessels under sail.
   Old courtiers know this; therefore set out so,
   As all the day thou may'st hold out to go.

In clothes, cheap handsomeness doth bear the bell.
Wisdom's a trimmer thing than shop e'er gave.
Say not then, This with that lace will do well;
But, This with my discretion will be brave.
   Much curiousness is a perpetual wooing,
   Nothing with labour, folly long a doing.

Play not for gain, but sport. Who plays for more
Than he can lose with pleasure, stakes his heart:
Perhaps his wife's too, and whom she hath bore:
Servants and churches also play their part.
    Only a herald, who that way doth pass,
    Finds his crack'd name at length in the Church-glass.

If yet thou love game at so dear a rate,
Learn this, that hath old gamesters dearly cost:
Dost lose? rise up; dost win? rise in that state.
Who strive to sit out losing hands, are lost.
    Game is a civil gunpowder, in peace
    Blowing up houses with their whole increase.

In Conversation boldness now bears sway.
But know, that nothing can so foolish be,
As empty boldness: therefore first assay
To stuff thy mind with solid bravery;
    Then march on gallant: get substantial worth:
    Boldness gilds finely, and will set it forth.

Be sweet to all. Is thy complexion sour?
Then keep such company; make them thy allay:
Get a sharp wife, a servant that will lour.
A stumbler stumbles least in rugged way.
    Command thyself in chief. He life's war knows,
    Whom all his passions follow, as he goes.

Catch not at quarrels. He that dares not speak
Plainly and home, is coward of the two.
Think not thy fame at every twitch will break:
By great deeds show, that thou canst little do;
    And do them not: that shall thy wisdom be;
    And change thy temperance into bravery.

## THE CHURCH PORCH.

If that thy fame with every toy be posed,
'Tis a thin web, which poisonous fancies make ;
But the great soldier's honour was composed
Of thicker stuff, which would endure a shake.
   Wisdom picks friends ; civility plays the rest.
   A toy shunn'd cleanly passeth with the best.

Laugh not too much : the witty man laughs least :
For wit is news only to ignorance.
Less at thine own things laugh ; lest in the jest
Thy person share, and the conceit advance.
   Make not thy sport, abuses : for the fly,
   That feeds on dung, is coloured thereby.

Pick out of mirth, like stones out of thy ground,
Profaneness, filthiness, abusiveness.
These are the scum, with which coarse wits abound :
The fine may spare these well, yet not go less.
   All things are big with jest : nothing that's plain
   But may be witty, if thou hast the vein.

Wit's an unruly engine, wildly striking
Sometimes a friend, sometimes the engineer :
Hast thou the knack ? pamper it not with liking :
But if thou want it, buy it not too dear.
   Many affecting wit beyond their power,
   Have got to be a dear fool for an hour.

A sad wise valour is the brave complexion,
That leads the van, and swallows up the cities.
The giggler is a milk-maid, whom infection,
Or a fired beacon frighteth from his ditties.
   Then he's the sport : the mirth then in him rests,
   And the sad man is cock of all his jests.

Towards great persons use respective boldness :
That temper gives them theirs, and yet doth take
Nothing from thine : in service, care, or coldness,
Doth ratably thy fortunes mar or make.
    Feed no man in his sins : for adulation
    Doth make thee parcel-devil in damnation.

Envy not greatness : for thou makest thereby
Thyself the worse, and so the distance greater.
Be not thine own worm : yet such jealousy,
As hurts not others, but may make thee better,
    Is a good spur. Correct thy passion's spite ;
    Then may the beasts draw thee to happy light.

When baseness is exalted, do not bate
The place its honour for the person's sake.
The shrine is that which thou dost venerate ;
And not the beast, that bears it on his back.
    I care not though the cloth of State should be
    Not of rich arras, but mean tapestry.

Thy friend put in thy bosom : wear his eyes
Still in thy heart, that he may see what's there.
If cause require, thou art his sacrifice ;
Thy drops of blood must pay down all his fear ;
    But love is lost ; the way of friendship's gone ;
    Though David had his Jonathan, Christ his John.

Yet be not surety, if thou be a father.
Love is a personal debt. I cannot give
My children's right, nor ought he take it : rather
Both friends should die, than hinder them to live.
    Fathers first enter bonds to nature's ends ;
    And are her sureties, ere they are a friend's.

## THE CHURCH PORCH.                13

If thou be single, all thy goods and ground
Submit to love ; but yet not more than all.
Give one estate, as one life.  None is bound
To work for two, who brought himself to thrall.
    God made me one man ; love makes me no more,
    Till labour come, and make my weakness score.

In thy Discourse, if thou desire to please :
All such is courteous, useful, new, or witty :
Usefulness comes by labour, wit by ease ,
Courtesy grows in court ; news in the city.
    Get a good stock of these, then draw the card
    That suits him best, of whom thy speech is heard.

Entice all neatly to what they know best ;
For so thou dost thyself and him a pleasure :
(But a proud ignorance will lose his rest,
Rather than show his cards), steal from his treasure
    What to ask further.  Doubts well-raised do lock
    The speaker to thee, and preserve thy stock.

If thou be Master-gunner, spend not all
That thou canst speak, at once ; but husband it,
And give men turns of speech : do not forestall
By lavishness thine own, and others' wit,
    As if thou madest thy will.  A civil guest
    Will no more talk all, than eat all the feast.

Be calm in arguing : for fierceness makes
Error a fault, and truth discourtesy.
Why should I feel another man's mistakes
More, than his sicknesses or poverty ?
    In love I should : but anger is not love,
    Nor wisdom neither ; therefore gently move.

Calmness is great advantage: he that lets
Another chafe, may warm him at his fire:
Mark all his wanderings, and enjoy his frets;
As cunning fencers suffer heat to tire.
    Truth dwells not in the clouds: the bow that's there
    Doth often aim at, never hit, the sphere.

Mark what another says: for many are
Full of themselves, and answer their own notion.
Take all into thee; then with equal care
Balance each dram of reason, like a potion.
    If truth be with thy friend, be with them both:
    Share in the conquest, and confess a troth.

Be useful where thou livest, that they may
Both want, and wish thy pleasing presence still.
Kindness, good parts, great places are the way
To compass this. Find out men's wants and will,
    And meet them there. All worldly joys go less
    To the one joy of doing kindnesses.

Pitch thy behaviour low, thy projects high;
So shalt thou humble and magnanimous be:
Sink not in spirit: who aimeth at the sky
Shoots higher much than he that means a tree.
    A grain of glory mixt with humbleness
    Cures both a fever and lethargickness.

Let thy mind still be bent, still plotting where,
And when, and how the business may be done.
Slackness breeds worms; but the sure traveller,
Though he alight sometimes, still goeth on.
    Active and stirring spirits live alone:
    Write on the others, *Here lies such a one.*

Slight not the smallest loss, whether it be
In love or honour; take account of all :
Shine like the sun in every corner : see
Whether thy stock of credit swell, or fall.
   Who say, *I care not*, those I give for lost ;
   And to instruct them, 'twill not quit the cost.

Scorn no man's love, though of a mean degree
(Love is a present for a mighty king) ;
Much less make any one thine enemy.
As guns destroy, so may a little sling.
   The cunning workman never doth refuse
   The meanest tool, that he may chance to use.

All foreign wisdom doth amount to this,
To take all that is given ; whether wealth,
Or love, or language ; nothing comes amiss :
A good digestion turneth all to health :
   And then as far as fair behaviour may,
   Strike off all scores ; none are so clear as they.

Keep all thy native good, and naturalize
All foreign of that name ; but scorn their ill :
Embrace their activeness, not vanities.
Who follows all things, forfeiteth his will.
   If thou observest strangers in each fit,
   In time they'll run thee out of all thy wit.

Affect in things about thee cleanliness,
That all may gladly board thee, as a flower.
Slovens take up their stock of noisomeness
Beforehand, and anticipate their last hour.
   Let thy mind's sweetness have his operation
   Upon thy body, clothes, and habitation.

In Alms regard thy means, and others' merit.
Think heaven a better bargain, than to give
Only thy single market-money for it.
Join hands with God to make a man to live.
   Give to all, something; to a good poor man,
   Till thou change names, and be where he began.

Man is God's image; but a poor man is
Christ's stamp to boot: both images regard.
God reckons for him, counts the favour his:
Write, *So much given to God;* thou shalt be heard.
   Let thy alms go before, and keep heaven's gate
   Open for thee; or both may come too late.

Restore to God his due in tithe and time:
A tithe purloin'd cankers the whole estate.
Sundays observe: think when the bells do chime,
'Tis angels' music; therefore come not late.
   God then deals blessings: if a King did so,
   Who would not haste, nay give, to see the show?

Twice on the day his due is understood;
For all the week thy food so oft he gave thee.
Thy cheer is mended; bate not of the food,
Because 'tis better, and perhaps may save thee.
   Thwart not th' Almighty God: O be not cross.
   Fast when thou wilt; but then 'tis gain, not loss.

Though private prayer be a brave design,
Yet public hath more promises, more love:
And love's a weight to hearts, to eyes a sign.
We all are but cold suitors; let us move
   Where it is warmest. Leave thy six and seven;
   Pray with the most: for where most pray, is heaven.

When once thy foot enters the Church, be bare.
God is more there, than thou: for thou art there
Only by his permission. Then beware,
And make thyself all reverence and fear.
   Kneeling ne'er spoil'd silk stocking: quit thy state.
   All equal are within the Church's gate.

Resort to sermons, but to prayers most:
Praying's the end of preaching. O be drest;
Stay not for th' other pin: why thou hast lost
A joy for it worth worlds. Thus hell doth jest
   Away thy blessings, and extremely flout thee,
   Thy clothes being fast, but thy soul loose about thee.

In time of service seal up both thine eyes,
And send them to thy heart; that spying sin,
They may weep out the stains by them did rise:
Those doors being shut, all by the ear comes in.
   Who marks in church-time others' symmetry,
   Makes all their beauty his deformity.

Let vain or busy thoughts have there no part:
Bring not thy plough, thy plots, thy pleasures thither.
Christ purged his temple; so must thou thy heart.
All worldly thoughts are but thieves met together
   To cozen thee. Look to thy actions well;
   For Churches either are our heaven or hell.

Judge not the preacher; for he is thy Judge:
If thou mislike him, thou conceivest him not.
God calleth preaching folly. Do not grudge
To pick out treasures from an earthen pot.
   The worst speak something good: if all want sense,
   God takes a text, and preacheth patience.

He that gets patience, and the blessing which
Preachers conclude with, hath not lost his pains.
He that by being at Church escapes the ditch,
Which he might fall in by companions, gains.
   He that loves God's abode, and to combine
   With saints on earth, shall one day with them shine.

Jest not at preachers' language, or expression :
How know'st thou, but thy sins made him miscarry ?
Then turn thy faults and his into confession :
God sent him, whatsoe'er he be : O tarry,
   And love him for his Master : his condition,
   Though it be ill, makes him no ill Physician.

None shall in hell such bitter pangs endure
As those, who mock at God's way of salvation.
Whom oil and balsams kill, what salve can cure ?
They drink with greediness a full damnation.
   The Jews refused thunder ; and we, folly.
   Though God do hedge us in, yet who is holy ?

Sum up at night, what thou hast done by day ;
And in the morning, what thou hast to do.
Dress and undress thy soul : mark the decay
And growth of it : if with thy watch, that too
   Be down, then wind up both ; since we shall be
   Most surely judged, make thy accounts agree.

In brief, acquit thee bravely ; play the man.
Look not on pleasures as they come, but go.
Defer not the least virtue : life's poor span
Make not an ell, by trifling in thy woe.
   If thou do ill, the joy fades, not the pains :
   If well, the pain doth fade, the joy remains.

## THE CHURCH.

### SUPERLIMINARE.

Thou, whom the former precepts have
Sprinkled and taught, how to behave
Thyself in Church ; approach, and taste
The Church's mystical repast.

Avoid profaneness ; come not here :
Nothing but holy, pure, and clear,
Or that which groaneth to be so,
May at his peril further go.

### THE ALTAR.

A broken Altar, Lord, thy servant rears,
Made of a heart, and cemented with tears :
  Whose parts are as thy hand did frame ;
  No workman's tool hath touch'd the same.
      A Heart alone
      Is such a stone,
      As nothing but
      Thy power doth cut.
      Wherefore each part
      Of my hard heart
      Meets in this frame,
      To praise thy name :
  That, if I chance to hold my peace,
  These stones to praise thee may not cease.
O let thy blessed Sacrifice be mine,
And sanctify this Altar to be thine.

## THE SACRIFICE.

*O all ye, who pass by,* whose eyes and mind
To worldly things are sharp, but to me blind;
To me, who took eyes that I might you find:
    *Was ever grief like mine?*

The Princes of my people make a head
Against their Maker: they do wish me dead,
Who cannot wish, except I give them bread:
    *Was ever grief like mine?*

Without me each one, who doth now me brave,
Had to this day been an Egyptian slave.
They use that power against me, which I gave:
    *Was ever grief like mine?*

Mine own Apostle, who the bag did bear,
Though he had all I had, did not forbear
To sell me also, and to put me there:
    *Was ever grief like mine?*

For thirty pence he did my death devise,
Who at three hundred did the ointment prize,
Not half so sweet as my sweet sacrifice:
    *Was ever grief like mine?*

Therefore my soul melts, and my heart's dear treasure
Drops blood (the only beads) my words to measure:
*O let this cup pass, if it be thy pleasure:*
    *Was ever grief like mine?*

## THE CHURCH.

These drops being temper'd with a sinner's tears,
A balsam are for both the Hemispheres,
Curing all wounds, but mine ; all, but my fears.
     *Was ever grief like mine ?*

Yet my Disciples sleep : I cannot gain
One hour of watching ; but their drowsy brain
Comforts not me, and doth my doctrine stain :
     *Was ever grief like mine ?*

Arise, arise, they come ! Look how they run !
Alas ! what haste they make to be undone !
How with their lanterns do they seek the sun !
     *Was ever grief like mine ?*

With clubs and staves they seek me, as a thief,
Who am the way of truth, the true relief,
Most true to those who are my greatest grief :
     *Was ever grief like mine ?*

Judas, dost thou betray me with a kiss ?
Canst thou find hell about my lips ? and miss
Of life, just at the gates of life and bliss ?
     *Was ever grief like mine ?*

See, they lay hold on me, not with the hands
Of faith, but fury ; yet at their commands
I suffer binding, who have loosed their bands :
     *Was ever grief like mine ?*

All my Disciples fly ; fear puts a bar
Betwixt my friends and me. They leave the star,
That brought the wise men of the East from far :
     *Was ever grief like mine ?*

## THE TEMPLE.

Then from one ruler to another bound
They lead me : urging, that it was not sound
What I taught :   Comments would the text confound.
     *Was ever grief like mine?*

The Priests and Rulers all false witness seek
'Gainst him, who seeks not life, but is the meek
And ready Paschal Lamb of this great week :
     *Was ever grief like mine?*

Then they accuse me of great blasphemy,
That I did thrust into the Deity,
Who never thought that any robbery :
     *Was ever grief like mine ?*

Some said, that I the Temple to the floor
In three days razed, and raised as before.
Why, he that built the world can do much more :
     *Was ever grief like mine ?*

Then they condemn me all with that same breath,
Which I do give them daily, unto death.
Thus Adam my first breathing rendereth :
     *Was ever grief like mine ?*

They bind, and lead me unto Herod : he
Sends me to Pilate.   This makes them agree ;
But yet their friendship is my enmity.
     *Was ever grief like mine ?*

Herod and all his bands do set me light,
Who teach all hands to war, fingers to fight,
And only am the Lord of hosts and might.
     *Was ever grief like mine ?*

Herod in judgment sits, while I do stand;
Examines me with a censorious hand:
I him obey, who all things else command:
    *Was ever grief like mine?*

The Jews accuse me with despitefulness;
And vying malice with my gentleness,
Pick quarrels with their only happiness:
    *Was ever grief like mine?*

I answer nothing, but with patience prove
If stony hearts will melt with gentle love.
But who does hawk at eagles with a dove?
    *Was ever grief like mine?*

My silence rather doth augment their cry;
My dove doth back into my bosom fly,
Because the raging waters still are high:
    *Was ever grief like mine?*

Hark how they cry aloud still, *Crucify:*
*It is not fit he live a day,* they cry,
Who cannot live less than eternally:
    *Was ever grief like mine?*

Pilate a stranger holdeth off; but they,
Mine own dear people, cry, *Away, away,*
With noises confused frighting the day:
    *Was ever grief like mine?*

Yet still they shout, and cry, and stop their ears,
Putting my life among their sins and fears,
And therefore with *my blood on them and theirs:*
    *Was ever grief like mine?*

See how spite cankers things. These words aright
Used, and wish'd, are the whole world's light:
But honey is their gall, brightness their night:
    *Was ever grief like mine?*

They choose a murderer, and all agree
In him to do themselves a courtesy;
For it was their own cause who killed me:
    *Was ever grief like mine?*

And a seditious murderer he was:
But I the Prince of Peace; peace that doth pass
All understanding, more than heaven doth glass:
    *Was ever grief like mine?*

Why, Cæsar is their only King, not I:
He clave the stony rock, when they were dry;
But surely not their hearts, as I well try:
    *Was ever grief like mine?*

Ah, how they scourge me! yet my tenderness
Doubles each lash: and yet their bitterness
Winds up my grief to a mysteriousness:
    *Was ever grief like mine?*

They buffet me, and box me as they list,
Who grasp the earth and heaven with my fist,
And never yet, whom I would punish, miss'd:
    *Was ever grief like mine?*

Behold, they spit on me in scornful wise;
Who with my spittle gave the blind man eyes,
Leaving his blindness to mine enemies:
    *Was ever grief like mine?*

## THE CHURCH.

My face they cover, though it be divine.
As Moses' face was veiled, so is mine,
Lest on their double-dark souls either shine :
    *Was ever grief like mine ?*

Servants and abjects flout me ; they are witty :
*Now prophesy who strikes thee,* is their ditty.
So they in me deny themselves all pity :
    *Was ever grief like mine ?*

And now I am deliver'd unto death,
Which each one calls for so with utmost breath,
That he before me well-nigh suffereth :
    *Was ever grief like mine ?*

Weep not, dear friends, since I for both have wept,
When all my tears were blood, the while you slept :
Your tears for your own fortunes should be kept :
    *Was ever grief like mine ?*

The soldiers lead me to the common hall ;
There they deride me, they abuse me all :
Yet for twelve heavenly legions I could call :
    *Was ever grief like mine ?*

Then with a scarlet robe they me array ;
Which shows my blood to be the only way,
And cordial left to repair man's decay :
    *Was ever grief like mine ?*

Then on my head a crown of thorns I wear ;
For these are all the grapes Sion doth bear,
Though I my vine planted and water'd there :
    *Was ever grief like mine ?*

So sits the earth's great curse in Adam's fall
Upon my head; so I remove it all
From th' earth unto my brows, and bear the thrall:
          *Was ever grief like mine?*

Then with the reed they gave to me before,
They strike my head, the rock from whence all store
Of heavenly blessings issue evermore:
          *Was ever grief like mine?*

They bow their knees to me, and cry, *Hail, King:*
Whatever scoffs or scornfulness can bring,
I am the floor, the sink, where they it fling:
          *Was ever grief like mine?*

Yet since man's sceptres are as frail as reeds,
And thorny all their crowns, bloody their weeds;
I, who am Truth, turn into truth their deeds:
          *Was ever grief like mine?*

The soldiers also spit upon that face
Which Angels did desire to have the grace,
And Prophets once to see, but found no place:
          *Was ever grief like mine?*

Thus trimmed, forth they bring me to the rout,
Who *Crucify him,* cry with one strong shout.
God holds his peace at man, and man cries out:
          *Was ever grief like mine?*

They lead me in once more, and putting then
Mine own clothes on, they lead me out again.
Whom devils fly, thus is he toss'd of men:
          *Was ever grief like mine?*

And now weary of sport, glad to engross
All spite in one, counting my life their loss,
They carry me to my most bitter cross :
    *Was ever grief like mine?*

My cross I bear myself, until I faint :
Then Simon bears it for me by constraint,
The decreed burden of each mortal Saint :
    *Was ever grief like mine?*

*O all ye who pass by, behold and see :*
Man stole the fruit, but I must climb the tree ;
The tree of life to all, but only me :
    *Was ever grief like mine?*

Lo, here I hang, charged with a world of sin,
The greater world o' the two ; for that came in
By words, but this by sorrow I must win :
    *Was ever grief like mine?*

Such sorrow, as if sinful man could feel,
Or feel his part, he would not cease to kneel,
Till all were melted, though he were all steel.
    *Was ever grief like mine?*

But, *O my God, my God!* why leavest thou me,
The Son, in whom thou dost delight to be ?
*My God, my God* ————
    *Never was grief like mine.*

Shame tears my soul, my body many a wound ;
Sharp nails pierce this, but sharper that confound ;
Reproaches, which are free, while I am bound :
    *Was ever grief like mine?*

Now heal thyself, Physician ; now come down.
Alas ! I do so, when I left my crown
And Father's smile for you, to feel his frown :
                *Was ever grief like mine ?*

In healing not myself, there doth consist
All that salvation, which ye now resist ;
Your safety in my sickness doth subsist :
                *Was ever grief like mine ?*

Betwixt two thieves I spend my utmost breath,
As he that for some robbery suffereth.
Alas ! what have I stolen from you ? death :
                *Was ever grief like mine ?*

A king my title is, prefix'd on high ;
Yet by my subjects I'm condemn'd to die
A servile death in servile company :
                *Was ever grief like mine ?*

They gave me vinegar mingled with gall,
But more with malice : yet, when they did call,
With Manna, Angels' food, I fed them all :
                *Was ever grief like mine ?*

They part my garments, and by lot dispose
My coat, the type of love, which once cured those
Who sought for help, never malicious foes :
                *Was ever grief like mine ?*

Nay, after death their spite shall further go ;
For they will pierce my side, I full well know ;
That as sin came, so Sacraments might flow :
                *Was ever grief like mine ?*

But now I die ; now all is finished.
My woe, man's weal: and now I bow my head:
Only let others say, when I am dead,
              *Never was grief like mine.*

## THE THANKSGIVING.

O KING of grief! (a title strange, yet true,
    To thee of all kings only due)
O King of wounds! how shall I grieve for thee,
    Who in all grief preventest me?
Shall I weep blood? why, thou hast wept such store,
    That all thy body was one door. .
Shall I be scourged, flouted, boxed, sold?
    'Tis but to tell the tale is told.
*My God, my God, why dost thou part from me ?*
    Was such a grief as cannot be.
Shall I then sing, skipping, thy doleful story,
    And side with thy triumphant glory?
Shall thy strokes be my stroking? thorns, my flower?
    Thy rod, my posie? cross, my bower?
But how then shall I imitate thee, and
    Copy thy fair, though bloody hand?
Surely I will revenge me on thy love,
    And try who shall victorious prove.
If thou dost give me wealth ; I will restore
    All back unto thee by the poor.
If thou dost give me honour ; men shall see,
    The honour doth belong to thee.
I will not marry ; or, if she be mine,
    She and her children shall be thine.
My bosom-friend, if he blaspheme thy name,
    I will tear thence his love and fame.

One half of me being gone, the rest I give
    Unto some Chapel, die or live.
As for thy passion—but of that anon,
    When with the other I have done.
For thy predestination, I'll contrive,
    That three years hence, if I survive,
I'll build a spital, or mend common ways,
    But mend my own without delays.
Then I will use the works of thy creation,
    As if I used them but for fashion.
The world and I will quarrel; and the year
    Shall not perceive, that I am here.
My music shall find thee, and every string
    Shall have his attribute to sing;
That altogether may accord in thee,
    And prove one God, one harmony.
If thou shalt give me wit, it shall appear,
    If thou hast given it me, 'tis here.
Nay, I will read thy book, and never move
    Till I have found therein thy love;
Thy art of love, which I'll turn back on thee,
    O my dear Saviour, Victory!
Then for thy passion—I will do for that—
    Alas! my God, I know not what.

## THE REPRISAL.

I HAVE consider'd it, and find
There is no dealing with thy mighty passion:
For though I die for thee, I am behind;
    My sins deserve the condemnation.

O make me innocent, that I
May give a disentangled state and free;
And yet thy wounds still my attempts defy,
    For by thy death I die for thee.

Ah! was it not enough that thou
By thy eternal glory didst outgo me?
Could'st thou not grief's sad conquests me allow,
    But in all victories overthrow me?

Yet by confession will I come
Into the conquest. Though I can do nought
Against thee, in thee I will overcome
    The man, who once against thee fought.


## THE AGONY.

PHILOSOPHERS have measured mountains,
Fathom'd the depths of seas, of states, and kings,
Walk'd with a staff to heaven, and traced fountains:
    But there are two vast, spacious things,
The which to measure it doth more behove:
Yet few there are that sound them; Sin and Love.

Who would know Sin, let him repair
Unto Mount Olivet; there shall he see
A man, so wrung with pains, that all his hair,
    His skin, his garments, bloody be.
Sin is that Press and Vice, which forceth pain
To hunt his cruel food through every vein.

    Who knows not Love, let him assay,
  And taste that juice, which on the cross a pike
  Did set again abroach ; then let him say
      If ever he did taste the like.
Love is that liquor sweet and most divine,
Which my God feels as blood ; but I, as wine.


## THE SINNER.

Lord, how I am all ague, when I seek
    What I have treasured in my memory!
    Since, if my soul make even with the week,
Each seventh note by right is due to thee.

I find there quarries of piled vanities,
    But shreds of holiness, that dare not venture
    To show their face, since cross to thy decrees :
There the circumference earth is, heaven the centre.

In so much dregs the quintessence is small :
    The spirit and good extract of my heart
    Comes to about the many hundredth part.
Yet, Lord, restore thine image, hear my call :

    And though my hard heart scarce to thee can groan,
    Remember that thou once didst write in stone.

## GOOD FRIDAY.

O MY chief good,
How shall I measure out thy blood?
How shall I count what thee befell,
    And each grief tell?

Shall I thy woes
Number according to thy foes?
Or, since one star show'd thy first breath,
    Shall all thy death?

Or shall each leaf,
Which falls in Autumn, score a grief?
Or cannot leaves, but fruit, be sign,
    Of the true vine?

Then let each hour
Of my whole life one grief devour;
That thy distress through-all may run,
    And be my sun.

Or rather let
My several sins their sorrows get;
That, as each beast his cure doth know,
    Each sin may so.


SINCE blood is fittest, Lord, to write
Thy sorrows in, and bloody fight;
My heart hath store; write there, where in
One box doth lie both ink and sin:

That when Sin spies so many foes,
Thy whips, thy nails, thy wounds, thy woes,
All come to lodge there, Sin may say,
*No room for me*, and fly away.

Sin being gone, O fill the place,
And keep possession with thy grace ;
Lest sin take courage and return,
And all the writings blot or burn.


## REDEMPTION.

HAVING been tenant long to a rich Lord,
    Not thriving, I resolved to be bold,
    And make a suit unto him, to afford
A new small-rented lease, and cancel th' old.

In Heaven at his manor I him sought :
    They told me there, that he was lately gone
    About some land, which he had dearly bought
Long since on earth, to take possession.

I straight return'd, and knowing his great birth,
    Sought him accordingly in great resorts ;
    In cities, theatres, gardens, parks, and courts :
At length I heard a ragged noise and mirth

    Of thieves and murderers : there I him espied,
    Who straight, *Your suit is granted*, said, and died.

## SEPULCHRE.

O BLESSED body! whither art thou thrown?
No lodging for thee, but a cold hard stone?
So many hearts on earth, and yet not one
                      Receive thee?

Sure there is room within our hearts good store;
For they can lodge transgressions by the score:
Thousands of toys dwell there, yet out of door
                      They leave thee.

But that which shows them large, shows them unfit.
Whatever sin did this pure rock commit,
Which holds thee now? Who hath indited it
                      Of murder?

Where our hard hearts took up of stones to brain thee,
And missing this, most falsely did arraign thee;
Only these stones in quiet entertain thee,
                      And order.

And as of old, the Law by heavenly art
Was writ in stone; so thou, which also art
The letter of the word, find'st no fit heart
                      To hold thee.

Yet do we still persist as we began,
And so should perish, but that nothing can,
Though it be cold, hard, foul, from loving man
                      Withhold thee.

## EASTER.

Rise, heart ; thy Lord is risen.  Sing his praise
        Without delays,
Who takes thee by the hand, that thou likewise
        With him may'st rise :
That, as his death calcined thee to dust,
His life may make thee gold, and much more, Just.

Awake, my lute, and struggle for thy part
        With all thy art.
The cross taught all wood to resound his name
        Who bore the same.
His stretched sinews taught all strings, what key
Is best to celebrate this most high day.

Consort both heart and lute, and twist a song
        Pleasant and long :
Or since all music is but three parts vied,
        And multiplied ;
O let thy blessed Spirit bear a part,
And make up our defects with his sweet art.


   I got me flowers to strew thy way ;
   I got me boughs off many a tree :
   But thou wast up by break of day,
   And brought'st thy sweets along with thee.

   The Sun arising in the East,
   Though he give light, and th' East perfume ;
   If they should offer to contest
   With thy arising, they presume.

Can there be any day but this,
Though many suns to shine endeavour?
We count three hundred, but we miss:
There is but one, and that one ever.


## EASTER WINGS.

LORD, WHO CREATEDST MAN IN WEALTH AND STORE,
  THOUGH FOOLISHLY HE LOST THE SAME,
    DECAYING MORE AND MORE,
      TILL HE BECAME
       MOST POOR:

       WITH THEE
      OH LET ME RISE
    AS LARKS, HARMONIOUSLY,
  AND SING THIS DAY THY VICTORIES:
THEN SHALL THE FALL FURTHER THE FLIGHT IN ME.


MY TENDER AGE IN SORROW DID BEGIN:
  AND STILL WITH SICKNESSES AND SHAME
    THOU DID'ST SO PUNISH SIN,
      THAT I BECAME
       MOST THIN.

       WITH THEE
     LET ME COMBINE,
   AND FEEL THIS DAY THY VICTORY,
 FOR, IF I IMP MY WING ON THINE,
AFFLICTION SHALL ADVANCE THE FLIGHT IN ME.

## HOLY BAPTISM.

As he that sees a dark and shady grove,
    Stays not, but looks beyond it on the sky ;
    So when I view my sins, mine eyes remove
More backward still, and to that water fly,

Which is above the heavens, whose spring and vent
    Is in my dear Redeemer's pierced side.
    O blessed streams ! either ye do prevent
And stop our sins from growing thick and wide,

Or else give tears to drown them, as they grow.
    In you Redemption measures all my time,
    And spreads the plaster equal to the crime :
You taught the book of life my name, that so,

    Whatever future sins should me miscall,
    Your first acquaintance might discredit all.


## HOLY BAPTISM.

    Since, Lord, to thee
  A narrow way and little gate
Is all the passage, on my infancy
    Thou didst lay hold, and antedate
      My faith in me.

      O let me still
  Write thee great God, and me a child :

Let me be soft and supple to thy will,
    Small to myself, to others mild,
    Behither ill.

    Although by stealth
  My flesh get on; yet let her sister
My soul bid nothing, but preserve her wealth:
  The growth of flesh is but a blister;
    Childhood is health.


## NATURE.

FULL of rebellion, I would die,
Or fight, or travel, or deny
That thou hast aught to do with me.
    O tame my heart;
    It is thy highest art
To captivate strong holds to thee.

If thou shalt let this venom lurk,
And in suggestions fume and work,
My soul will turn to bubbles straight,
    And thence by kind
    Vanish into a wind,
Making thy workmanship deceit.

O smooth my rugged heart, and there
Engrave thy reverend law and fear;
Or make a new one, since the old
    Is sapless grown,
    And a much fitter stone
To hide my dust, than thee to hold.

## SIN.

Lord, with what care hast thou begirt us round!
  Parents first season us : then schoolmasters
  Deliver us to laws ; they send us bound
To rules of reason, holy messengers,

Pulpits and Sundays, sorrow dogging sin,
  Afflictions sorted, anguish of all sizes.
  Fine nets and stratagems to catch us in,
Bibles laid open, millions of surprises,

Blessings beforehand, ties of gratefulness,
  The sound of glory ringing in our ears ;
  Without, our shame ; within, our consciences ;
Angels and grace, eternal hopes and fears.

  Yet all these fences and their whole array
  One cunning bosom-sin blows quite away.


## AFFLICTION.

When first thou didst entice to thee my heart,
    I thought the service brave :
So many joys I writ down for my part,
    Besides what I might have
Out of my stock of natural delights,
Augmented with thy gracious benefits.

I looked on thy furniture so fine,
               And made it fine to me ;
Thy glorious household-stuff did me entwine,
               And 'tice me unto thee.
Such stars I counted mine : both heaven and earth
Paid me my wages in a world of mirth.

What pleasures could I want, whose King I served,
               Where joys my fellows were ?
Thus argued into hopes, my thoughts reserved
               No place for grief or fear ;
Therefore my sudden soul caught at the place,
And made her youth and fierceness seek thy face :

At first thou gavest me milk and sweetnesses ;
               I had my wish and way :
My days were strew'd with flowers and happiness :
               There was no month but May.
But with my years sorrow did twist and grow,
And made a party unawares for woe.

My flesh began unto my soul in pain,
               Sicknesses cleave my bones,
Consuming agues dwell in every vein,
               And tune my breath to groans :
Sorrow was all my soul ; I scarce believed,
Till grief did tell me roundly, that I lived.

When I got health, thou took'st away my life,
               And more ; for my friends die :
My mirth and edge was lost ; a blunted knife
               Was of more use than I.
Thus thin and lean, without a fence or friend,
I was blown through with every storm and wind.

Whereas my birth and spirit rather took
    The way that takes the town ;
Thou didst betray me to a lingering book,
    And wrap me in a gown.
I was entangled in the world of strife,
Before I had the power to change my life.

Yet, for I threaten'd oft the siege to raise,
    Not simpering all mine age,
Thou often didst with Academic praise
    Melt and dissolve my rage.
I took thy sweeten'd pill, till I came near ;
I could not go away, nor persevere.

Yet lest perchance I should too happy be
    In my unhappiness,
Turning my purge to food, thou throwest me
    Into more sicknesses.
Thus doth thy power cross-bias me, not making
Thine own gift good, yet me from my ways taking.

Now I am here, what thou wilt do with me
    None of my books will show :
I read, and sigh, and wish I were a tree ;
    For sure then I should grow
To fruit or shade : at least some bird would trust
Her household to me, and I should be just.

Yet, though thou troublest me, I must be meek ;
    In weakness must be stout.
Well, I will change the service, and go seek
    Some other Master out.
Ah, my dear God ! though I am clean forgot,
Let me not love thee, if I love thee not.

## REPENTANCE.

Lord, I confess my sin is great;
Great is my sin. Oh! gently treat
With thy quick flower, thy momentary bloom;
Whose life still pressing
Is one undressing,
A steady aiming at a tomb.

Man's age is two hours' work, or three;
Each day doth round about us see.
Thus are we to delights: but we are all
To sorrows old,
If life be told
From what life feeleth, Adam's fall.

O let thy height of mercy then
Compassionate short-breathed men,
Cut me not off for my most foul transgression:
I do confess
My foolishness;
My God, accept of my confession.

Sweeten at length this bitter bowl,
Which thou hast pour'd into my soul;
Thy wormwood turn to health, winds to fair weather:
For if thou stay,
I and this day,
As we did rise, we die together.

When thou for sin rebukest man,
Forthwith he waxeth woe and wan :
Bitterness fills our bowels ; all our hearts
    Pine, and decay,
    And drop away,
And carry with them th' other parts.

But thou wilt sin and grief destroy ;
That so the broken bones may joy,
And tune together in a well-set song,
    Full of his praises
    Who dead men raises.
Fractures well cured make us more strong.


## FAITH.

LORD, how couldst thou so much appease
Thy wrath for sin, as, when man's sight was dim,
And could see little, to regard his ease,
    And bring by Faith all things to him ?

Hungry I was, and had no meat :
I did conceit a most delicious feast ;
I had it straight, and did as truly eat,
    As ever did a welcome guest.

There is a rare outlandish root,
Which when I could not get, I thought it here :
That apprehension cured so well my foot,
    That I can walk to heaven well near.

I owed thousands and much more :
I did believe that I did nothing owe,
And lived accordingly ; my creditor
    Believes so too, and lets me go.

Faith makes me anything, or all
That I believe is in the sacred story :
And when sin placeth me in Adam's fall,
    Faith sets me higher in his glory.

If I go lower in the book,
What can be lower than the common manger?
Faith puts me there with Him, who sweetly took
    Our flesh and frailty, death and danger.

If bliss had lien in art or strength,
None but the wise and strong had gained it :
Where now by Faith all arms are of a length ;
    One size doth all conditions fit.

A peasant may believe as much
As a great Clerk, and reach the highest stature.
Thus dost thou make proud knowledge bend and crouch,
    While Grace fills up uneven Nature.

When creatures had no real light
Inherent in them, thou didst make the sun,
Impute a lustre, and allow them bright :
    And in this show what Christ hath done.

That which before was darken'd clean
With bushy groves, pricking the looker's eye,
Vanish'd away, when Faith did change the scene :
    And then appear'd a glorious sky.

What though my body run to dust?
Faith cleaves unto it, counting every grain,
With an exact and most particular trust,
Reserving all for flesh again.


## PRAYER.

Prayer, the Church's banquet, Angel's age,
   God's breath in man returning to his birth,
   The soul in paraphrase, heart in pilgrimage,
The Christian plummet sounding heaven and earth;

Engine against th' Almighty, sinner's tower,
   Reversed thunder, Christ-side-piercing spear,
   The six days' world-transposing in an hour,
A kind of tune, which all things hear and fear;

Softness, and peace, and joy, and love, and bliss,
   Exalted Manna, gladness of the best,
   Heaven in ordinary, men well drest,
The Milky Way, the bird of Paradise,

   Church-bells beyond the stars heard, the soul's blood,
   The land of spices, something understood.


## HOLY COMMUNION.

Not in rich furniture, or fine array,
   Nor in a wedge of gold,
   Thou, who from me wast sold,
To me dost now thyself convey;

For so thou should'st without me still have been,
    Leaving within me sin :

But by the way of nourishment and strength,
    Thou creep'st into my breast ;
    Making thy way my rest,
  And thy small quantities my length ;
Which spread their forces into every part,
    Meeting sin's force and art.

Yet can these not get over to my soul,
    Leaping the wall that parts
    Our souls and fleshly hearts ;
  But as th' outworks, they may control
My rebel-flesh, and, carrying thy name,
    Affright both sin and shame.

Only thy grace, which with these elements comes,
    Knoweth the ready way,
    And hath the privy key,
  Opening the soul's most subtile rooms :
While those to spirits refined, at door attend
    Despatches from their friend.


    Give me my captive soul, or take
      My body also thither.
    Another lift like this will make
      Them both to be together.


Before that sin turn'd flesh to stone,
    And all our lump to leaven ;
A fervent sigh might well have blown
    Our innocent earth to heaven.

For sure, when Adam did not know
    To sin, or sin to smother ;
He might to heaven from Paradise go,
    As from one room t' another.

Thou hast restored us to this ease
    By this thy heavenly blood,
Which I can go to, when I please,
    And leave th' earth to their food.


## ANTIPHON.

Cho.   Let all the world in every corner sing,
        *My God and King.*

Ver.    The heavens are not too high,
       His praise may thither fly :
       The earth is not too low,
       His praises there may grow.

Cho.   Let all the world in every corner sing,
        *My God and King.*

Ver.    The Church with Psalms must shout,
       No door can keep them out :
       But above all, the heart
       Must bear the longest part.

Cho.   Let all the world in every corner sing,
        *My God and King.*

## LOVE.

#### PART I.

IMMORTAL Love, author of this great frame,
   Sprung from that beauty which can never fade;
   How hath man parcell'd out thy glorious name,
And thrown it on that dust which thou hast made,

While mortal love doth all the title gain!
   Which siding with invention, they together
   Bear all the sway, possessing heart and brain
(Thy workmanship), and give thee share in neither.

Wit fancies beauty, beauty raiseth wit:
   The world is theirs; they two play out the game,
   Thou standing by: and though thy glorious name
Wrought our deliverance from th' infernal pit,

   Who sings thy praise? only a scarf or glove
   Doth warm our hands, and make them write of love.

#### PART II.

IMMORTAL Heat, O let thy greater flame
   Attract the lesser to it: let those fires
   Which shall consume the world, first make it tame,
And kindle in our hearts such true desires,

As may consume our lusts, and make thee way.
   Then shall our hearts pant thee; then shall our brain
   All her inventions on thine Altar lay,
And there in hymns send back thy fire again:

Our eyes shall see thee, which before saw dust;
   Dust blown by wit, till that they both were blind:
   Thou shalt recover all thy goods in kind,
Who wert disseized by usurping lust:

   All knees shall bow to thee; all wits shall rise,
   And praise Him who did make and mend our eyes.


## THE TEMPER.

How should I praise thee, Lord! how should my rhymes
   Gladly engrave thy love in steel,
   If what my soul doth feel sometimes,
      My soul might ever feel!

Although there were some forty heavens, or more,
   Sometimes I peer above them all;
   Sometimes I hardly reach a score,
      Sometimes to hell I fall.

O rack me not to such a vast extent;
   Those distances belong to thee:
   The world's too little for thy tent,
      A grave too big for me.

Wilt thou meet arms with man, that thou dost stretch
   A crumb of dust from heaven to hell?
   Will great God measure with a wretch?
      Shall he thy stature spell?

O let me, when thy roof my soul hath hid,
   O let me roost and nestle there :
Then of a sinner thou art rid,
   And I of hope and fear.

Yet take thy way ; for sure thy way is best :
   Stretch or contract me thy poor debtor :
This is but tuning of my breast,
   To make the music better.

Whether I fly with angels, fall with dust,
   Thy hands made both, and I am there.
Thy power and love, my love and trust,
   Make one place every where.


## THE TEMPER.

It cannot be. Where is that mighty joy,
   Which just now took up all my heart ?
   Lord ! if thou must needs use thy dart,
Save that, and me ; or sin for both destroy.

The grosser world stands to thy word and art ;
   But thy diviner world of grace
   Thou suddenly dost raise and raze,
And every day a new Creator art.

O fix thy chair of grace, that all my powers
   May also fix their reverence :
   For when thou dost depart from hence,
They grow unruly, and sit in thy bowers.

Scatter, or bind them all to bend to thee :
　　Though elements change, and heaven move ;
　　Let not thy higher Court remove,
But keep a standing Majesty in me.


## JORDAN.

Who says that fictions only and false hair
Become a verse ?　Is there in truth no beauty ?
Is all good structure in a winding stair ?
May no lines pass, except they do their duty
　　Not to a true, but painted chair ?

Is it not verse, except enchanted groves
And sudden arbours shadow coarse-spun lines ?
Must purling streams refresh a lover's loves ?
Must all be veil'd, while he that reads, divines,
　　Catching the sense at two removes ?

Shepherds are honest people ; let them sing :
Riddle who list, for me, and pull for Prime :
I envy no man's nightingale or spring ;
Nor let them punish me with loss of rhyme,
　　Who plainly say, *My God, my King.*


## EMPLOYMENT.

If as a flower doth spread and die,
　　Thou wouldst extend me to some good,
Before I were by frost's extremity
　　　　Nipt in the bud ;

The sweetness and the praise were thine ;
But the extension and the room,
Which in thy garland I should fill, were mine
        At thy great doom.

For as thou dost impart thy grace,
The greater shall our glory be.
The measure of our joys is in this place,
        The stuff with thee.

Let me not languish then, and spend
A life as barren to thy praise
As is the dust, to which that life doth tend,
        But with delays.

All things are busy : only I
Neither bring honey with the bees,
Nor flowers to make that, nor the husbandry
        To water these.

I am no link of thy great chain,
But all my company is a weed.
Lord, place me in thy consort; give one strain
        To my poor reed.

## THE HOLY SCRIPTURES.

### PART I.

O BOOK! infinite sweetness! let my heart
    Suck every letter, and a honey gain,
    Precious for any grief in any part ;
To clear the breast, to mollify all pain.

Thou art all health, health thriving, till it make
    A full eternity : thou art a mass
    Of strange delights, where we may wish and take.
Ladies, look here ; this is the thankful glass,

That mends the looker's eyes : this is the well
    That washes what it shows. Who can endear
    Thy praise too much ? thou art Heaven's Lieger here,
Working against the states of death and hell.

    Thou art joy's handsel : heaven lies flat in thee,
    Subject to every mounter's bended knee.


### PART II.

OH that I knew how all thy lights combine,
    And the configurations of their glory!
    Seeing not only how each verse doth shine,
But all the constellations of the story.

This verse marks that, and both do make a motion
    Unto a third, that ten leaves off doth lie :
    Then as dispersed herbs do watch a potion,
These three make up some Christian's destiny.

Such are thy secrets, which my life makes good,
    And comments on thee : for in every thing
    Thy words do find me out, and parallels bring,
And in another make me understood.

    Stars are poor books, and oftentimes do miss :
    This book of stars lights to eternal bliss.

## WHITSUNDAY.

Listen, sweet Dove, unto my song,
   And spread thy golden wings in me;
   Hatching my tender heart so long,
Till it get wing, and fly away with thee.

Where is that fire which once descended
   On thy Apostles? thou didst then
   Keep open house, richly attended,
Feasting all comers by twelve chosen men.

Such glorious gifts thou didst bestow,
   That th' earth did like a heaven appear:
   The stars were coming down to know
If they might mend their wages, and serve here.

The Sun, which once did shine alone,
   Hung down his head, and wish'd for night,
   When he beheld twelve Suns for one
Going about the world, and giving light.

But since those pipes of gold, which brought
   That cordial water to our ground,
   Were cut and martyr'd by the fault
Of those who did themselves through their side wound;

Thou shutt'st the door, and keep'st within;
   Scarce a good joy creeps through the chink:
   And if the braves of conquering sin
Did not excite thee, we should wholly sink.

Lord, though we change, thou art the same;
The same sweet God of love and light:
Restore this day, for thy great Name,
Unto his ancient and miraculous right.


## GRACE.

My stock lies dead, and no increase
Doth my dull husbandry improve:
O let thy graces without cease
              Drop from above!

If still the Sun should hide his face,
Thy house would but a dungeon prove,
Thy works night's captives: O let grace
              Drop from above!

The dew doth every morning fall;
And shall the dew outstrip thy Dove?
The dew, for which grass cannot call,
              Drop from above.

Death is still working like a mole,
And digs my grave at each remove:
Let grace work too, and on my soul
              Drop from above.

Sin is still hammering my heart
Unto a hardness, void of love:
Let suppling grace, to cross his art,
              Drop from above.

O come! for thou dost know the way.
Or if to me thou wilt not move,
Remove me where I need not say—
*Drop from above.*


## PRAISE.

To write a verse or two, is all the praise
        That I can raise:
    Mend my estate in any ways,
        Thou shalt have more.

I go to Church; help me to wings, and I
        Will thither fly;
    Or, if I mount unto the sky,
        I will do more.

Man is all weakness; there is no such thing
        As Prince or King:
    His arm is short; yet with a sling
        He may do more.

An herb distill'd, and drunk, may dwell next door,
        On the same floor,
    To a brave soul: Exalt the poor,
        They can do more.

O raise me, then! poor bees, that work all day,
        Sting my delay,
    Who have a work, as well as they,
        And much, much more.

## AFFLICTION.

Kill me not every day,
Thou Lord of life ; since thy one death for me
    Is more than all my deaths can be,
      Though I in broken pay
Die over each hour of Methusalem's stay.

    If all men's tears were let
Into one common sewer, sea, and brine ;
    What were they all, compared to thine ?
      Wherein if they were set,
They would discolour thy most bloody sweat.

    Thou art my grief alone,
Thou Lord conceal it not : and as thou art
    All my delight, so all my smart :
      Thy cross took up in one,
By way of imprest, all my future moan.


## MATINS.

    I cannot ope mine eyes,
  But thou art ready there to catch
  My morning-soul and sacrifice :
Then we must needs for that day make a match.

    My God, what is a heart ?
  Silver, or gold, or precious stone,
  Or star, or rainbow, or a part
Of all these things, or all of them in one ?

My God, what is a heart,
That thou shouldst it so eye, and woo,
Pouring upon it all thy art,
As if that thou hadst nothing else to do?

Indeed, man's whole estate
Amounts (and richly) to serve thee:
He did not heaven and earth create,
Yet studies them, not Him by whom they be.

Teach me thy love to know;
That this new light, which now I see,
May both the work and workman show:
Then by a Sunbeam I will climb to thee.


## SIN.

O THAT I could a sin once see!
We paint the devil foul, yet he
Hath some good in him, all agree.
Sin is flat opposite to th' Almighty, seeing
It wants the good of *virtue*, and of *being*.

But God more care of us hath had,
If apparitions make us sad,
By sight of sin we should grow mad.
Yet as in sleep we see foul death, and live;
So devils are our sins in prospective.

### EVEN-SONG.

Blest be the God of love,
Who gave me eyes, and light, and power this day,
Both to be busy and to play.
But much more blest be God above,

Who gave me sight alone,
Which to himself he did deny :
For when he sees my ways, I die :
But I have got his Son, and he hath none.

What have I brought thee home
For this thy love ? have I discharged the debt,
Which this day's favour did beget ?
I ran ; but all I brought, was foam.

Thy diet, care, and cost
Do end in bubbles, balls of wind ;
Of wind to thee whom I have crost,
But balls of wild-fire to my troubled mind.

Yet still thou goest on,
And now with darkness closest weary eyes,
Saying to man, *It doth suffice :*
*Henceforth repose ; your work is done.*

Thus in thy Ebony box
Thou dost enclose us, till the day
Put our amendment in our way,
And give new wheels to our disorder'd clocks.

I muse, which shows more love,
The day or night : that is the gale, this th' harbour ;
That is the walk, and this the arbour ;
Or that the garden, this the grove.

My God, thou art all love.
Not one poor minute 'scapes thy breast,
But brings a favour from above ;
And in this love, more than in bed, I rest.


## CHURCH MONUMENTS.

WHILE that my soul repairs to her devotion,
Here I entomb my flesh, that it betimes
May take acquaintance of this heap of dust ;
To which the blast of death's incessant motion,
Fed with the exhalation of our crimes,
Drives all at last.   Therefore I gladly trust

My body to this school, that it may learn
To spell his elements, and find his birth
Written in dusty heraldry and lines ;
Which dissolution sure doth best discern,
Comparing dust with dust, and earth with earth.
These laugh at Jet, and Marble put for signs,

To sever the good fellowship of dust,
And spoil the meeting.   What shall point out them,
When they shall bow, and kneel, and fall down flat
To kiss those heaps, which now they have in trust ?
Dear flesh, while I do pray, learn here thy stem
And true descent ; that when thou shalt grow fat,

And wanton in thy cravings, thou may'st know,
That flesh is but the glass, which holds the dust
That measures all our time ; which also shall
Be crumbled into dust.  Mark here below,
How tame these ashes are, how free from lust,
That thou may'st fit thyself against thy fall.


## CHURCH MUSIC.

SWEETEST of sweets, I thank you : when displeasure
    Did through my body wound my mind,
You took me thence ; and in your house of pleasure
    A dainty lodging me assign'd.

Now I in you without a body move,
    Rising and falling with your wings :
We both together sweetly live and love,
    Yet say sometimes, *God help poor kings.*

Comfort, I'll die ; for if you post from me,
    Sure I shall do so, and much more :
But if I travel in your company,
    You know the way to heaven's door.


## CHURCH LOCK AND KEY.

I KNOW it is my sin, which locks thine ears,
        And binds thy hands !
Out-crying my requests, drowning my tears ;
Or else the chillness of my faint demands.

But as cold hands are angry with the fire,
                And mend it still;
So I do lay the want of my desire,
Not on my sins, or coldness, but thy will.

Yet hear, O God, only for His blood's sake,
                Which pleads for me:
For though sins plead too, yet like stones they make
His blood's sweet current much more loud to be.


## THE CHURCH FLOOR.

MARK you the floor? that square and speckled stone,
      Which looks so firm and strong,
          Is *Patience:*

And th' other black and grave, wherewith each one
      Is chequer'd all along,
          *Humility:*

The gentle rising, which on either hand
      Leads to the quire above,
          Is *Confidence:*

But the sweet cement, which in one sure band
      Ties the whole frame, is *Love*
          And *Charity.*


    HITHER sometimes Sin steals, and stains
      The Marble's neat and curious veins:
But all is cleansed when the Marble weeps.

Sometimes Death, puffing at the door,
    Blows all the dust about the floor :
But while he thinks to spoil the room, he sweeps.

    Blest be the *Architect*, whose art
    Could build so strong in a weak heart.


## THE WINDOWS.

Lord, how can man preach thy eternal word ?
    He is a brittle crazy glass :
Yet in thy Temple thou dost him afford
    This glorious and transcendent place,
    To be a window, through thy grace.

But when thou dost anneal in glass thy story,
    Making thy life to shine within
The holy Preachers, then the light and glory
    More reverend grows, and more doth win ;
    Which else shows waterish, bleak, and thin.

Doctrine and life, colours and light, in one
    When they combine and mingle, bring
A strong regard and awe : but speech alone
    Doth vanish like a flaring thing,
    And in the ear, not conscience ring.


## TRINITY SUNDAY.

Lord, who hast form'd me out of mud,
    And hast redeem'd me through thy blood,
    And sanctified me to do good ;

Purge all my sins done heretofore;
For I confess my heavy score,
And I will strive to sin no more.

Enrich my heart, mouth, hands in me,
With faith, with hope, with charity;
That I may run, rise, rest with thee.

## CONTENT.

Peace, muttering thoughts, and do not grudge to keep
    Within the walls of your own breast.
Who cannot on his own bed sweetly sleep,
    Can on another's hardly rest.

Gad not abroad at every quest and call
    Of an untrained hope or passion.
To court each place or fortune that doth fall,
    Is wantonness in contemplation.

Mark how the fire in flints doth quiet lie,
    Content and warm to itself alone:
But when it would appear to other's eye,
    Without a knock it never shone.

Give me the pliant mind, whose gentle measure
    Complies and suits with all estates;
Which can let loose to a crown, and yet with pleasure
    Take up within a cloister's gates.

This soul doth span the world, and hang content
    From either pole unto the centre:
Where in each room of the well-furnish'd tent
    He lies warm, and without adventure.

The brags of life are but a nine days' wonder:
    And after death the fumes that spring
From private bodies, make as big a thunder
    As those which rise from a huge King.

Only thy Chronicle is lost: and yet
    Better by worms be all once spent,
Than to have hellish moths still gnaw and fret
    Thy name in books, which may not vent.

When all thy deeds, whose brunt thou feel'st alone,
    Are chaw'd by others' pens and tongue,
And as their wit is, their digestion,
    Thy nourish'd fame is weak or strong.

Then cease discoursing, soul, till thine own ground;
    Do not thyself or friends importune.
He that by seeking hath himself once found,
    Hath ever found a happy fortune.


## THE QUIDDITY.

My God, a verse is not a crown;
No point of honour, or gay suit,
No hawk, or banquet, or renown,
Nor a good sword, nor yet a lute:

It cannot vault, or dance, or play;
It never was in France or Spain;
Nor can it entertain the day
With a great stable or domain.

It is no office, art, or news ;
Nor the Exchange, or busy Hall :
But it is that, which while I use,
I am with thee, and *Most take all.*

## HUMILITY.

I SAW the Virtues sitting hand in hand
In several ranks upon an azure throne,
Where all the beasts and fowls, by their command,
Presented tokens of submission.
Humility, who sat the lowest there
    To execute their call,
When by the beasts the presents tender'd were,
    Gave them about to all.

The angry Lion did present his paw,
Which by consent was given to Mansuetude.
The fearful Hare her ears, which by their law
Humility did reach to Fortitude.
The jealous Turkey brought his coral chain,
    That went to Temperance.
On Justice was bestow'd the Fox's brain,
    Kill'd in the way by chance.

At length the Crow, bringing the Peacock's plume
(For he would not), as they beheld the grace
Of that brave gift, each one began to fume,
And challenge it, as proper to his place,
Till they fell out ; which when the beasts espied,
    They leapt upon the throne ;
And if the Fox had lived to rule their side,
    They had deposed each one.

Humility, who held the plume, at this
Did weep so fast, that the tears trickling down
Spoil'd all the train : then saying, *Here it is,
For which ye wrangle,* made them turn their frown
Against the beasts : so jointly bandying,
    They drive them soon away ;
And then amerced them, double gifts to bring
    At the next Session-day.


## FRAILTY.

Lord, in my silence how do I despise
    What upon trust
Is styled *honour, riches,* or *fair eyes;*
    But is—*fair dust!*
  I surname them *gilded clay,*
  *Dear earth, fine grass,* or *hay;*
In all, I think my foot doth ever tread
    Upon their head.

But when I view abroad both Regiments,
    The world's, and thine ;
Thine clad with simpleness, and sad events ;
    The other fine,
  Full of glory and gay weeds,
  Brave language, braver deeds :
That which was dust before, doth quickly rise,
    And prick mine eyes.

O brook not this, lest if what even now
    My foot did tread,

Affront those joys, wherewith thou didst endow,
   And long since wed
 My poor soul, e'en sick of love;
 It may a Babel prove,
Commodious to conquer heaven and thee
   Planted in me.


## CONSTANCY.

  Who is the honest man?
He that doth still and strongly good pursue,
To God, his neighbour, and himself most true:
 Whom neither force nor fawning can
Unpin, or wrench from giving all their due.

  Whose honesty is not
So loose or easy, that a ruffling wind
Can blow away, or glittering look it blind:
 Who rides his sure and even trot,
While the world now rides by, now lags behind.

  Who, when great trials come,
Nor seeks, nor shuns them; but doth calmly stay,
Till he the thing and the example weigh:
 All being brought into a sum,
What place or person calls for, he doth pay.

  Whom none can work or woo,
To use in any thing a trick or sleight;
For above all things he abhors deceit:
 His words and works and fashion too
All of a piece, and all are clear and straight.

>    Who never melts or thaws
> At close temptations : when the day is done,
> His goodness sets not, but in dark can run ;
>    The sun to others writeth laws,
> And is their virtue ; Virtue is his Sun.
>
>    Who, when he is to treat
> With sick folks, women, those whom passions sway,
> Allows for that, and keeps his constant way :
>    Whom others' faults do not defeat ;
> But though men fail him, yet his part doth play.
>
>    Whom nothing can procure,
> When the wide world runs bias, from his will
> To writhe his limbs, and share, not mend the ill.
>    This is the Marksman, safe and sure,
> Who still is right, and prays to be so still.

## AFFLICTION.

> My heart did heave, and there came forth, *O God!*
> By that I knew that thou wast in the grief,
> To guide and govern it to my relief,
>         Making a sceptre of the rod :
>         Hadst thou not had thy part,
> Sure the unruly sigh had broke my heart.
>
> But since thy breath gave me both life and shape,
> Thou know'st my tallies ; and when there's assign'd
> So much breath to a sigh, what's then behind ?
>         Or if some years with it escape,
>         The sigh then only is
> A gale to bring me sooner to my bliss.

Thy life on earth was grief, and thou art still
Constant unto it, making it to be
A point of honour, now to grieve in me,
    And in thy members suffer ill.
    They who lament one cross,
Thou dying daily, praise thee to thy loss.

## THE STAR.

Bright spark, shot from a brighter place,
  Where beams surround my Saviour's face,
    Canst thou be any where
    So well as there?

Yet, if thou wilt from thence depart,
  Take a bad lodging in my heart;
    For thou canst make a debtor,
    And make it better.

First with thy fire-work burn to dust
  Folly, and worse than folly, lust:
    Then with thy light refine,
    And make it shine.

So disengaged from sin and sickness,
  Touch it with thy celestial quickness,
    That it may hang and move
    After thy love.

Then with our trinity of light,
  Motion, and heat, let's take our flight
    Unto the place where thou
    Before didst bow.

Get me a standing there, and place
   Among the beams, which crown the face
     Of Him who died to part
       Sin and my heart:

That so among the rest I may
   Glitter, and curl, and wind as they:
     That winding is their fashion
       Of adoration.

Sure thou wilt joy, by gaining me
   To fly home like a laden bee
     Unto that hive of beams
       And garland-streams.

## SUNDAY.

    O DAY most calm, most bright,
The fruit of this, the next world's bud,
Th' indorsement of supreme delight,
Writ by a friend, and with his blood;
The couch of time; care's balm and bay;
The week were dark, but for thy light:
    Thy Torch doth show the way.

    The other days and thou
Make up one man; whose face thou art,
Knocking at heaven with thy brow:
The working-days are the back-part;
The burden of the week lies there,
Making the whole to stoop and bow,
    Till thy release appear.

## THE CHURCH.

    Man had straight forward gone
To endless death ; but thou dost pull
And turn us round to look on one,
Whom, if we were not very dull,
We could not choose but look on still ;
Since there is no place so alone
        The which he doth not fill.

    Sundays the pillars are,
On which heaven's palace arched lies :
The other days fill up the spare
And hollow room with vanities.
They are the fruitful beds and borders
In God's rich garden : that is bare
        Which parts their ranks and orders.

    The Sundays of man's life,
Threaded together on time's string,
Make bracelets to adorn the wife
Of the eternal glorious King.
On Sunday heaven's gate stands ope ;
Blessings are plentiful and rife,
        More plentiful than hope.

    This day my Saviour rose,
And did enclose this light for his :
That, as each beast his manger knows,
Man might not of his fodder miss.
Christ hath took in this piece of ground,
And made a garden there for those
        Who want herbs for their wound.

    The Rest of our Creation
Our great Redeemer did remove

With the same shake, which at his passion
Did th' earth and all things with it move.
As Samson bore the doors away,
Christ's hands, though nail'd, wrought our salvation,
    And did unhinge that day.

    The brightness of that day
We sullied by our foul offence :
Wherefore that robe we cast away,
Having a new at his expense,
Whose drops of blood paid the full price,
That was required to make us gay,
    And fit for Paradise.

    Thou art a day of mirth :
And where the week-days trail on ground,
Thy flight is higher, as thy birth :
O let me take thee at the bound,
Leaping with thee from seven to seven,
Till that we both, being toss'd from earth,
    Fly hand in hand to heaven !

## AVARICE.

Money, thou bane of bliss, and source of woe,
    Whence comest thou, that thou art so fresh and fine ?
    I know thy parentage is base and low :
Man found thee poor and dirty in a mine.

Surely thou didst so little contribute
    To this great kingdom, which thou now hast got,
    That he was fain, when thou wast destitute,
To dig thee out of thy dark cave and grot.

Then forcing thee, by fire he made thee bright :
   Nay, thou hast got the face of man ; for we
   Have with our stamp and seal transferr'd our right ;
Thou art the man, and man but dross to thee.

   Man calleth thee his wealth, who made thee rich ;
   And while he digs out thee, falls in the ditch.

## ANA-{MARY/ARMY}GRAM.

How well her name an *Army* doth present,
In whom the *Lord of hosts* did pitch his tent !

## TO ALL ANGELS AND SAINTS.

O GLORIOUS spirits, who after all your bands
See the smooth face of God, without a frown,
              Or strict commands ;
Where every one is king, and hath his crown,
If not upon his head, yet in his hands :

Not out of envy or maliciousness
Do I forbear to crave your special aid.
              I would address
My vows to thee most gladly, blessed Maid,
And Mother of my God, in my distress :

Thou art the holy mine, whence came the gold,
The great restorative for all decay
              In young and old ;
Thou art the cabinet where the jewel lay :
Chiefly to thee would I my soul unfold.

But now, alas! I dare not; for our King,
Whom we do all jointly adore and praise,
                    Bids no such thing :
And where his pleasure no injunction lays
('Tis your own case), ye never move a wing.

All worship is prerogative, and a flower
Of his rich crown, from whom lies no appeal
                    At the last hour :
Therefore we dare not from his garland steal,
To make a posie for inferior power.

Although then others court you, if ye know
What's done on earth, we shall not fare the worse
                    Who do not so ;
Since we are ever ready to disburse,
If any one our Master's hand can show.


### EMPLOYMENT.

He that is weary, let him sit.
                    My soul would stir
And trade in courtesies and wit,
                    Quitting the fur,
To cold complexions needing it.

Man is no star, but a quick coal
                    Of mortal fire :
Who blows it not, nor doth control
                    A faint desire,
Lets his own ashes choke his soul.

When th' elements did for place contest
           With Him, whose will
Ordain'd the highest to be best:
           The earth sat still,
And by the others is opprest.

Life is a business, not good cheer;
           Ever in wars.
The sun still shineth there or here,
           Whereas the stars
Watch an advantage to appear.

O that I were an Orange-tree,
           That busy plant!
Then I should ever laden be,
           And never want
Some fruit for him that dresseth me.

But we are still too young or old;
           The man is gone,
Before we do our wares unfold:
           So we freeze on,
Until the grave increase our cold.


## DENIAL.

WHEN my devotions could not pierce
           Thy silent ears;
Then was my heart broken, as was my verse;
           My breast was full of fears
                    And disorder,

My bent thoughts, like a brittle bow,
        Did fly asunder:
Each took his way; some would to pleasures go,
    Some to the wars and thunder
        Of alarms.

As good go any where, they say,
        As to benumb
Both knees and heart, in crying night and day,
    *Come, come, my God, O come,*
        But no hearing.

O Thou that shouldst give dust a tongue
        To cry to thee,
And then not hear it crying! all day long
    My heart was in my knee,
        But no hearing.

Therefore my soul lay out of sight,
        Untuned, unstrung:
My feeble spirit, unable to look right,
    Like a nipt blossom, hung
        Discontented.

O cheer and tune my heartless breast,
        Defer no time;
That so thy favours granting my request,
    They and my mind may chime,
        And mend my rhyme.

## CHRISTMAS.

ALL after pleasures as I rid one day,
  My horse and I, both tired, body and mind,
  With full cry of affections, quite astray;
I took up in the next Inn I could find.

There when I came, whom found I but my dear,
  My dearest Lord, expecting till the grief
  Of pleasures brought me to him, ready there
To be all passengers' most sweet relief?

O Thou, whose glorious, yet contracted light,
  Wrapt in night's mantle, stole into a manger;
  Since my dark soul and brutish is thy right,
To Man of all beasts be not thou a stranger:

Furnish and deck my soul, that thou may'st have
A better lodging, than a rack, or grave.

THE shepherds sing; and shall I silent be?
    My God, no hymn for thee?
My soul's a shepherd too: a flock it feeds
    Of thoughts, and words, and deeds.
The pasture is thy word; the streams, thy grace
    Enriching all the place.

Shepherd and flock shall sing, and all my powers
    Out-sing the daylight hours.
Then we will chide the Sun for letting night
    Take up his place and right:
We sing one common Lord; wherefore he should
    Himself the candle hold.

I will go searching, till I find a Sun
    Shall stay, till we have done ;
A willing shiner, that shall shine as gladly,
    As frost-nipt Suns look sadly.
Then we will sing, and shine all our own day,
    And one another pay :

His beams shall cheer my breast, and both so twine,
Till even his beams sing, and my music shine.


## UNGRATEFULNESS.

LORD, with what bounty and rare clemency
    Hast thou redeem'd us from the grave!
        If thou hadst let us run,
    Gladly had man adored the Sun,
        And thought his god most brave ;
Where now we shall be better gods than he.

Thou hast but two rare Cabinets full of treasure,
    The *Trinity*, and *Incarnation :*
        Thou hast unlock'd them both,
    And made them jewels to betroth
        The work of thy creation
Unto thyself in everlasting pleasure.

The statelier Cabinet is the *Trinity*,
    Whose sparkling light access denies :
        Therefore thou dost not show
    This fully to us, till death blow
        The dust into our eyes ;
For by that powder thou wilt make us see.

But all thy sweets are pack'd up in the other;
　　Thy mercies thither flock and flow;
　　　That, as the first affrights,
　　　This may allure us with delights;
　　　　Because this box we know;
For we have all of us just such another.

But man is close, reserved, and dark to thee;
　　When thou demandest but a heart,
　　　He cavils instantly.
　　　In his poor cabinet of bone
　　　　Sins have their box apart,
Defrauding thee, who gavest two for one.

## SIGHS AND GROANS.

　　　　O DO not use me
After my sins! look not on my desert,
But on thy glory! then thou wilt reform,
And not refuse me: for thou only art
The mighty God, but I a silly worm:
　　　　O do not bruise me!

　　　　O do not urge me!
For what account can thy ill steward make?
I have abused thy stock, destroy'd thy woods,
Suck'd all thy magazines: my head did ache,
Till it found out how to consume thy goods:
　　　　O do not scourge me!

　　　　O do not blind me!
I have deserved that an Egyptian night
Should thicken all my powers; because my lust

Hath still sew'd fig-leaves to exclude thy light:
But I am frailty, and already dust:
   O do not grind me!

   O do not fill me
With the turn'd vial of thy bitter wrath!
For thou hast other vessels full of blood,
A part whereof my Saviour emptied hath,
Even unto death: since he died for my good,
   O do not kill me!

   But O, reprieve me!
For thou hast *life* and *death* at thy command;
Thou art both *Judge* and *Saviour, feast* and *rod,*
*Cordial* and *Corrosive:* put not thy hand
Into the bitter box; but, O my God,
   My God, relieve me!


## THE WORLD.

Love built a stately house; where *Fortune* came:
And spinning fancies, she was heard to say,
That her fine cobwebs did support the frame,
Whereas they were supported by the same:
But *Wisdom* quickly swept them all away.

Then *Pleasure* came, who, liking not the fashion,
Began to make *Balconies, Terraces,*
Till she had weaken'd all by alteration:
But reverend *laws,* and many a *proclamation*
Reformed all at length with menaces.

THE CHURCH.                83

Then enter'd *Sin*, and with that Sycamore,
Whose leaves first shelter'd man from drought and dew,
Working and winding slily evermore,
The inward walls and summers cleft and tore :
But *Grace* shored these, and cut that as it grew.

Then *Sin* combined with *Death* in a firm band,
To raze the building to the very floor :
Which they effected, none could them withstand ;
But *Love* and *Grace* took *Glory* by the hand,
And built a braver palace than before.


COLOSSIANS III. 3.

" OUR LIFE IS HID WITH CHRIST IN GOD."

*My* words and thoughts do both express this notion,
That *Life* hath with the sun a double motion.
The first *Is* straight, and our diurnal friend ,
The other *Hid*, and doth obliquely bend.
One life is wrapt *In* flesh, and tends to earth :
The other winds toward *Him*, whose happy birth
Taught me to live here so, *That* still one eye
Should aim and shoot at that which *Is* on high ;
Quitting with daily labour all *My* pleasure,
To gain at harvest an eternal *Treasure*.

## VANITY.

The fleet Astronomer can bore
And thread the spheres with his quick-piercing mind :
He views their stations, walks from door to door,
    Surveys, as if he had design'd
To make a purchase there : he sees their dances
        And knoweth long before,
Both their full-eyed aspects, and secret glances.

    The nimble Diver with his side
Cuts through the working waves, that he may fetch
His dearly-earned pearl, which God did hide
    On purpose from the venturous wretch ;
That he might save his life, and also hers,
        Who with excessive pride
Her own destruction and his danger wears.

    The subtle Chymic can divest
And strip the creature naked, till he find
The callow principles within their nest :
    There he imparts to them his mind,
Admitted to their bed-chamber, before
        They appear trim and drest
To ordinary suitors at the door.

    What hath not man sought out and found,
But his dear God ? who yet his glorious law
Embosoms in us, mellowing the ground
    With showers and frosts, with love and awe ;
So that we need not say, Where's this command ?
        Poor man ! thou searchest round
To find out *death*, but missest *life* at hand.

## LENT.

WELCOME, dear feast of Lent : who loves not thee,
He loves not Temperance, or Authority,
    But is composed of passion.
The Scriptures bid us *fast*; the Church says, Now:
Give to thy Mother what thou wouldst allow
    To every Corporation.

The humble soul, composed of love and fear,
Begins at home, and lays the burden there,
    When doctrines disagree :
He says, In things which use hath justly got,
I am a scandal to the Church, and not
    The Church is so to me.

True Christians should be glad of an occasion
To use their temperance, seeking no evasion,
    When good is seasonable ;
Unless Authority, which should increase
The obligation in us, make it less,
    And Power itself disable.

Besides the cleanness of sweet abstinence,
Quick thoughts and motions at a small expense,
    A face not fearing light :
Whereas in fulness there are sluttish fumes,
Sour exhalations, and dishonest rheums,
    Revenging the delight.

Then those same pendent profits, which the spring
And Easter intimate, enlarge the thing,
    And goodness of the deed.

Neither ought other men's abuse of Lent
Spoil the good use ; lest by that argument
    We forfeit all our Creed.

'Tis true, we cannot reach Christ's fortieth day;
Yet to go part of that religious way
    Is better than to rest :
We cannot reach our Saviour's purity;
Yet are we bid, *Be holy even as he.*
    In both let's do our best.

Who goeth in the way which Christ hath gone,
Is much more sure to meet with him, than one
    That travelleth by-ways.
Perhaps my God, though he be far before,
May turn, and take me by the hand, and more,
    May strengthen my decays.

Yet, Lord, instruct us to improve our fast
By starving sin, and taking such repast
    As may our faults control :
That every man may revel at his door,
Not in his parlour ; banqueting the poor,
    And among those his soul.


## VIRTUE.

Sweet Day, so cool, so calm, so bright,
  The bridal of the earth and sky,
  The dew shall weep thy fall to-night;
        For thou must die.

Sweet Rose, whose hue angry and brave
Bids the rash gazer wipe his eye,
Thy root is ever in its grave,
   And thou must die.

Sweet Spring, full of sweet days and roses,
A box where sweets compacted lie,
My Music shows ye have your closes,
   And all must die.

Only a sweet and virtuous soul,
Like season'd timber, never gives;
But though the whole world turn to coal,
   Then chiefly lives.


## THE PEARL.

#### MATT. XIII.

I KNOW the ways of Learning; both the head
And Pipes that feed the press, and make it run;
What Reason hath from Nature borrowed,
Or of itself, like a good housewife, spun
In laws and policy; what the stars conspire,
What willing Nature speaks, what forced by fire;
Both th' old discoveries, and the new-found seas,
The stock and surplus, cause and history:
All these stand open, or I have the keys:
   Yet I love thee.

I know the ways of Honour, what maintains
The quick returns of courtesy and wit:

In vies of favours whether party gains,
When glory swells the heart, and mouldeth it
To all expressions both of hand and eye,
Which on the world a true-love-knot may tie,
And bear the bundle, wheresoe'er it goes:
How many drams of spirit there must be
To sell my life unto my friends or foes:
    Yet I love thee.

I know the ways of Pleasure, the sweet strains,
The lullings and the relishes of it;
The propositions of hot blood and brains;
What mirth and music mean; what love and wit
Have done these twenty hundred years, and more:
I know the projects of unbridled store:
My stuff is flesh, not brass; my senses live,
And grumble oft, that they have more in me
Than he that curbs them, being but one to five:
    Yet I love thee.

I know all these, and have them in my hand:
Therefore not sealed, but with open eyes
I fly to thee, and fully understand
Both the main sale, and the commodities;
And at what rate and price I have thy love;
With all the circumstances that may move:
Yet through the labyrinths, not my grovelling wit,
But thy silk-twist let down from heaven to me,
Did both conduct and teach me, how by it
    To climb to thee.

## AFFLICTION.

Broken in pieces all asunder,
      Lord, hunt me not,
      A thing forgot,
Once a poor creature, now a wonder,
    A wonder tortured in the space
    Betwixt this world and that of grace.

My thoughts are all a case of knives,
      Wounding my heart
      With scatter'd smart;
As watering-pots give flowers their lives.
    Nothing their fury can control,
    While they do wound and prick my soul.

All my attendants are at strife,
      Quitting their place
      Unto my face:
Nothing performs the task of life:
    The elements are let loose to fight,
    And while I live, try out their right.

Oh, help, my God! let not their plot
      Kill them and me,
      And also thee,
Who art my life: dissolve the knot,
    As the sun scatters by his light
    All the rebellions of the night.

Then shall those powers, which work for grief,
      Enter thy pay,
      And day by day

Labour thy praise and my relief ;
    With care and courage building me,
    Till I reach heaven, and much more, thee.

## MAN.

    My God, I heard this day,
That none doth build a stately habitation
    But he that means to dwell therein.
    What house more stately hath there been,
Or can be, than is Man ? to whose creation
    All things are in decay.

    For Man is every thing,
And more : He is a tree, yet bears no fruit ;
    A beast, yet is, or should be more :
    Reason and speech we only bring.
Parrots may thank us, if they are not mute,
    They go upon the score.

    Man is all symmetry,
Full of proportions, one limb to another,
    And all to all the world besides :
    Each part may call the farthest, brother :
For head with foot hath private amity,
    And both with moons and tides.

    Nothing hath got so far,
But Man hath caught and kept it, as his prey.
    His eyes dismount the highest star
    He is in little all the sphere.
Herbs gladly cure our flesh, because that they
    Find their acquaintance there.

For us the winds do blow ;
The earth doth rest, heaven move, and fountains flow.
Nothing we see, but means our good,
As our *delight*, or as our *treasure* :
The whole is, either our cupboard of *food*,
Or cabinet of *pleasure*.

The stars have us to bed ;
Night draws the curtain, which the Sun withdraws :
Music and light attend our head.
All things unto our *flesh* are kind
In their *descent* and *being* ; to our *mind*
In their *ascent* and *cause*.

Each thing is full of duty :
Waters united, are our navigation ;
Distinguished,[1] our habitation ;
Below, our drink ; above, our meat :
Both are our cleanliness. Hath one such beauty ?
Then how are all things neat !

More servants wait on Man,
Than he'll take notice of : in every path
He treads down that which doth befriend him,
When sickness makes him pale and wan.
Oh, mighty love ! Man is one world, and hath
Another to attend him.

Since then, my God, thou hast
So brave a Palace built ; O dwell in it,
That it may dwell with thee at last !
Till then, afford us so much wit,
That, as the world serves us, we may serve thee,
And both thy servants be.

[1] 'Distinguished,' *i. e.*, when marked by an island.

## ANTIPHON.

Chor. Praised be the God of love,
    Men. Here below,
    Angels. And here above:

Chor. Who hath dealt his mercies so,
    Ang. To his friend,
    Men. And to his foe;

Chor. That both grace and glory tend
    Ang. Us of old,
    Men. And us in the end.

Chor. The great Shepherd of the fold
    Ang. Us did make,
    Men. For us was sold.

Chor. He our foes in pieces brake:
    Ang. Him we touch;
    Men. And him we take.

Chor. Wherefore since that he is such,
    Ang. We adore,
    Men. And we do crouch.

Chor. Lord, thy praises shall be more.
    Men. We have none,
    Ang. And we no store.

Chor. Praised be the God alone
    Who hath made of two folds one.

## UNKINDNESS.

Lord, make me coy and tender to offend:
In friendship, first I think, if that agree,
                Which I intend,
    Unto my friend's intent and end.
I would not use a friend, as I use Thee.

If any touch my friend, or his good name,
It is my honour and my love to free
                His blasted fame
    From the least spot or thought of blame.
I could not use a friend, as I use Thee.

My friend may spit upon my curious floor:
Would he have gold? I lend it instantly;
                But let the poor,
    And thou within them, starve at door.
I cannot use a friend, as I use Thee.

When that my friend pretendeth to a place,
I quit my interest, and leave it free:
                But when thy grace
    Sues for my heart, I thee displace;
Nor would I use a friend, as I use Thee.

Yet can a friend what Thou hast done fulfil?
O write in brass, *My God upon a tree*
                *His blood did spill,*
    *Only to purchase my good-will:*
*Yet use I not my foes, as I use Thee.*

## LIFE.

I MADE a posie, while the day ran by:
Here will I smell my remnant out, and tie
   My life within this band.
But time did beckon to the flowers, and they
By noon most cunningly did steal away,
   And wither'd in my hand.

My hand was next to them, and then my heart;
I took, without more thinking, in good part
   Time's gentle admonition;
Who did so sweetly death's sad taste convey,
Making my mind to smell my fatal day,
   Yet sugaring the suspicion.

Farewell, dear flowers, sweetly your time ye spent,
Fit, while ye lived, for smell or ornament,
   And after death for cures.
I follow straight without complaints or grief,
Since if my scent be good, I care not if
   It be as short as yours.


## SUBMISSION.

BUT that thou art my wisdom, Lord,
 And both mine eyes are thine,
My mind would be extremely stirr'd
 For missing my design.

Were it not better to bestow
 Some place and power on me?

Then should thy praises with me grow,
  And share in my degree.

But when I thus dispute and grieve,
  I do resume my sight;
And pilfering what I once did give,
  Disseize thee of thy right.

How know I, if thou shouldst me raise,
  That I should then raise thee?
Perhaps great places and thy praise
  Do not so well agree.

Wherefore unto my gift I stand;
  I will no more advise:
Only do thou lend me a hand,
  Since thou hast both mine eyes.

## JUSTICE.

I CANNOT skill of these thy ways:
*Lord, thou didst make me, yet thou woundest me:*
*Lord, thou dost wound me, yet thou dost relieve me:*
*Lord, thou relievest, yet I die by thee:*
*Lord, thou dost kill me, yet thou dost reprieve me.*

But when I mark my life and praise,
  Thy justice me most fitly pays:
For, *I do praise thee, yet I praise thee not:*
*My prayers mean thee, yet my prayers stray:*
*I would do well, yet sin the hand hath got:*
*My soul doth love thee, yet it loves delay.*
  I cannot skill of these my ways.

## CHARMS AND KNOTS.

Who read a Chapter when they rise,
Shall ne'er be troubled with ill eyes.

A poor man's rod, when thou dost ride,
Is both a weapon and a guide.

Who shuts his hand, hath lost his gold:
Who opens it, hath it twice told.

Who goes to bed, and doth not pray,
Maketh two nights to every day.

Who by aspersions throw a stone
At the head of others, hit their own.

Who looks on ground with humble eyes,
Finds himself there, and seeks to rise.

When the hair is sweet through pride or lust,
The powder doth forget the dust.

Take one from ten, and what remains?
Ten still, if Sermons go for gains.

In shallow waters heaven doth show:
But who drinks on, to hell may go.

## AFFLICTION.

My God, I read this day,
That planted Paradise was not so firm
As was and is thy floating Ark ; whose stay
And anchor thou art only, to confirm
    And strengthen it in every age,
    When waves do rise, and tempests rage.

At first we lived in pleasure ;
Thine own delights thou didst to us impart :
When we grew wanton, thou didst use displeasure
To make us thine : yet that we might not part,
    As we at first did board with thee,
    Now thou wouldst taste our misery.

There is but joy and grief ;
If either will convert us, we are thine :
Some angels used the first; if our relief
Take up the second, then thy double line
    And several baits in either kind
    Furnish thy table to thy mind.

Affliction then is ours ;
We are the trees, whom shaking fastens more,
While blustering winds destroy the wanton bowers,
And ruffle all their curious knots and store.
    My God, so temper joy and woe,
    That thy bright beams may tame thy bow.

## MORTIFICATION.

How soon doth man decay!
When clothes are taken from a chest of sweets
    To swaddle infants, whose young breath
        Scarce knows the way;
    Those clouts are little winding-sheets,
Which do consign and send them unto death.

    When boys go first to bed,
They step into their voluntary graves;
    Sleep binds them fast; only their breath
        Makes them not dead.
    Successive nights, like rolling waves,
Convey them quickly, who are bound for death.

    When youth is frank and free,
And calls for music, while his veins do swell,
    All day exchanging mirth and breath
        In company;
    That music summons to the knell,
Which shall befriend him at the house of death.

    When man grows staid and wise,
Getting a house and home, where he may move
    Within the circle of his breath,
        Schooling his eyes;
    That dumb enclosure maketh love
Unto the coffin, that attends his death.

    When age grows low and weak,
Marking his grave, and thawing every year,
    Till all do melt, and drown his breath

When he would speak ;
A chair or litter shows the bier
Which shall convey him to the house of death.

Man, ere he is aware,
Hath put together a solemnity,
And dress'd his hearse, while he has breath
As yet to spare.
Yet, Lord, instruct us so to die,
That all these dyings may be life in death.

### DECAY.

Sweet were the days, when thou didst lodge with *Lot*,
Struggle with *Jacob*, sit with *Gideon*,
Advise with *Abraham*, when thy power could not
Encounter *Moses*' strong complaints and moan :
    Thy words were then, *Let me alone.*

One might have sought and found thee presently
At some fair oak, or bush, or cave, or well :
Is my God this way ? No, they would reply ;
He is to *Sinai* gone, as we heard tell :
    List, ye may hear great *Aaron's* bell.

But now thou dost thyself immure and close
In some one corner of a feeble heart :
Where yet both Sin and Satan, thy old foes,
Do pinch and straiten thee, and use much art
    To gain thy thirds and little part.

I see the world grows old, when as the heat
Of thy great love once spread, as in an urn

Doth closet up itself, and still retreat,
Cold sin still forcing it, till it return,
    And calling Justice, all things burn.


## MISERY.

L<small>ORD</small>, let the Angels praise thy name.
Man is a foolish thing, a foolish thing;
  Folly and Sin play all his game.
His house still burns; and yet he still doth sing,
    *Man is but grass,*
  *He knows it, fill the glass.*

How canst thou brook his foolishness?
Why, he'll not lose a cup of drink for thee:
  Bid him but temper his excess;
Not he: he knows, where he can better be,
    As he will swear,
  Than to serve thee in fear.

What strange pollutions doth he wed,
And make his own? as if none knew, but he.
  No man shall beat into his head
That thou within his curtains drawn canst see:
    They are of cloth,
  Where never yet came moth.

The best of men, turn but thy hand
For one poor minute, stumble at a pin:
  They would not have their actions scann'd,
Nor any sorrow tell them that they sin,
    Though it be small,
  And measure not their fall.

They quarrel thee, and would give over
The bargain made to serve thee : but thy love
  Holds them unto it, and doth cover
Their follies with the wing of thy mild Dove,
      Not suffering those
      Who would, to be thy foes.

  My God, Man cannot praise thy name :
Thou art all brightness, perfect purity ;
  The Sun holds down his head for shame,
Dead with eclipses, when we speak of thee.
      How shall infection
      Presume on thy perfection ?

  As dirty hands foul all they touch,
And those things most, which are most pure and fine :
  So our clay hearts, even when we crouch
To sing thy praises, make them less divine.
      Yet either this
      Or none thy portion is.

  Man cannot serve thee ; let him go
And serve the swine : there, there is his delight :
  He doth not like this virtue, no ;
Give him his dirt to wallow in all night ;
      These Preachers make
      His head to shoot and ache.

  O foolish man ! where are thine eyes ?
How hast thou lost them in a crowd of cares ?
  Thou pull'st the rug, and wilt not rise,
No, not to purchase the whole pack of stars ·
      There let them shine,
      Thou must go sleep, or dine.

The bird that sees a dainty bower
Made in the tree, where she was wont to sit,
Wonders and sings, but not his power
Who made the arbour : this exceeds her wit.
    But Man doth know
     The spring whence all things flow :

And yet, as though he knew it not,
His knowledge winks, and lets his humours reign:
They make his life a constant blot,
And all the blood of God to run in vain.
     Ah, wretch! what verse
     Can thy strange ways rehearse ?

Indeed at first Man was a treasure,
A box of jewels, shop of rarities,
 A ring, whose posie was, *My pleasure*:
He was a garden in a Paradise :
     Glory and grace
     Did crown his heart and face.

But sin hath fool'd him. Now he is
A lump of flesh, without a foot or wing
 To raise him to the glimpse of bliss :
A sick toss'd vessel, dashing on each thing ;
     Nay, his own shelf :
     My God, I mean myself.


## JORDAN.

When first my lines of heavenly joys made mention,
Such was their lustre, they did so excel,
That I sought out quaint words, and trim invention ;

My thoughts began to burnish, sprout, and swell,
Curling with metaphors a plain intention,
Decking the sense, as if it were to sell.

Thousands of notions in my brain did run,
Offering their service, if I were not sped:
I often blotted what I had begun;
This was not quick enough, and that was dead.
Nothing could seem too rich to clothe the Sun,
Much less those joys which trample on his head.

As flames do work and wind, when they ascend;
So did I weave myself into the sense.
But while I bustled, I might hear a friend
Whisper, *How wide is all this long pretence!*
*There is in love a sweetness ready penn'd:*
*Copy out only that, and save expense.*


## PRAYER.

Of what an easy quick access,
My blessed Lord, art thou! how suddenly
May our requests thine ear invade!
To show that state dislikes not easiness,
If I but lift mine eyes, my suit is made:
Thou canst no more not hear, than thou canst die.

Of what supreme Almighty power
Is thy great arm which spans the East and West,
And tacks the Centre to the Sphere!
By it do all things live their measured hour:
We cannot ask the thing, which is not there,
Blaming the shallowness of our request.

Of what unmeasurable love
Art thou possest, who, when thou couldst not die,
    Wert fain to take our flesh and curse,
And for our sakes in person sin reprove ;
That by destroying that which tied thy purse,
Thou might'st make way for liberality !

    Since then these three wait on thy throne,
*Ease, Power,* and *Love* ; I value Prayer so,
    That were I to leave all but one,
Wealth, fame, endowments, virtues, all should go ;
I and dear Prayer would together dwell,
And quickly gain, for each inch lost, an ell.

## OBEDIENCE.

    My God, if writings may
  Convey a lordship any way
Whither the buyer and the seller please ;
    Let it not thee displease ;
If this poor paper do as much as they.

    On it my heart doth bleed
  As many lines, as there doth need
To pass itself and all it hath to thee.
    To which I do agree,
And here present it as my special deed.

    If that hereafter Pleasure
  Cavil, and claim her part and measure,
As if this passed with a reservation,
    Or some such words in fashion ;
I here exclude the wrangler from thy treasure.

## THE CHURCH.

      O let thy sacred will
   All thy delight in me fulfil!
Let me not think an action mine own way,
    But as thy love shall sway,
Resigning up the rudder to thy skill.

    Lord, what is man to thee,
  That thou shouldst mind a rotten tree?
Yet since thou canst not choose but see my actions;
    So great are thy perfections,
Thou may'st as well my actions guide, as see.

    Besides, thy death and blood
  Show'd a strange love to all our good:
Thy sorrows were in earnest; no faint proffer,
    Or superficial offer
Of what we might not take, or be withstood.

    Wherefore I all forego:
  To one word only I say, No:
Where in the deed there was an intimation
    Of a *gift* or *donation,*
Lord, let it now by way of *purchase* go.

    He that will pass his land,
  As I have mine, may set his hand
And heart unto this deed, when he hath read;
    And make the purchase spread
To both our goods, if he to it will stand.

    How happy were my part,
  If some kind man would thrust his heart
Into these lines; till in Heaven's court of rolls
    They were by winged souls
Enter'd for both, far above their desert!

### CONSCIENCE.

Peace, prattler, do not lour:
Not a fair look, but thou dost call it foul:
Not a sweet dish, but thou dost call it sour:
    Music to thee doth howl.
By listening to thy chatting fears
I have both lost mine eyes and ears.

    Prattler, no more, I say:
My thoughts must work, but like a noiseless sphere.
Harmonious peace must rock them all the day:
    No room for prattlers there.
If thou persistest, I will tell thee,
That I have physic to expel thee.

    And the receipt shall be
My Saviour's blood: whenever at his board
I do but taste it, straight it cleanseth me,
    And leaves thee not a word;
No, not a tooth or nail to scratch,
And at my actions carp, or catch.

    Yet if thou talkest still,
Besides my physic, know there's some for thee:
Some wood and nails to make a staff or bill
    For those that trouble me:
The bloody cross of my dear Lord
Is both my physic and my sword.

## SION.

Lord, with what glory wast thou served of old,
   When *Solomon's* temple stood and flourished!
Where most things were of purest gold;
   The wood was all embellished
With flowers and carvings, mystical and rare:
All show'd the builder's, craved the seer's care.

Yet all this glory, all this pomp and state,
   Did not affect thee much, was not thy aim;
Something there was that sow'd debate:
   Wherefore thou quitt'st thy ancient claim:
And now thy Architecture meets with sin;
For all thy frame and fabric is within.

There thou art struggling with a peevish heart,
   Which sometimes crosseth thee, thou sometimes it:
The fight is hard on either part.
   Great God doth fight, he doth submit.
All *Solomon's* sea of brass and world of stone
Is not so dear to thee as one good groan.

And truly brass and stones are heavy things,
   Tombs for the dead, not temples fit for thee:
But groans are quick, and full of wings,
   And all their motions upward be;
And ever as they mount, like larks they sing:
The note is sad, yet music for a king.

## HOME.

Come, Lord, my head doth burn, my heart is sick,
    While thou dost ever, ever stay:
Thy long deferrings wound me to the quick,
    My spirit gaspeth night and day.
        O show thyself to me,
        Or take me up to thee!

How canst thou stay, considering the pace
    The blood did make, which thou didst waste?
When I behold it trickling down thy face,
    I never saw thing make such haste.
        O show thyself, &c.

When man was lost, thy pity look'd about,
    To see what help in th' earth or sky:
But there was none; at least no help without:
    The help did in thy bosom lie.
        O show thyself, &c.

There lay thy Son: and must he leave that nest,
    That hive of sweetness, to remove
Thraldom from those, who would not at a feast
    Leave one poor apple for thy love?
        O show thyself, &c.

He did, he came: O my Redeemer dear,
    After all this canst thou be strange?
So many years baptized, and not appear;
    As if thy love could fail or change?
        O show thyself, &c.

Yet if thou stayest still, why must I stay?
  My God, what is this world to me?
This world of woe? Hence, all ye clouds, away,
  Away; I must get up and see.
    O show thyself, &c.

What is this weary world; this meat and drink,
  That chains us by the teeth so fast?
What is this woman-kind, which I can wink
  Into a blackness and distaste?
    O show thyself, &c.

With one small sigh thou gavest me th' other day
  I blasted all the joys about me:
And scowling on them as they pined away,
  Now come again, said I, and flout me.
    O show thyself, &c.

Nothing but drought and dearth, but bush and brake,
  Which way soe'er I look, I see.
Some may dream merrily, but when they wake,
  They dress themselves and come to thee.
    O show thyself, &c.

We talk of harvests; there are no such things,
  But when we leave our corn and hay:
There is no fruitful year, but that which brings
  The last and loved, though dreadful day.
    O show thyself, &c.

O loose this frame, this knot of man untie,
  That my free soul may use her wing,
Which now is pinion'd with mortality,
  As an entangled, hamper'd thing.
    O show thyself, &c.

What have I left, that I should stay and groan?
    The most of me to heaven is fled :
My thoughts and joys are all pack'd up and gone,
    And for their old acquaintance plead.
        O show thyself, &c.

Come, dearest Lord, pass not this holy season,
    My flesh and bones and joints do pray :
And even my verse, when by the rhyme and reason
    The word is *Stay*, says ever, *Come*.
        O show thyself to me,
        Or take me up to thee !

## THE BRITISH CHURCH.

I JOY, dear Mother, when I view
Thy perfect lineaments and hue
    Both sweet and bright :
Beauty in thee takes up her place,
And dates her letters from thy face,
    When she doth write.

A fine aspect in fit array,
Neither too mean, nor yet too gay,
    Shows who is best :
Outlandish looks may not compare ;
For all they either painted are,
    Or else undrest.

She on the hills, which wantonly
Allureth all in hope to be
    By her preferr'd,

Hath kiss'd so long her painted shrines,
That even her face by kissing shines,
    For her reward.

She in the valley is so shy
Of dressing, that her hair doth lie
    About her ears :
While she avoids her neighbour's pride,
She wholly goes on th' other side,
    And nothing wears.

But, dearest Mother (what those miss),
The mean thy praise and glory is,
    And long may be.
Blessed be God, whose love it was
To double-moat thee with his grace,
    And none but thee.


## THE QUIP.

THE merry world did on a day
With his train-bands and mates agree
To meet together, where I lay,
And all in sport to jeer at me.

First, Beauty crept into a Rose ;
Which when I pluck'd not, Sir, said she,
Tell me, I pray, whose hands are those ?
*But thou shalt answer, Lord, for me.*

Then Money came, and chinking still,
What tune is this, poor man ? said he :

I heard in Music you had skill :
*But thou shalt answer, Lord, for me.*

Then came brave Glory puffing by
In silks that whistled, who but he!
He scarce allow'd me half an eye :
*But thou shalt answer, Lord, for me.*

Then came quick Wit and Conversation,
And he would needs a comfort be,
And, to be short, make an oration.
*But thou shalt answer, Lord, for me.*

Yet when the hour of thy design
To answer these fine things shall come ;
Speak not at large, say, I am thine,
And then they have their answer home.

## VANITY.

Poor silly soul, whose hope and head lies low ;
Whose flat delights on earth do creep and grow :
To whom the stars shine not so fair, as eyes ;
Nor solid work, as false embroideries ;
Hark and beware, lest what you now do measure,
And write for sweet, prove a most sour displeasure.
  O hear betimes, lest thy relenting
   May come to late!
  To purchase heaven for repenting
   Is no hard rate.
  If souls be made of earthly mould,
   Let them love gold ;

If born on high,
Let them unto their kindred fly:
For they can never be at rest,
Till they regain their ancient nest.
Then silly soul, take heed; for earthly joy
Is but a bubble, and makes thee a boy.

## THE DAWNING.

AWAKE, sad heart, whom sorrow ever drowns:
　Take up thine eyes, which feed on earth,
Unfold thy forehead gather'd into frowns:
　Thy Saviour comes, and with him mirth:
　　　　　Awake, awake;
And with a thankful heart his comforts take.
　But thou dost still lament, and pine, and cry;
　And feel his death, but not his victory.

Arise, sad heart; if thou dost not withstand,
　Christ's resurrection thine may be:
Do not by hanging down break from the hand,
　Which, as it riseth, raiseth thee:
　　　　　Arise, arise;
And with his burial-linen dry thine eyes.
　Christ left his grave-clothes, that we might, when grief
　Draws tears, or blood, not want a handkerchief.

## JESU.

JESU is in my heart, his sacred name
Is deeply carved there: but the other week
A great affliction broke the little frame,
Even all to pieces; which I went to seek:

And first I found the corner where was J,
After, where ES, and next where U was graved.
When I had got these parcels, instantly
I sat me down to spell them, and perceived
That to my broken heart he was *I ease you*,
   And to my whole is *JESU*.

## BUSINESS.

  C<small>ANST</small> be idle ? canst thou play,
  Foolish soul who sinn'd to-day ?

Rivers run, and springs each one
Know their home, and get them gone :
Hast thou tears, or hast thou none ?

If, poor soul, thou hast no tears,
Would thou hadst no faults or fears!
Who hath these, those ills forbears.

Winds still work : it is their plot,
Be the season cold or hot :
Hast thou sighs, or hast thou not ?

If thou hast no sighs or groans,
Would thou hadst no flesh and bones!
Lesser pains 'scape greater ones.

  But if yet thou idle be,
  Foolish soul, who died for thee ?

Who did leave his Father's throne,
To assume thy flesh and bone ?
Had he life, or had he none ?

If he had not lived for thee,
Thou hadst died most wretchedly;
And two deaths had been thy fee.

He so far thy good did plot,
That his own self he forgot.
Did he die, or did he not?

If he had not died for thee,
Thou hadst lived in misery.
Two lives worse than ten deaths be.

 And hath any space of breath
 'Twixt his sins and Saviour's death?

He that loseth gold, though dross,
Tells to all he meets, his cross:
He that sins, hath he no loss?

He that finds a silver vein,
Thinks on it, and thinks again:
Brings thy Saviour's death no gain?

 Who in heart not ever kneels,
 Neither sin nor Saviour feels.


## DIALOGUE.

Sweetest Saviour, if my soul
 Were but worth the having,
Quickly should I then control
 Any thought of waving.

But when all my care and pains
Cannot give the name of gains
To thy wretch so full of stains ;
What delight or hope remains ?

*What (Child), is the balance thine ?*
   *Thine the poise and measure ?*
*If I say, Thou shalt be mine,*
   *Finger not my treasure.*
*What the gains in having thee*
*Do amount to, only he,*
*Who for man was sold, can see,*
*That transferr'd the accounts to me.*

But as I can see no merit,
   Leading to this favour :
So the way to fit me for it,
   Is beyond my savour.
As the reason then is thine ;
So the way is none of mine :
I disclaim the whole design :
Sin disclaims and I resign.

*That is all, if that I could*
   *Get without repining ;*
*And my clay my creature would*
   *Follow my resigning :*
*That as I did freely part*
*With my glory and desert,*
*Left all joys to feel all smart*——
Ah ! no more : thou break'st my heart.

## DULNESS.

Why do I languish thus, drooping and dull,
    As if I were all earth?
O give me quickness, that I may with mirth
    Praise thee brimful!

The wanton lover in a curious strain
    Can praise his fairest fair;
And with quaint metaphors her curled hair
    Curl o'er again:

Thou art my loveliness, my life, my light,
    Beauty alone to me:
Thy bloody death and undeserved, makes thee
    Pure red and white.

When all perfections as but one appear,
    That those thy form doth show,
The very dust, where thou dost tread and go,
    Makes beauties here;

Where are my lines then? my approaches? views?
    Where are my window-songs?
Lovers are still pretending, and even wrongs
    Sharpen their Muse.

But I am lost in flesh, whose sugar'd lies
    Still mock me, and grow bold:
Sure thou didst put a mind there, if I could
    Find where it lies.

Lord, clear thy gift, that with a constant wit
    I may but look towards thee :
*Look* only ; for to *love* thee, who can be,
    What angel, fit ?

## LOVE-JOY.

As on a window late I cast mine eye,
I saw a vine drop grapes with J and C
Anneal'd on every bunch.  One standing by
Ask'd what it meant.  I (who am never loth
To spend my judgment) said, it seem'd to me
To be the body and the letters both
Of *Joy* and *Charity*.  Sir, you have not miss'd,
The man replied ; It figures JESUS CHRIST.

## PROVIDENCE.

O SACRED Providence, who from end to end
Strongly and sweetly movest ! shall I write,
And not of thee, through whom my fingers bend
To hold my quill ? shall they not do thee right ?

Of all the creatures both in sea and land,
Only to Man thou hast made known thy ways,
And put the pen alone into his hand,
And made him Secretary of thy praise.

Beasts fain would sing ; birds ditty to their notes;
Trees would be tuning on their native lute
To thy renown : but all their hands and throats
Are brought to Man, while they are lame and mute.

Man is the world's High Priest: he doth present
The sacrifice for all; while they below
Unto the service mutter an assent,
Such as springs use that fall, and winds that blow.

He that to praise and laud thee doth refrain,
Doth not refrain unto himself alone,
But robs a thousand who would praise thee fain;
And doth commit a world of sin in one.

The beasts say, Eat me; but, if beasts must teach,
The tongue is yours to eat, but mine to praise.
The trees say, Pull me: but the hand you stretch
Is mine to write, as it is yours to raise.

Wherefore, most sacred Spirit, I here present
For me and all my fellows praise to thee:
And just it is that I should pay the rent,
Because the benefit accrues to me.

We all acknowledge both thy power and love
To be exact, transcendent, and divine;
Who dost so strongly and so sweetly move,
While all things have their will, yet none but thine.

For either thy *command*, or thy *permission*
Lay hands on all: they are thy *right* and *left*:
The first puts on with speed and expedition;
The other curbs sin's stealing pace and theft;

Nothing escapes them both: all must appear,
And be disposed, and dress'd, and tuned by thee,
Who sweetly temper'st all. If we could hear
Thy skill and art, what music would it be!

Thou art in small things great, not small in any :
Thy even praise can neither rise nor fall.
Thou art in all things one, in each thing many :
For thou art infinite in one and all.

Tempests are calm to thee, they know thy hand,
And hold it fast, as children do their father's,
Which cry and follow.  Thou hast made poor sand
Check the proud sea, even when it swells and gathers.

Thy cupboard serves the world : the meat is set
Where all may reach : no beast but knows his feed.
Birds teach us hawking : fishes have their net :
The great prey on the less, they on some weed.

Nothing engender'd doth prevent his meat ;
Flies have their table spread, ere they appear ;
Some creatures have in winter what to eat ;
Others do sleep, and envy not their cheer.

How finely dost thou times and seasons spin,
And make a twist checker'd with night and day !
Which as it lengthens, winds, and winds us in,
As bowls go on, but turning all the way.

Each creature hath a wisdom for his good.
The pigeons feed their tender offspring crying,
When they are callow ; but withdraw their food,
When they are fledged, that need may teach them flying.

Bees work for man ; and yet they never bruise
Their master's flower, but leave it, having done,
As fair as ever, and as fit to use :
So both the flower doth stay, and honey run.

Sheep eat the grass, and dung the ground for more :
Trees after bearing drop their leaves for soil :
Springs vent their streams, and by expense get store :
Clouds cool by heat, and baths by cooling boil.

Who hath the virtue to express the rare
And curious virtues both of herbs and stones ?
Is there an herb for that ?   O that thy care
Would show a root, that gives expressions !

And if an herb hath power, what have the stars ?
A rose, besides his beauty, is a cure.
Doubtless our plagues and plenty, peace and wars,
Are there much surer than our art is sure.

Thou hast hid metals : man may take them thence ;
But at his peril : when he digs the place,
He makes a grave : as if the thing had sense,
And threaten'd man, that he should fill the space.

Even poisons praise thee.   Should a thing be lost ?
Should creatures want, for want of heed, their due ?
Since where are poisons, antidotes are most ;
The help stands close, and keeps the fear in view.

The sea, which seems to stop the traveller,
Is by a ship the speedier passage made.
The winds, who think they rule the mariner,
Are ruled by him, and taught to serve his trade.

And as thy house is full, so I adore
Thy curious art in marshalling thy goods
The hills with health abound, the vales with store ;
The South with marble ; North with furs and woods.

Hard things are glorious; easy things good cheap;
The common all men have; that which is rare,
Men therefore seek to have, and care to keep.
The healthy frosts with summer-fruits compare.

Light without wind is glass: warm without weight
Is wool and furs: cool without closeness, shade:
Speed without pains, a horse: tall without height,
A servile hawk: low without loss, a spade.

All countries have enough to serve their need:
If they seek fine things, thou dost make them run
For their offence; and then dost turn their speed
To be commerce and trade from sun to sun.

Nothing wears clothes, but Man; nothing doth need
But he to wear them. Nothing useth fire,
But Man alone, to show his heavenly breed:
And only he hath fuel in desire.

When th' earth was dry, thou madest a sea of wet:
When that lay gather'd, thou didst broach the mountains:
When yet some places could no moisture get,
The winds grew gardeners, and the clouds good fountains.

Rain, do not hurt my flowers; but gently spend
Your honey drops: press not to smell them here;
When they are ripe, their odour will ascend,
And at your lodging with their thanks appear.

How harsh are thorns to pears! and yet they make
A better hedge, and need less reparation.
How smooth are silks, compared with a stake,
Or with a stone! yet make no good foundation.

Sometimes thou dost divide thy gifts to man,
Sometimes unite.  The Indian nut alone
Is clothing, meat and trencher, drink and can,
Boat, cable, sail and needle, all in one.

Most herbs that grow in brooks, are hot and dry.
Cold fruit's warm kernels help against the wind.
The lemon's juice and rind cure mutually.
The whey of milk doth loose, the milk doth bind.

Thy creatures leap not, but express a feast,
Where all the guests sit close, and nothing wants.
Frogs marry fish and flesh ; bats, bird and beast ;
Sponges, nonsense and sense ; mines, th' earth and plants.

To show thou art not bound, as if thy lot
Were worse than ours, sometimes thou shiftest hands.
Most things move th' under-jaw ; the Crocodile not.
Most things sleep lying, th' Elephant leans or stands.

But who hath praise enough ? nay, who hath any ?
None can express thy works, but he that knows them ;
And nono can know thy works, which are so many,
And so complete, but only he that owes them.

All things that are, though they have several ways,
Yet in their being join with one advice
To honour thee : and so I give thee praise
In all my other hymns, but in this twice.

Each thing that is, although in use and name
It go for one, hath many ways in store
To honour thee ; and so each hymn thy fame
Extolleth many ways, yet this one more.

## HOPE.

I GAVE to Hope a Watch of mine : but he
    An Anchor gave to me.
Then an old Prayer-book I did present :
    And he an Optic sent.

With that I gave a Phial full of tears :
    But he a few green ears.
Ah, loiterer! I'll no more, no more I'll bring :
    I did expect a Ring.

## SINS ROUND.

SORRY I am, my God, sorry I am,
That my offences course it in a ring.
My thoughts are working like a busy flame,
Until their Cockatrice they hatch and bring :
And when they once have perfected their draughts,
My words take fire from my inflamed thoughts.

My words take fire from my inflamed thoughts,
Which spit it forth like the Sicilian hill.
They vent the wares, and pass them with their faults,
And by their breathing ventilate the ill.
But words suffice not, where are lewd intentions :
My hands do join to finish the inventions :

My hands do join to finish the inventions :
And so my sins ascend three storeys high,
As Babel grew, before there were dissensions.

Yet ill deeds loiter not : for they supply
New thoughts of sinning ; wherefore, to my shame,
Sorry I am, my God, sorry I am.


## TIME.

MEETING with Time, Slack thing, said I,
Thy scythe is dull ; whet it for shame.
No marvel, Sir, he did reply,
If it at length deserve some blame :
 But where one man would have me grind it,
 Twenty for one too sharp do find it.

Perhaps some such of old did pass,
Who above all things loved this life ;
To whom thy scythe a hatchet was,
Which now is but a pruning-knife.
 Christ's coming hath made Man thy debtor,
 Since by thy cutting he grows better.

And in his blessing thou art blest :
For where thou only wert before
An executioner at best,
Thou art a gardener now, and more.
 An usher to convey our souls
 Beyond the utmost stars and poles.

And this is that makes life so long,
While it detains us from our God.
Even pleasures here increase the wrong :
And length of days lengthen the rod.
 Who wants the place, where God doth dwell,
 Partakes already half of hell.

Of what strange length must that needs be,
Which even eternity excludes!
Thus far Time heard me patiently:
Then chafing said, This man deludes:
   What do I here before his door?
   He doth not crave less time, but more.


## GRATEFULNESS.

Thou that hast given so much to me,
Give one thing more, a grateful heart.
See how thy beggar works on thee
                By art.

He makes thy gifts occasion more,
And says, If he in this be crost,
All thou hast given him heretofore
                Is lost.

But thou didst reckon, when at first
Thy word our hearts and hands did crave,
What it would come to at the worst
                To save.

Perpetual knockings at thy door,
Tears sullying thy transparent rooms,
Gift upon gift; much would have more,
                And comes.

This notwithstanding, thou went'st on,
And didst allow us all our noise:
Nay, thou hast made a sigh and groan
                Thy joys.

Not that thou hast not still above
Much better tunes, than groans can make ;
But that these country-airs thy love
    Did take.

Wherefore I cry, and cry again ;
And in no quiet canst thou be,
Till I a thankful heart obtain
    Of thee :

Not thankful, when it pleaseth me :
As if thy blessings had spare days :
But such a heart, whose pulse may be
    Thy praise.


## PEACE.

Sweet Peace, where dost thou dwell ? I humbly crave,
    Let me once know.
 I sought thee in a secret cave,
    And ask'd, if Peace were there.
A hollow wind did seem to answer, No :
    Go seek elsewhere.

I did ; and going did a rainbow note :
    Surely, thought I,
  This is the lace of Peace's coat :
    I will search out the matter.
But while I look'd, the clouds immediately
    Did break and scatter.

Then went I to a garden, and did spy
    A gallant flower,

The Crown Imperial: Sure, said I,
    Peace at the root must dwell.
But when I digg'd, I saw a worm devour
    What show'd so well.

At length I met a reverend good old man:
    Whom when for Peace
I did demand, he thus began:
    There was a Prince of old
At Salem dwelt, who lived with good increase
    Of flock and fold.

He sweetly lived; yet sweetness did not save
    His life from foes.
But after death out of his grave
    There sprang twelve stalks of wheat:
Which many wondering at, got some of those
    To plant and set.

It prosper'd strangely, and did soon disperse
    Through all the earth:
For they that taste it do rehearse,
    That virtue lies therein;
A secret virtue, bringing peace and mirth
    By flight of sin.

Take of this grain, which in my garden grows,
    And grows for you;
Make bread of it: and that repose
    And peace, which every where
With so much earnestness you do pursue,
    Is only there.

## CONFESSION.

Oh, what a cunning guest
Is this same grief! within my heart I made
    Closets; and in them many a chest;
    And like a master in my trade,
In those chests, boxes; in each box, a till:
Yet grief knows all, and enters when he will.

    No screw, no piercer can
Into a piece of timber work and wind,
    As God's afflictions into man,
    When he a torture hath design'd.
They are too subtle for the subtlest hearts;
And fall, like rheums, upon the tenderest parts.

    We are the earth; and they,
Like moles within us, heave, and cast about:
    And till they foot and clutch their prey,
    They never cool, much less give out.
No Smith can make such locks, but they have keys;
Closets are Halls to them; and hearts, highways.

    Only an open breast
Doth shut them out, so that they cannot enter;
    Or, if they enter, cannot rest,
    But quickly seek some new adventure.
Smooth open hearts no fastening have; but fiction
Doth give a hold and handle to affliction.

    Wherefore my faults and sins,
Lord, I acknowledge; take thy plagues away:

For since confession pardon wins,
    I challenge here the brightest day,
The clearest diamond : let them do their best,
They shall be thick and cloudy to my breast.


## GIDDINESS.

Oh, what a thing is Man ! how far from power,
    From settled peace and rest !
He is some twenty several men at least
    Each several hour.

One while he counts of heaven, as of his treasure :
    But then a thought creeps in,
And calls him coward, who for fear of sin
    Will lose a pleasure.

Now he will fight it out, and to the wars ;
    Now eat his bread in peace,
And snudge in quiet : now he scorns increase ;
    Now all day spares.

He builds a house, which quickly down must go,
    As if a whirlwind blew
And crush'd the building : and 'tis partly true,
    His mind is so.

Oh, what a sight were Man, if his attires
    Did alter with his mind ;
And, like a Dolphin's skin, his clothes combined
    With his desires !

Surely if each one saw another's heart,
    There would be no commerce,
No Sale or Bargain pass : all would disperse,
      And live apart.

Lord, mend or rather make us : one creation
    Will not suffice our turn :
Except thou make us daily, we shall spurn
      Our own salvation.

## THE BUNCH OF GRAPES.

Joy, I did lock thee up : but some bad man
      Hath let thee out again :
And now, methinks, I am where I began
    Seven years ago : one vogue and vein,
    One air of thoughts usurps my brain.
I did toward Canaan draw ; but now I am
Brought back to the Red Sea, the sea of shame.

For as the Jews of old by God's command
      Travell'd, and saw no town ;
So now each Christian hath his journeys spann'd :
    Their story pens and sets us down.
    A single deed is small renown.
God's works are wide, and let in future times ;
His ancient justice overflows our crimes.

Then have we too our guardian fires and clouds ;
    Our Scripture-dew drops fast :
We have our sands and serpents, tents and shrouds ;—
    Alas ! our murmurings come not last.
    But where's the cluster ? where's the taste

Of mine inheritance ?   Lord, if I must borrow,
Let me as well take up their joy, as sorrow.

But can he want the grape, who hath the wine ?
        I have their fruit, and more.
Blessed be God, who prosper'd *Noah's* vine,
    And made it bring forth grapes good store.
      But much more Him I must adore,
Who of the law's sour juice sweet wine did make,
Even God himself, being pressed for my sake.


## LOVE UNKNOWN.

Dear friend, sit down, the tale is long and sad :
And in my faintings I presume your love
Will more comply, than help.  A Lord I had,
And have, of whom some grounds, which may improve,
I hold for two lives, and both lives in me.
To him I brought a dish of fruit one day,
And in the middle placed my heart.  But he
        (I sigh to say)
Look'd on a servant, who did know his eye
Better than you know me, or (which is one)
Than I myself.  The servant instantly
Quitting the fruit, seized on my heart alone
And threw it in a font, wherein did fall
A stream of blood, which issued from the side
Of a great rock :  I well remember all,
And have good cause : there it was dipt and dyed,
And wash'd, and wrung : the very wringing yet
Enforceth tears.  *Your heart was foul, I fear.*
Indeed 'tis true.  I did and do commit
Many a fault more than my lease will bear ;

Yet still ask'd pardon, and was not denied.
But you shall hear. After my heart was well,
And clean and fair, as I one even-tide
<blockquote>(I sigh to tell)</blockquote>
Walk'd by myself abroad, I saw a large
And spacious furnace flaming, and thereon
A boiling caldron, round about whose verge
Was in great letters set AFFLICTION.
The greatness show'd the owner. So I went
To fetch a sacrifice out of my fold,
Thinking with that, which I did thus present,
To warm his love, which I did fear grew cold.
But as my heart did tender it, the man
Who was to take it from me, slipt his hand,
And threw my heart into the scalding pan ;
My heart, that brought it (do you understand ?),
The offerer's heart. *Your heart was hard, I fear.*
Indeed 'tis true. I found a callous matter
Began to spread and to expatiate there :
But with a richer drug, than scalding water,
I bathed it often, even with holy blood,
Which at a board, while many drank bare wine,
A friend did steal into my cup for good,
Even taken inwardly, and most divine
To supple hardnesses. But at the length
Out of the caldron getting, soon I fled
Unto my house, where to repair the strength
Which I had lost, I hasted to my bed :
But when I thought to sleep out all these faults,
<blockquote>(I sigh to speak)</blockquote>
I found that some had stuff'd the bed with thoughts,
I would say *thorns.* Dear, could my heart not break,
When with my pleasures even my rest was gone ?
Full well I understood, who had been there :

For I had given the key to none, but one :
It must be he.  *Your heart was dull, I fear.*
Indeed a slack and sleepy state of mind
Did oft possess me, so that when I pray'd,
Though my lips went, my heart did stay behind.
But all my scores were by another paid,
Who took the debt upon him.  *Truly, Friend,
For ought I hear, your Master shows to you
More favour than you wot of.  Mark the end.
The Font did only, what was old, renew :
The Caldron suppled, what was grown too hard :
The Thorns did quicken, what was grown too dull :
All did but strive to mend, what you had marr'd.
Wherefore be cheer'd, and praise him to the full
Each day, each hour, each moment of the week,
Who fain would have you be, new, tender, quick.*

## MAN'S MEDLEY.

HARK, how the birds do sing,
  And woods do ring.
All creatures have their joy, and man hath his.
  Yet if we rightly measure,
   Man's joy and pleasure
Rather hereafter, than in present, is.

  To this life things of sense
   Make their pretence :
In th' other Angels have a right by birth :
  Man ties them both alone,
   And makes them one,
With th' one hand touching heaven, with the other earth.

In soul he mounts and flies,
In flesh he dies.
He wears a stuff whose thread is coarse and round,
But trimm'd with curious lace,
And should take place
After the trimming, not the stuff and ground.

Not, that he may not here
Taste of the cheer:
But as birds drink, and straight lift up their head;
So must he sip, and think
Of better drink
He may attain to, after he is dead.

But as his joys are double,
So is his trouble.
He hath two winters, other things but one:
Both frosts and thoughts do nip,
And bite his lip;
And he of all things fears two deaths alone.

Yet even the greatest griefs
May be reliefs,
Could he but take them right, and in their ways.
Happy is he, whose heart
Hath found the art
To turn his double pains to double praise.

## THE STORM.

If as the winds and waters here below
Do fly and flow,
My sighs and tears as busy were above;

                Sure they would move
And much affect thee, as tempestuous times
Amaze poor mortals, and object their crimes.

Stars have their storms, even in a high degree,
                As well as we.
A throbbing conscience spurred by remorse
                Hath a strange force:
It quits the earth, and mounting more and more,
Dares to assault thee, and besiege thy door.

There it stands knocking, to thy music's wrong,
                And drowns the song.
Glory and honour are set by till it
                An answer get.
Poets have wrong'd poor storms: such days are best;
They purge the air without, within the breast.


## PARADISE.

I BLESS thee, Lord, because I GROW
Among thy trees, which in a ROW
To thee both fruit and order OW.

What open force, or hidden CHARM
Can blast my fruit, or bring me HARM,
While the enclosure is thine ARM?

Enclose me still, for fear I START.
Be to me rather sharp and TART,
Than let me want thy hand and ART.

When thou dost greater judgments SPARE,
And with thy knife but prune and PARE,
Even fruitful trees more fruitful ARE.

Such sharpness shows the sweetest FRIEND:
Such cuttings rather heal than REND:
And such beginnings touch their END.

## THE METHOD.

POOR heart, lament,
For since thy God refuseth still,
There is some rub, some discontent,
    Which cools his will.

Thy Father *could*
Quickly effect, what thou dost move;
For he is *Power:* and sure he *would;*
    For he is *Love.*

Go search this thing,
Tumble thy breast, and turn thy book:
If thou hadst lost a glove or ring,
    Wouldst thou not look?

What do I see
Written above there? *Yesterday
I did behave me carelessly,
    When I did pray.*

And should God's ear
To such indifferents chained be,
Who do not their own motions hear?
    Is God less free?

But stay! what's there?
*Late when I would have something done,*
*I had a motion to forbear,*
*Yet I went on.*

And should God's ear,
Which needs not man, be tied to those
Who hear not him, but quickly hear
His utter foes?

Then once more pray:
Down with thy knees, up with thy voice:
Seek pardon first, and God will say,
*Glad heart, rejoice.*


## DIVINITY.

As men, for fear the stars should sleep and nod,
    And trip at night, have spheres supplied;
As if a star were duller than a clod,
    Which knows his way without a guide:

Just so the other heaven they also serve,
    Divinity's transcendent sky:
Which with the edge of wit they cut and carve.
    Reason triumphs, and Faith lies by.

Could not that wisdom, which first broach'd the wine,
    Have thicken'd it with definitions?
And jagg'd his seamless coat, had that been fine,
    With curious questions and divisions?

But all the doctrine, which he taught and gave,
    Was clear as heaven, from whence it came.
At least those beams of truth, which only save,
    Surpass in brightness any flame.

*Love God, and love your neighbour.  Watch and pray.*
    *Do as you would be done unto.*
O dark instructions, even as dark as day!
    Who can these Gordian knots undo?

But he doth bid us take his blood for wine.
    Bid what he please; yet I am sure,
To take and taste what he doth there design,
    Is all that saves, and not obscure.

Then burn thy Epicycles, foolish man;
    Break all thy spheres, and save thy head;
Faith needs no staff of flesh, but stoutly can
    To Heaven alone both go, and lead.


## EPHESIANS IV. 30.

"GRIEVE NOT THE HOLY SPIRIT," ETC.

AND art thou grieved, sweet and sacred Dove,
    When I am sour,
    And cross thy love?
Grieved for me? the God of strength and power
    Grieved for a worm, which when I tread,
    I pass away and leave it dead?

Then weep, mine eyes, the God of love doth grieve:
    Weep foolish heart,

And weeping live;
For death is dry as dust. Yet if we part,
End as the night, whose sable hue
Your sins express; melt into dew.

When saucy Mirth shall knock or call at door,
Cry out, Get hence,
Or cry no more.
Almighty God doth grieve, he puts on sense:
I sin not to my grief alone,
But to my God's too; he doth groan.

O take thy lute, and tune it to a strain,
Which may with thee
All day complain.
There can no discord but in ceasing be.
Marbles can weep; and surely strings
More bowels have, than such hard things.

Lord, I adjudge myself to tears and grief,
Even endless tears
Without relief.
If a clear spring for me no time forbears,
But runs, although I be not dry;
I am no Crystal, what shall I?

Yet if I wail not still, since still to wail
Nature denies;
And flesh would fail,
If my deserts were masters of mine eyes:
Lord, pardon, for thy Son makes good
My want of tears with store of blood.

## THE FAMILY.

WHAT doth this noise of thoughts within my heart,
    As if they had a part?
What do these loud complaints and pulling fears,
    As if there were no rule or ears?

But, Lord, the house and family are thine,
    Though some of them repine.
Turn out these wranglers, which defile thy seat:
    For where thou dwellest all is neat.

First Peace and Silence all disputes control,
    Then Order plays the soul;
And giving all things their set forms and hours,
    Makes of wild woods sweet walks and bowers.

Humble Obedience near the door doth stand,
    Expecting a command:
Than whom in waiting nothing seems more slow,
    Nothing more quick when she doth go.

Joys oft are there, and griefs as oft as joys;
    But griefs without a noise:
Yet speak they louder, than distemper'd fears:
    What is so shrill as silent tears?

This is thy house, with these it doth abound:
    And where these are not found,
Perhaps thou comest sometimes, and for a day;
    But not to make a constant stay.

## THE SIZE.

  Content thee, greedy heart.
Modest and moderate joys to those, that have
Title to more hereafter when they part,
   Are passing brave.
  Let th' upper springs into the low
  Descend and fall, and thou dost flow.

  What though some have a fraught
Of cloves and nutmegs, and in cinnamon sail?
If thou hast wherewithal to spice a draught,
   When griefs prevail,
  And for the future time art heir
  To th' Isle of Spices, is't not fair?

  To be in both worlds full
Is more than God was, who was hungry here.
Wouldst thou his laws of fasting disannul?
   Enact good cheer?
  Lay out thy joy, yet hope to save it?
  Wouldst thou both eat thy cake, and have it?

  Great joys are all at once;
But little do reserve themselves for more:
Those have their hopes; these what they have renounce,
   And live on score:
  Those are at home; these journey still,
  And meet the rest on *Sion's* hill.

  Thy Saviour sentenced joy,
And in the flesh condemn'd it as unfit,

At least in lump : for such doth oft destroy;
        Whereas a bit
    Doth 'tice us on to hopes of more,
    And for the present health restore.

        A Christian's state and case
Is not a corpulent, but a thin and spare,
Yet active strength : whose long and bony face
        Content and care
    Do seem to equally divide,
    Like a pretender, not a bride.

        Wherefore sit down, good heart;
Grasp not at much, for fear thou losest all.
If comforts fell according to desert,
    They would great frosts and snows destroy :
    For we should count, Since the last joy.

        Then close again the seam,
Which thou hast open'd ; do not spread thy robe
In hope of great things. Call to mind thy dream,
        An earthly globe,
    On whose meridian was engraven,
    *These Seas are tears, and Heaven the haven.*


## ARTILLERY.

As I one evening sat before my cell,
Methought a star did shoot into my lap.
I rose, and shook my clothes, as knowing well,
That from small fires comes oft no small mishap :

When suddenly I heard one say,
*Do as thou usest, disobey,*
*Expel good motions from thy breast,*
*Which have the face of fire, but end in rest.*

I, who had heard of music in the spheres,
But not of speech in stars, began to muse :
But turning to my God, whose ministers
The stars and all things are ; If I refuse,
    Dread Lord, said I, so oft my good ;
    Then I refuse not even with blood
    To wash away my stubborn thought :
For I will do, or suffer what I ought.

But I have also stars and shooters too,
Born where thy servants both artilleries use.
My tears and prayers night and day do woo,
And work up to thee ; yet thou dost refuse.
    Not but I am (I must say still)
    Much more obliged to do thy will,
    Than thou to grant mine : but because
Thy promise now hath even set thee thy laws.

Then we are shooters both, and thou dost deign
To enter combat with us, and contest
With thine own clay. But I would parley fain :
Shun not my arrows, and behold my breast.
    Yet if thou shunnest, I am thine :
    I must be so, if I am mine.
    There is no articling with thee :
I am but finite, yet thine infinitely.

## CHURCH-RENTS AND SCHISMS.

BRAVE rose, (alas!) where art thou? in the chair,
Where thou didst lately so triumph and shine,
A worm doth sit, whose many feet and hair
Are the more foul, the more thou wert divine.
This, this hath done it, this did bite the root
And bottom of the leaves: which when the wind
Did once perceive, it blew them under foot,
Where rude unhallow'd steps do crush and grind
   Their beauteous glories. Only shreds of thee,
   And those all bitten, in thy chair I see.

Why doth my Mother blush? is she the rose,
And shows it so? Indeed Christ's precious blood
Gave you a colour once; which when your foes
Thought to let out, the bleeding did you good,
And made you look much fresher than before.
But when debates and fretting jealousies
Did worm and work within you more and more,
Your colour faded, and calamities
   Turned your ruddy into pale and bleak:
   Your health and beauty both began to break.

Then did your several parts unloose and start:
Which when your neighbours saw. like a north wind
They rushed in, and cast them in the dirt
Where Pagans tread. O Mother dear and kind,
Where shall I get me eyes enough to weep,
As many eyes as stars? since it is night,
And much of *Asia* and *Europe* fast asleep,
And even all *Africk;* would at least I might
With these two poor ones lick up all the dew,
Which falls by night, and pour it out for you!

K

## JUSTICE.

O DREADFUL Justice, what a fright and terror
    Wast thou of old,
    When Sin and Error
  Did show and shape thy looks to me,
  And through their glass discolour thee!
He that did but look up, was proud and bold.

The dishes of thy balance seem'd to gape,
    Like two great pits;
    The beam and scape
  Did like some tottering engine show:
  Thy hand above did burn and glow,
Daunting the stoutest hearts, the proudest wits.

But now that Christ's pure veil presents the sight,
    I see no fears:
    Thy hand is white,
  Thy scales like buckets, which attend
  And interchangeably descend,
Lifting to heaven from this well of tears.

For where before thou still didst call on me,
    Now I still touch
    And harp on thee.
  God's promises have made thee mine:
  Why should I justice now decline?
Against me there is none, but for me much.

## THE PILGRIMAGE.

I travell'd on, seeing the hill, where lay
    My expectation.
  A long it was and weary way.
  The gloomy cave of Desperation
I left on the one, and on the other side
    The rock of Pride.

And so I came to Fancy's meadow strew'd
    With many a flower:
  Fain would I here have made abode,
  But I was quicken'd by the hour.
So to Care's copse I came, and there got through
    With much ado.

That led me to the wild of Passion; which
    Some call the wold;
  A wasted place, but sometimes rich.
  Here I was robb'd of all my gold,
Save one good Angel, which a friend had tied
    Close to my side.

At length I got unto the gladsome hill,
    Where lay my hope,
  Where lay my heart; and climbing still,
  When I had gain'd the brow and top,
A lake of brackish waters on the ground
    Was all I found.

With that abash'd and struck with many a sting
    Of swarming fears,

I fell, and cried, Alas! my King;
　　Can both the way and end be tears?
Yet taking heart I rose, and then perceived
　　　　I was deceived:

My hill was further: so I flung away,
　　　　Yet heard a cry
　　Just as I went, *None goes that way
　　And lives:* If that be all, said I,
After so foul a journey death is fair,
　　　　And but a chair.


## THE HOLD-FAST.

I THREATEN'D to observe the strict decree
　　Of my dear God with all my power and might:
　　But I was told by one, it could not be;
Yet I might trust in God to be my light.

Then will I trust, said I, in him alone.
　　Nay, even to trust in him, was also his:
　　We must confess, that nothing is our own.
Then I confess that he my succour is:

But to have nought is ours, not to confess
　　That we have nought.  I stood amazed at this,
　　Much troubled, till I heard a friend express,
That all things were more ours by being his.

　　What *Adam* had, and forfeited for all,
　　*Christ* keepeth now, who cannot fail or fall.

## COMPLAINING.

Do not beguile my heart,
  Because thou art
My power and wisdom.  Put me not to shame,
  Because I am
Thy clay that weeps, thy dust that calls.

Thou art the Lord of glory;
  The deed and story
Are both thy due : but I a silly fly,
  That live or die,
According as the weather falls.

Art thou all justice, Lord?
  Shows not thy word
More attributes?  Am I all throat or eye,
  To weep or cry?
Have I no parts but those of grief?

Let not thy wrathful power
  Afflict my hour,
My inch of life : or let thy gracious power
  Contract my hour,
That I may climb and find relief.

## THE DISCHARGE.

Busy inquiring heart, what wouldst thou know?
        Why dost thou pry,
And turn, and leer, and with a licorous eye
        Look high and low;
And in thy lookings stretch and grow?

Hast thou not made thy counts, and summ'd up all?
        Did not thy heart
Give up the whole, and with the whole depart?
        Let what will fall:
That which is past who can recall?

Thy life is God's, thy time to come is gone,
        And is his right.
He is thy night at noon: he is at night
        Thy noon alone.
The crop is his, for he hath sown.

And well it was for thee, when this befell,
        That God did make
Thy business his, and in thy life partake:
        For thou canst tell,
If it be his once, all is well.

Only the present is thy part and fee.
        And happy thou,
If, though thou didst not beat thy future brow,
        Thou couldst well see
What present things required of thee.

They ask enough; why shouldst thou further go?
    Raise not the mud
Of future depths, but drink the clear and good.
    Dig not for woe
  In times to come; for it will grow.

Man and the present fit: if he provide,
    He breaks the square.
This hour is mine: if for the next I care,
    I grow too wide,
  And do encroach upon death's side:

For death each hour environs and surrounds.
    He that would know
And care for future chances, cannot go,
    Unto those grounds,
  But through a Churchyard which them bounds.

Things present shrink and die: but they that spend
    Their thoughts and sense
On future grief, do not remove it thence,
    But it extend,
  And draw the bottom out an end.

God chains the dog till night: wilt loose the chain,
    And wake thy sorrow?
Wilt thou forestall it, and now grieve to-morrow,
    And then again
  Grieve over freshly all thy pain?

Either grief will not come: or if it must,
    Do not forecast:
And while it cometh, it is almost past.
    Away distrust:
  My God hath promised; he is just.

## PRAISE.

King of glory, King of peace,
    I will love thee :
And that love may never cease,
    I will move thee.

Thou hast granted my request,
    Thou hast heard me :
Thou didst note my working breast,
    Thou hast spared me.

Wherefore with my utmost art
    I will sing thee,
And the cream of all my heart
    I will bring thee.

Though my sins against me cried,
    Thou didst clear me ;
And alone, when they replied,
    Thou didst hear me.

Seven whole days, not one in seven,
    I will praise thee.
In my heart, though not in heaven,
    I can raise thee.

Thou grew'st soft and moist with tears,
    Thou relentedst.
And when Justice call'd for fears,
    Thou dissentedst.

Small it is, in this poor sort
    To enrol thee :
Even eternity is too short
    To extol thee.


## AN OFFERING.

COME, bring thy gift. If blessings were as slow
As men's returns, what would become of fools?
What hast thou there? a heart? but is it pure?
Search well and see; for hearts have many holes.
Yet one pure heart is nothing to bestow :
In Christ two natures met to be thy cure.

O that within us hearts had propagation,
Since many gifts do challenge many hearts!
Yet one, if good, may title to a number;
And single things grow fruitful by deserts.
In public judgments one may be a nation,
And fence a plague, while others sleep and slumber.

But all I fear is, lest thy heart displease,
As neither good, nor one : so oft divisions
Thy lusts have made, and not thy lusts alone ;
Thy passions also have their set partitions.
These parcel out thy heart : recover these,
And thou may'st offer many gifts in one

There is a balsam, or indeed a blood,
Dropping from heaven, which doth both cleanse and close
All sorts of wounds ; of such strange force it is.
Seek out this All-heal, and seek no repose,

Until thou find, and use it to thy good :
Then bring thy gift ; and let thy hymn be this :

    SINCE my sadness
    Into gladness,
Lord, thou dost convert,
    O accept
    What thou hast kept,
As thy due desert.

    Had I many,
    Had I any
(For this heart is none),
    All were thine
    And none of mine,
Surely thine alone.

    Yet thy favour
    May give savour
To this poor oblation ;
    And it raise
    To be thy praise,
And be my salvation.


## LONGING.

WITH sick and famish'd eyes,
With doubling knees and weary bones,
    To thee my cries,
    To thee my groans,
To thee my sighs, my tears ascend :
      No end ?

My throat, my soul is hoarse;
My heart is wither'd like a ground
  Which thou dost curse.
   My thoughts turn round,
And make me giddy: Lord, I fall,
     Yet call.


From thee all pity flows.
Mothers are kind, because thou art,
  And dost dispose
  To them a part:
Their infants, them; and they suck thee
     More free.


Bowels of pity, hear!
Lord of my soul, love of my mind,
  Bow down thine ear!
  Let not the wind
Scatter my words, and in the same
     Thy name!


Look on my sorrows round!
Mark well my furnace! O what flames,
  What heats abound!
  What griefs, what shames!
Consider, Lord; Lord, bow thine ear,
     And hear!


Lord JESU, thou didst bow
Thy dying head upon the tree:
  O be not now
  More dead to me!
Lord, hear! *Shall he that made the ear*
     *Not hear?*

Behold, thy dust doth stir ;
It moves, it creeps, it aims at thee :
   Wilt thou defer
    To succour me,
Thy pile of dust, wherein each crumb
        Says, Come ?

To thee help appertains.
Hast thou left all things to their course,
   And laid the reins
   Upon the horse ?
Is all lock'd ? hath a sinner's plea
        No key ?

Indeed the world's thy book,
Where all things have their leaf assign'd :
   Yet a meek look
   Hath interlined.
Thy board is full, yet humble guests
        Find nests.

Thou tarriest, while I die,
And fall to nothing : thou dost reign,
   And rule on high,
   While I remain
In bitter grief : yet am I styled
        Thy child.

Lord, didst thou leave thy throne,
Not to relieve ? how can it be,
   That thou art grown
   Thus hard to me ?
Were sin alive, good cause there were
        To bear.

But now both Sin is dead,
And all thy promises live and bide.
　　That wants his head ;
　　These speak and chide,
And in thy bosom pour my tears,
　　　　　As theirs.


Lord JESU, hear my heart,
Which hath been broken now so long,
　　That every part
　　Hath got a tongue !
Thy beggars grow ; rid them away
　　　　　To-day.


My love, my sweetness, hear !
By these thy feet, at which my heart
　　Lies all the year,
　　Pluck out thy dart,
And heal my troubled breast which cries,
　　　　　Which dies.


## THE BAG.

AWAY despair ; my gracious Lord doth hear,
　　Though winds and waves assault my keel,
　　He doth preserve it : he doth steer,
　　Even when the boat seems most to reel.
　　Storms are the triumph of his art :
Well may he close his eyes, but not his heart.

Hast thou not heard, that my Lord JESUS died ?
　　Then let me tell thee a strange story.
　　The God of power, as he did ride

In his majestic robes of glory,
  Resolved to light; and so one day
He did descend, undressing all the way.

The stars his tire of light and rings obtain'd,
  The cloud his bow, the fire his spear,
  The sky his azure mantle gain'd.
  And when they ask'd, what he would wear;
  He smiled, and said as he did go,
He had new clothes a making here below.

When he was come, as travellers are wont,
  He did repair unto an inn.
  Both then, and after, many a brunt
  He did endure to cancel sin :
  And having given the rest before,
Here he gave up his life to pay our score.

But as he was returning, there came one
  That ran upon him with a spear.
  He, who came hither all alone,
  Bringing nor man, nor arms, nor fear,
  Received the blow upon his side,
And straight he turn'd, and to his brethren cried,

If ye have any thing to send or write
  (I have no bag, but here is room)
  Unto my Father's hands and sight,
  (Believe me) it shall safely come.
  That I shall mind, what you impart;
Look, you may put it very near my heart.

Or if hereafter any of my friends
  Will use me in this kind, the door

Shall still be open ; what he sends
I will present, and somewhat more,
Not to his hurt.  Sighs will convey
Anything to me.  Hark despair, away.

### THE JEWS.

POOR nation, whose sweet sap and juice
Our scions have purloin'd, and left you dry :
Whose streams we got by the Apostles' sluice,
And use in baptism, while ye pine and die :
Who by not keeping once, became a debtor ;
    And now by keeping lose the letter :

    O that my prayers ! mine, alas !
O that some Angel might a trumpet sound :
At which the Church falling upon her face
Should cry so loud, until the trump were drown'd,
And by that cry of her dear Lord obtain,
    That your sweet sap might come again !

### THE COLLAR.

    I STRUCK the board, and cried, No more ;
        I will abroad.
    What ? shall I ever sigh and pine ?
My lines and life are free ; free as the road,
    Loose as the wind, as large as store.
        Shall I be still in suit ?
    Have I no harvest but a thorn
    To let me blood, and not restore
What I have lost with cordial fruit ?

Sure there was wine,
Before my sighs did dry it: there was corn,
Before my tears did drown it.
Is the year only lost to me?
Have I no bays to crown it?
No flowers, no garlands gay? all blasted?
All wasted?
Not so, my heart: but there is fruit,
And thou hast hands.
Recover all thy sigh-blown age
On double pleasures: leave thy cold dispute
Of what is *fit, and not:* forsake thy cage,
Thy rope of sands,
Which petty thoughts have made, and made to thee
Good cable, to enforce and draw,
And be thy law,
While thou didst wink and wouldst not see.
Away; take heed:
I will abroad.
Call in thy death's-head there: tie up thy fears.
He that forbears
To suit and serve his need,
Deserves his load.
But as I raved and grew more fierce and wild
At every word,
Methought I heard one calling, *Child:*
And I replied, *My Lord.*


## THE GLIMPSE.

WHITHER away delight?
Thou camest but now; wilt thou so soon depart,
And give me up to-night?

For many weeks of lingering pain and smart
But one half hour of comfort for my heart?

  Methinks delight should have
More skill in music, and keep better time.
  Wert thou a wind or wave,
They quickly go and come with lesser crime:
Flowers look about, and die not in their prime.

  Thy short abode and stay
Feeds not, but adds to the desire of meat.
  Lime begg'd of old (they say)
A neighbour spring to cool his inward heat;
Which by the spring's access grew much more great.

  In hope of thee my heart
Pick'd here and there a crumb, and would not die;
  But constant to his part,
When as my fears foretold this, did reply,
A slender thread a gentle guest will tie.

  Yet if the heart that wept
Must let thee go, return when it doth knock.
  Although thy heap be kept
For future times, the droppings of the stock
May oft break forth, and never break the lock.

  If I have more to spin,
The wheel shall go, so that thy stay be short.
  Thou know'st how grief and sin
Disturb the work. O make me not their sport,
Who by thy coming may be made a Court!

## ASSURANCE.

O SPITEFUL bitter thought!
Bitterly spiteful thought! Couldst thou invent
So high a torture? Is such poison bought?
Doubtless, but in the way of punishment,
   When wit contrives to meet with thee,
   No such rank poison can there be.

Thou saidst but even now,
That all was not so fair, as I conceived,
Betwixt my God and me; that I allow
And coin large hopes; but, that I was deceived:
   Either the league was broke, or near it;
   And, that I had great cause to fear it.

And what to this? what more
Could poison, if it had a tongue, express?
What is thy aim? wouldst thou unlock the door
To cold despairs, and gnawing pensiveness?
   Wouldst thou raise devils? I see, I know,
   I writ thy purpose long ago.

But I will to my Father,
Who heard thee say it. O most gracious Lord,
If all the hope and comfort that I gather,
Were from myself, I had not half a word,
   Not half a letter to oppose
   What is objected by my foes.

But thou art my desert:
And in this League, which now my foes invade,
Thou art not only to perform thy part,
But also mine; as when the league was made,
  Thou didst at once thyself indite,
  And hold my hand, while I did write.

Wherefore if thou canst fail,
Then can thy truth and I: but while rocks stand,
And rivers stir, thou canst not shrink or quail:
Yea, when both rocks and all things shall disband,
  Then shalt thou be my rock and tower,
  And make their ruin praise thy power.

Now foolish thought go on,
Spin out thy thread, and make thereof a coat
To hide thy shame: for thou hast cast a bone,
Which bounds on thee, and will not down thy throat.
  What for itself love once began,
  Now love and truth will end in man.

## THE CALL.

Come, my Way, my Truth, my Life:
Such a Way, as gives us breath:
Such a Truth, as ends all strife:
Such a Life, as killeth death.

Come, my Light, my Feast, my Strength:
Such a Light, as shows a feast:
Such a Feast, as mends in length:
Such a Strength, as makes his guest.

Come, my Joy, my Love, my Heart:
Such a Joy, as none can move:
Such a Love, as none can part:
Such a Heart, as joys in love.

## CLASPING OF HANDS.

Lord, thou art mine, and I am thine,
If mine I am: and thine much more,
Than I or ought, or can be mine.
Yet to be thine, doth me restore;
So that again I now am mine,
And with advantage mine the more.
Since this being mine, brings with it thine,
And thou with me dost thee restore.
    If I without thee would be mine,
    I neither should be mine nor thine.

Lord, I am thine, and thou art mine:
So mine thou art, that something more
I may presume thee mine, than thine.
For thou didst suffer to restore
Not thee, but me, and to be mine:
And with advantage mine the more,
Since thou in death wast none of thine,
Yet then as mine didst me restore.
    O be mine still! still make me thine;
    Or rather make no Thine and Mine!

## PRAISE.

Lord, I will mean and speak thy praise,
    Thy praise alone.
My busy heart shall spin it all my days :
    And when it stops for want of store,
Then will I wring it with a sigh or groan,
    That thou may'st yet have more.

When thou dost favour any action,
    It runs, it flies :
All things concur to give it a perfection.
    That which had but two legs before,
When thou dost bless, hath twelve : one wheel doth rise
    To twenty then, or more.

But when thou dost on business blow,
    It hangs, it clogs :
Not all the teams of Albion in a row
    Can hale or draw it out of door.
Legs are but stumps, and Pharaoh's wheels but logs,
    And struggling hinders more.

Thousands of things do thee employ
    In ruling all
This spacious Globe : Angels must have their joy,
    Devils their rod, the sea his shore,
The winds their stint : and yet when I did call,
    Thou heardst my call, and more.

I have not lost one single tear :
　　　　But when mine eyes
Did weep to heaven, they found a bottle there
　　(As we have boxes for the poor)
Ready to take them in ; yet of a size
　　That would contain much more.

But after thou hadst slipt a drop
　　　　From thy right eye
(Which there did hang like streamers near the top
　　Of some fair Church, to show the sore
And bloody battle which thou once didst try),
　　The glass was full, and more.

Wherefore I sing.　Yet since my heart,
　　　　Though press'd, runs thin ;
O that I might some other hearts convert,
　　And so take up at use good store :
That to thy chests there might be coming in
　　Both all my praise, and more !


## JOSEPH'S COAT.

　Wounded I sing, tormented I indite,
Thrown down I fall into a bed, and rest :
Sorrow hath changed its note : such is His will
Who changeth all things, as him pleaseth best.

　For well he knows, if but one grief and smart
Among my many had his full career,
Sure it would carry with it even my heart,
And both would run until they found a bier

To fetch the body; both being due to grief.
But he hath spoil'd the race; and given to anguish
One of Joy's coats, 'ticing it with relief
To linger in me, and together languish.

I live to show his power, who once did bring
My *joys to weep*, and now *my griefs to sing*.


## THE PULLEY.

WHEN God at first made man,
Having a glass of blessings standing by;
Let us (said he) pour on him all we can:
Let the world's riches, which dispersed lie,
  Contract into a span.

So strength first made a way;
Then beauty flow'd, then wisdom, honour, pleasure:
When almost all was out, God made a stay,
Perceiving that alone, of all his treasure,
  Rest in the bottom lay.

For if I should (said he)
Bestow this jewel also on my creature,
He would adore my gifts instead of me,
And rest in Nature, not the God of Nature:
  So both should losers be.

Yet let him keep the rest,
But keep them with repining restlessness:
Let him be rich and weary, that at least,
If goodness lead him not, yet weariness
  May toss him to my breast.

## THE PRIESTHOOD.

BLEST Order, which in power dost so excel,
That with the one hand thou liftest to the sky,
And with the other throwest down to hell,
In thy just censures; fain would I draw nigh;
Fain put thee on, exchanging my lay-sword
  For that of the holy Word.

But thou art fire, sacred and hallow'd fire;
And I but earth and clay: should I presume
To wear thy habit, the severe attire
My slender compositions might consume.
I am both foul and brittle, much unfit
  To deal in holy Writ.

Yet have I often seen, by cunning hand
And force of fire, what curious things are made
Of wretched earth. Where once I scorn'd to stand,
That earth is fitted by the fire and trade
Of skilful Artists, for the boards of those
  Who make the bravest shows.

But since those great ones, be they ne'er so great,
Come from the earth, from whence those vessels come;
So that at once both feeder, dish, and meat,
Have one beginning and one final sum:
I do not greatly wonder at the sight,
  If earth in earth delight.

But the holy men of God such vessels are,
As serve him up, who all the world commands.

When God vouchsafeth to become our fare,
Their hands convey him, who conveys their hands:
O what pure things, most pure must those things be,
    Who bring my God to me!

Wherefore I dare not, I, put forth my hand
To hold the Ark, although it seem to shake
Through th' old sins and new doctrines of our land.
Only, since God doth often vessels make
Of lowly matter for high uses meet,
    I throw me at his feet.

There will I lie, until my Maker seek
For some mean stuff whereon to show his skill:
Then is my time. The distance of the meek
Doth flatter power. Lest good come short of ill
In praising might, the poor do by submission
    What pride by opposition.


## THE SEARCH.

Whither, O, whither art thou fled,
    My Lord, my love?
My searches are my daily bread;
    Yet never prove.

My knees pierce th' earth, mine eyes the sky:
    And yet the sphere
And centre both to me deny
    That thou art there.

Yet can I mark how herbs below
        Grow green and gay;
As if to meet thee they did know,
        While I decay.

Yet can I mark how stars above
        Simper and shine,
As having keys unto thy love,
        While poor I pine.

I sent a sigh to seek thee out,
        Deep drawn in pain,
Wing'd like an arrow: but my scout
        Returns in vain.

I turn'd another (having store)
        Into a groan,
Because the search was dumb before:
        But all was one.

Lord, dost thou some new fabric mould
        Which favour wins,
And keeps thee present, leaving th' old
        Unto their sins?

Where is my God? what hidden place
        Conceals thee still?
What covert dare eclipse thy face?
        Is it thy will?

O let not that of any thing:
        Let rather brass,
Or steel, or mountains be thy ring,
        And I will pass.

Thy will such an intrenching is,
                As passeth thought:
To it all strength, all subtilties
                Are things of nought.

Thy will such a strange distance is,
                As that to it
East and West touch, the poles do kiss,
                And parallels meet.

Since then my grief must be as large
                As is thy space,
Thy distance from me; see my charge,
                Lord, see my case.

O take these bars, these lengths, away;
                Turn, and restore me:
Be not Almighty, let me say,
                *Against*, but *for* me.

When thou dost turn, and wilt be near:
                What edge so keen,
What point so piercing can appear
                To come between?

For as thy absence doth excel
                All distance known:
So doth thy nearness bear the bell,
                Making two one.

## GRIEF.

O who will give me tears ? Come, all ye springs,
Dwell in my head and eyes : come, clouds, and rain :
My grief hath need of all the watery things,
That Nature hath produced. Let every vein
Suck up a river to supply mine eyes,
My weary weeping eyes too dry for me,
Unless they get new conduits, new supplies,
To bear them out, and with my state agree.
What are two shallow fords, two little spouts
Of a less world ? the greater is but small,
A narrow cupboard for my griefs and doubts,
Which want provision in the midst of all.
Verses, ye are too fine a thing, too wise
For my rough sorrows : cease, be dumb and mute,
Give up your feet and running to mine eyes,
And keep your measures for some lover's lute,
Whose grief allows him music and a rhyme :
For mine excludes both measure, tune, and time.
          Alas, my God !


## THE CROSS.

  What is this strange and uncouth thing
To make me sigh, and seek, and faint, and die,
Until I had some place, where I might sing,
    And serve thee ; and not only I,
But all my wealth, and family might combine
To set thy honour up, as our design ?

And then when after much delay,
Much wrestling, many a combat, this dear end,
So much desired, is given, to take away
    My power to serve thee : to unbend
All my abilities, my designs confound,
And lay my threatenings bleeding on the ground.

    One ague dwelleth in my bones,
Another in my soul (the memory
What I would do for thee, if once my groans
    Could be allow'd for harmony);
I am in all a weak disabled thing,
Save in the sight thereof, where strength doth sting.

    Besides, things sort not to my will,
Even when my will doth study thy renown :
Thou turn'st the edge of all things on me still,
    Taking me up to throw me down :
So that, even when my hopes seem to be sped,
I am to grief alive, to them as dead.

    To have my aim, and yet to be
Farther from it than when I bent my bow :
To make my hopes my torture, and the fee
    Of all my woes another woe,
Is in the midst of delicates to need,
And even in Paradise to be a weed.

    Ah, my dear Father, ease my smart !
These contrarieties crush me : these cross actions
Do wind a rope about, and cut my heart :
    And yet since these thy contradictions
Are properly a Cross felt by thy Son,
With but four words, my words, *Thy will be done.*

## THE FLOWER.

How fresh, O Lord, how sweet and clean
Are thy returns! even as the flowers in spring;
　To which, besides their own demean,
The late-past frosts tributes of pleasure bring.
　　　Grief melts away
　　　Like snow in May,
As if there were no such cold thing.

Who would have thought my shrivell'd heart
Could have recover'd greenness? It was gone
　Quite under ground; as flowers depart
To see their Mother-root, when they have blown:
　　　Where they together
　　　All the hard weather,
Dead to the world, keep house unknown.

These are thy wonders, Lord of power,
Killing and quickening, bringing down to hell
　And up to heaven in an hour;
Making a chiming of a passing bell.
　　　We say amiss,
　　　This or that is:
Thy Word is all, if we could spell.

O that I once past changing were,
Fast in thy Paradise, where no flower can wither!
　Many a spring I shoot up fair,
Offering at heaven, growing and groaning thither:
　　　Nor doth my flower
　　　Want a spring-shower,
My sins and I joining together.

But while I grow in a straight line,
Still upwards bent, as if heaven were mine own,
   Thy anger comes, and I decline :
What frost to that ? what pole is not the zone
      Where all things burn,
      When thou dost turn,
   And the least frown of thine is shown ?


   And now in age I bud again,
After so many deaths I live and write ;
   I once more smell the dew and rain,
And relish versing : O my only light,
      It cannot be
      That I am he,
   On whom thy tempests fell at night.


   These are thy wonders, Lord of love,
To make us see we are but flowers that glide :
   Which when we once can find and prove,
Thou hast a garden for us, where to bide.
      Who would be more,
      Swelling through store,
   Forfeit their Paradise by their pride.


## DOTAGE.

FALSE glozing pleasures, casks of happiness,
Foolish night-fires, women's and children's wishes,
Chases in arras, gilded emptiness,
Shadows well mounted, dreams in a career,
Embroider'd lies, nothing between two dishes ;
         These are the pleasures here.

True earnest sorrows, rooted miseries,
Anguish in grain, vexations ripe and blown,
Sure-footed griefs, solid calamities,
Plain demonstrations, evident and clear,
Fetching their proofs even from the very bone ;
    These are the sorrows here.

But oh the folly of distracted men,
Who griefs in earnest, joys in jest pursue ;
Preferring, like brute beasts, a loathsome den
Before a court, even that above so clear,
Where are no sorrows, but delights more true
    Than miseries are here !

## THE SON.

Let foreign nations of their language boast,
What fine variety each tongue affords :
I like our language, as our men and coast ;
Who cannot dress it well, want wit, not words.
How neatly do we give one only name
To Parent's issue and the Sun's bright star !
A Son is light and fruit ; a fruitful flame
Chasing the Father's dimness, carried far
From the first man in the East, to fresh and new
Western discoveries of posterity.
So in one word our Lord's humility
We turn upon him in a sense most true :
    For what Christ once in humbleness began,
    We him in glory call, *The Son of Man.*

## A TRUE HYMN.

My joy, my life, my crown!
  My heart was meaning all the day,
    Somewhat it fain would say:
And still it runneth muttering up and down
With only this, *My joy, my life, my crown!*

Yet slight not these few words;
  If truly said, they may take part
    Among the best in art.
The fineness which a Hymn or Psalm affords,
Is, when the soul unto the lines accords.

He who craves all the mind,
  And all the soul, and strength, and time,
    If the words only rhyme,
Justly complains, that somewhat is behind
To make his Verse, or write a Hymn in kind.

Whereas if the heart be moved,
  Although the Verse be somewhat scant,
    God doth supply the want.
As when the heart says (sighing to be approved),
*Oh, could I love!* and stops; God writeth, *Loved.*


## THE ANSWER.

My comforts drop and melt away like snow:
I shake my head, and all the thoughts and ends,
Which my fierce youth did bandy, fall and flow
Like leaves about me, or like summer friends,

Flies of estates and sunshine.  But to all,
Who think me eager, hot, and undertaking,
But in my prosecutions slack and small ;
As a young exhalation, newly waking,
Scorns his first bed of dirt, and means the sky;
But cooling by the way, grows pursy and slow,
And settling to a cloud, doth live and die
In that dark state of tears : to all, that so
Show me, and set me, I have one reply,
Which they that know the rest, know more than I.

## A DIALOGUE-ANTHEM.

CHRISTIAN, DEATH.

CHR. Alas, poor Death ! where is thy glory ?
 Where is thy famous force, thy ancient sting ?

DEA. *Alas! poor mortal, void of story,*
 *Go spell and read how I have kill'd thy King.*

CHR. Poor Death ! and who was hurt thereby ?
 Thy curse being laid on him makes thee accurst.

DEA. *Let losers talk, yet thou shalt die ;*
 *These arms shall crush thee.*

                        CHR. Spare not, do thy worst
 I shall be one day better than before :
 Thou so much worse, that thou shalt be no more.

## THE WATER-COURSE.

Thou who dost dwell and linger here below,
Since the condition of this world is frail,
Where of all plants afflictions soonest grow;
If troubles overtake thee, do not wail:
   For who can look for less that loveth $\begin{cases} \text{Life?} \\ \text{Strife?} \end{cases}$

But rather turn the pipe, and water's course
To serve thy sins, and furnish thee with store
Of sovereign tears, springing from true remorse:
That so in pureness thou may'st him adore
   Who gives to man, as he sees fit, $\begin{cases} \text{Salvation.} \\ \text{Damnation.} \end{cases}$

## SELF-CONDEMNATION.

Thou who condemnest Jewish hate,
For choosing *Barabbas* a murderer
   Before the Lord of glory;
Look back upon thine own estate,
Call home thine eye (that busy wanderer),
   That choice may be thy story.

He that doth love, and love amiss,
This world's delights before true Christian joy,
   Hath made a Jewish choice:
The world an ancient murderer is;
Thousands of souls it hath and doth destroy
   With her enchanting voice.

He that hath made a sorry wedding
Between his soul and gold, and hath preferr'd
    False gain before the true,
  Hath done what he condemns in reading :
For he hath sold for money his dear Lord,
    And is a Judas-Jew.

  Thus we prevent the last great day,
And judge ourselves.  That light which sin and passion
    Did before dim and choke,
  When once those snuffs are ta'en away,
Shines bright and clear, even unto condemnation,
    Without excuse or cloak.

### BITTER-SWEET.

    Ah, my dear angry Lord,
  Since thou dost love, yet strike ;
  Cast down, yet help afford :
    Sure I will do the like.

  I will complain, yet praise ;
  I will bewail, approve .
  And all my sour-sweet days
  I will lament, and love.

### THE GLANCE.

  When first thy sweet and gracious eye
Vouchsafed even in the midst of youth and night
To look upon me, who before did lie
    Weltering in sin ;

I felt a sugar'd strange delight,
Passing all Cordials made by any Art,
Bedew, embalm, and overrun my heart,
    And take it in.

Since that time many a bitter storm
My soul hath felt, even able to destroy,
Had the malicious and ill-meaning harm
    His swing and sway :
But still thy sweet original joy,
Sprung from thine eye, did work within my soul,
And surging griefs, when they grew bold, control,
    And got the day.

If thy first glance so powerful be,
A mirth but open'd, and seal'd up again ;
What wonders shall we feel, when we shall see
    Thy full-eyed love !
When thou shalt look us out of pain,
And one aspect of thine spend in delight
More than a thousand suns disburse in light,
    In Heaven above.


## THE TWENTY-THIRD PSALM.

The God of love my shepherd is,
    And he that doth me feed :
While he is mine, and I am his,
    What can I want or need ?

He leads me to the tender grass,
    Where I both feed and rest ;
Then to the streams that gently pass :
    In both I have the best.

Or if I stray, he doth convert,
    And bring my mind in frame :
And all this not for my desert,
    But for his holy name.

Yea, in death's shady, black abode
    Well may I walk, not fear :
For thou art with me, and thy rod
    To guide, thy staff to bear.

Nay, thou dost make me sit and dine,
    Even in my enemies' sight ;
My head with oil, my cup with wine
    Runs over day and night.

Surely thy sweet and wondrous love
    Shall measure all my days ;
And as it never shall remove,
    So neither shall my praise.

## MARY MAGDALEN.

WHEN blessed *Mary* wiped her Saviour's feet
(Whose precepts she had trampled on before),
And wore them for a Jewel on her head,
    Showing his steps should be the street,
    Wherein she thenceforth evermore
With pensive humbleness would live and tread :

She being stain'd herself, why did she strive
To make him clean, who could not be defiled ?

Why kept she not her tears for her own faults,
   And not his feet? Though we could dive
   In tears like Seas, our sins are piled
Deeper than they, in words, and works, and thoughts.

Dear soul, she knew who did vouchsafe and deign
To bear her filth: and that her sins did dash
Even God himself: wherefore she was not loath,
   As she had brought wherewith to stain,
   So to bring in wherewith to wash:
And yet in washing one, she washed both.


## AARON.

    HOLINESS on the head,
  Light and perfections on the breast,
Harmonious bells below, raising the dead
  To lead them unto life and rest.
    Thus are true *Aarons* drest.

    Profaneness in my head,
  Defects and darkness in my breast,
A noise of passions ringing me for dead
  Unto a place where is no rest:
    Poor Priest thus am I drest.

    Only another head
  I have, another heart and breast,
Another music, making live, not dead,
  Without whom I could have no rest:
    In him I am well drest.

Christ is my only head,
My alone only heart and breast,
My only music, striking me even dead ;
That to the old man I may rest,
And be in him new drest.

So holy in my head,
Perfect and light in my dear breast,
My doctrine tuned by Christ (who is not dead,
But lives in me while I do rest),
Come, people ; *Aaron's* drest.

### THE ODOUR.

#### 2 Cor. ii.

How sweetly doth *My Master* sound ! *My Master !*
As ambergis leaves a rich scent
Unto the taster :
So do these words a sweet content,
An Oriental fragrancy, *My Master.*

With these all day I do perfume my mind,
My mind even thrust into them both ;
That I might find
What Cordials make this curious broth,
This broth of smells, that feeds and fats my mind.

*My Master*, shall I speak ? O that to thee
*My Servant* were a little so,
As flesh may be ;
That these two words might creep and grow
To some degree of spiciness to thee !

Then should the Pomander, which was before
　　A speaking sweet, mend by reflection,
　　　　And tell me more :
　　For pardon of my imperfection
Would warm and work it sweeter than before.

For when *My Master*, which alone is sweet,
　　And even in my unworthiness pleasing,
　　　　Shall call and meet,
　　*My Servant*, as thee not displeasing,
That call is but the breathing of the sweet.

This breathing would with gains by sweetening me
　　(As sweet things traffic when they meet)
　　　　Return to thee.
　　And so this new commerce and sweet
Should all my life employ, and busy me.


## THE FOIL.

　　　　If we could see below
　　The sphere of virtue, and each shining grace,
　　　　As plainly as that above doth show ;
　　This were the better sky, the brighter place.

　　　　God hath made stars the foil
　　To set off virtues : griefs to set off sinning :
　　　　Yet in this wretched world we toil,
　　As if grief were not foul, nor virtue winning.

## THE FORERUNNERS.

The Harbingers are come. See, see their mark ;
White is their colour, and behold my head.
But must they have my brain ? must they dispark
Those sparkling notions, which therein were bred ?
    Must dulness turn me to a clod ?
Yet have they left me, *Thou art still my God.*

Good men ye be, to leave me my best room,
Even all my heart, and what is lodged there :
I pass not, I, what of the rest become,
So, *Thou art still my God*, be out of fear.
    He will be pleased with that ditty;
And if I please him, I write fine and witty.

Farewell sweet phrases, lovely metaphors :
But will ye leave me thus ? when ye before
Of stews and brothels only knew the doors,
Then did I wash you with my tears, and more,
    Brought you to Church well drest and clad .
My God must have my best, even all I had.

Lovely enchanting language, sugar-cane,
Honey of roses, whither wilt thou fly ?
Hath some fond lover 'ticed thee to thy bane ?
And wilt thou leave the Church, and love a sty ?
    Fie, thou wilt soil thy broider'd coat,
And hurt thyself, and him that sings the note.

Let foolish lovers, if they will love dung,
With Canvas, not with Arras, clothe their shame:
Let Folly speak in her own native tongue.
True beauty dwells on high: ours is a flame
    But borrow'd thence to light us thither.
Beauty and beauteous words should go together.

Yet if you go, I pass not; take your way:
For, *Thou art still my God*, is all that ye
Perhaps with more embellishment can say.
Go, birds of spring: let winter have his fee;
    Let a bleak paleness chalk the door,
So all within be livelier than before.


## THE ROSE.

    Press me not to take more pleasure
        In this world of sugar'd lies,
    And to use a larger measure
        Than my strict, yet welcome size.

    First, there is no pleasure here:
        Colour'd griefs indeed there are,
    Blushing woes, that look as clear,
        As if they could beauty spare.

    Or if such deceits there be,
        Such delights I mean to say;
    There are no such things to me,
        Who have pass'd my right away.

But I will not much oppose
    Unto what you now advise :
Only take this gentle Rose,
    And therein my answer lies.

What is fairer than a rose ?
    What is sweeter ? yet it purgeth.
Purgings enmity disclose,
    Enmity forbearance urgeth.

If then all that worldlings prize
    Be contracted to a rose ;
Sweetly there indeed it lies,
    But it biteth in the close.

So this flower doth judge and sentence
    Worldly joys to be a scourge :
For they all produce repentance,
    And repentance is a purge.

But I health, not physic choose :
    Only though I you oppose,
Say that fairly I refuse,
    For my answer is a rose.

## DISCIPLINE.

Throw away thy rod,
Throw away thy wrath :
    O my God,
Take the gentle path.

For my heart's desire
Unto thine is bent :
    I aspire
To a full consent.

Not a word or look
I affect to own,
    But by book,
And thy book alone.

Though I fail, I weep :
Though I halt in pace,
    Yet I creep
To the throne of grace.

Then let wrath remove ;
Love will do the deed :
    For with love
Stony hearts will bleed.

Love is swift of foot ;
Love's a man of war,
    And can shoot,
And can hit from far.

Who can 'scape his bow ?
That which wrought on thee,
    Brought thee low,
Needs must work on me.

Throw away thy rod ;
Though man frailties hath,
    Thou art God :
Throw away thy wrath.

## THE INVITATION.

Come ye hither all, whose taste
   Is your waste ;
Save your cost, and mend your fare.
God is here prepared and dress'd,
   And the feast,
God, in whom all dainties are.

Come ye hither all, whom wine
   Doth define,
Naming you not to your good :
Weep what ye have drunk amiss,
   And drink this,
Which before ye drink is blood.

Come ye hither all, whom pain
   Doth arraign,
Bringing all your sins to sight :
Taste and fear not : God is here
   In this cheer,
And on sin doth cast the fright.

Come ye hither all, whom joy
   Doth destroy,
While ye graze without your bounds :
Here is joy that drowneth quite
   Your delight,
As a flood the lower grounds.

Come ye hither all, whose love
   Is your dove,
And exalts you to the sky:
Here is love, which, having breath
   Even in death,
After death can never die.

Lord, I have invited all,
   And I shall
Still invite, still call to thee:
For it seems but just and right
   In my sight,
Where is all, there all should be.

## THE BANQUET.

WELCOME sweet and sacred cheer,
   Welcome dear;
With me, in me, live and dwell:
For thy neatness passeth sight,
   Thy delight
Passeth tongue to taste or tell.

O what sweetness from the bowl
   Fills my soul,
Such as is, and makes divine!
Is some star (fled from the sphere)
   Melted there,
As we sugar melt in wine?

Or hath sweetness in the bread
    Made a head
To subdue the smell of sin,
Flowers, and gums, and powders giving
    All their living,
Lest the enemy should win?

Doubtless, neither star nor flower
    Hath the power
Such a sweetness to impart:
Only God, who gives perfumes,
    Flesh assumes,
And with it perfumes my heart.

But as Pomanders and wood
    Still are good,
Yet being bruised are better scented;
God, to show how far his love
    Could improve,
Here, as broken, is presented.

When I had forgot my birth,
    And on earth
In delights of earth was drown'd;
God took blood, and needs would be
    Spilt with me,
And so found me on the ground.

Having raised me to look up,
    In a cup
Sweetly he doth meet my taste.
But I still being low and short,
    Far from court,
Wine becomes a wing at last.

For with it alone I fly
        To the sky:
Where I wipe mine eyes, and see
What I seek, for what I sue;
        Him I view
Who hath done so much for me.

Let the wonder of this pity
        Be my ditty,
And take up my lines and life:
Hearken under pain of death,
        Hands and breath,
Strive in this, and love the strife.


## THE POSY.

LET wits contest,
And with their words and posies windows fill:
    *Less than the least*
*Of all thy mercies*, is my posy still.

This on my ring,
This by my picture, in my book I write;
    Whether I sing,
Or say, or dictate, this is my delight.

Invention rest;
Comparisons go play; wit use thy will:
    *Less than the least*
*Of all God's mercies*, is my posy still.

## A PARODY.

Soul's joy, when thou art gone,
    And I alone,
    Which cannot be,
Because thou dost abide in me,
    And I depend on thee;

Yet when thou dost suppress
    The cheerfulness
    Of thy abode,
And in my powers not stir abroad,
    But leave me to my load:

O what a damp and shade
    Doth me invade!
    No stormy night
Can so afflict or so affright
    As thy eclipsed light.

Ah, Lord! do not withdraw,
    Lest want of awe
    Make sin appear;
And when thou dost but shine less clear,
    Say, that thou art not here.

And then what life I have,
    While Sin doth rave,
    And falsely boast,
That I may seek, but thou art lost!
    Thou and alone thou know'st.

O what a deadly cold
    Doth me infold!
   I half believe,
That Sin says true: but while I grieve,
  Thou comest and dost relieve.


## THE ELIXIR.

T<small>EACH</small> me, my God and King,
  In all things thee to see,
And what I do in any thing,
  To do it as for thee :

Not rudely, as a beast,
  To run into an action ;
But still to make thee prepossest,
  And give it his perfection.

A man that looks on glass,
  On it may stay his eye ;
Or if he pleaseth, through it pass,
  And then the heaven espy.

All may of thee partake :
  Nothing can be so mean,
Which with his tincture (*for thy sake*)
  Will not grow bright and clean.

A servant with this clause
  Makes drudgery divine :
Who sweeps a room, as for thy laws,
  Makes that and th' action fine.

>    This is the famous stone
>    That turneth all to gold :
> For that which God doth touch and own
>    Cannot for less be told.

## A WREATH.

A WREATHED garland of deserved praise,
Of praise deserved, unto thee I give,
I give to thee, who knowest all my ways,
My crooked winding ways, wherein I live,
Wherein I die, not live ; for life is straight,
Straight as a line, and ever tends to thee,
To thee, who art more far above deceit,
Than deceit seems above simplicity.
Give me simplicity, that I may live,
So live and like, that I may know thy ways,
Know them and practise them : then shall I give
For this poor wreath, give thee a crown of praise.

## DEATH.

DEATH, thou wast once an uncouth hideous thing,
        Nothing but bones,
    The sad effect of sadder groans :
Thy mouth was open, but thou couldst not sing.

For we consider'd thee as at some six
        Or ten years hence,
    After the loss of life and sense,
Flesh being turn'd to dust, and bones to sticks.

We look'd on this side of thee, shooting short;
        Where we did find
   The shells of fledge souls left behind,
Dry dust, which sheds no tears, but may extort.

But since our Saviour's death did put some blood
        Into thy face:
   Thou art grown fair and full of grace,
Much in request, much sought for, as a good.

For we do now behold thee gay and glad,
        As at doomsday;
   When souls shall wear their new array,
And all thy bones with beauty shall be clad.

Therefore we can go die as sleep, and trust
        Half that we have
   Unto an honest faithful grave;
Making our pillows either down, or dust.

## DOOMSDAY.

        Come away,
       Make no delay.
Summon all the dust to rise,
Till it stir, and rub the eyes;
While this member jogs the other,
Each one whispering, *Live you, brother?*

        Come away,
      Make this the day.
Dust, alas! no music feels,

But thy trumpet : then it kneels,
As peculiar notes and strains
Cure Tarantula's raging pains.

Come away,
O make no stay !
Let the graves make their confession,
Lest at length they plead possession :
Flesh's stubbornness may have
Read that lesson to the grave.

Come away,
Thy flock doth stray.
Some to the winds their body lend,
And in them many drown a friend :
Some in noisome vapours grow
To a plague and public woe.

Come away,
Help our decay.
Man is out of order hurl'd,
Parcell'd out to all the world.
Lord, thy broken consort raise,
And the music shall be praise.

## JUDGMENT.

ALMIGHTY Judge, how shall poor wretches brook
Thy dreadful look,
Able a heart of iron to appal,
When thou shalt call
For every man's peculiar book ?

What others mean to do, I know not well;
    Yet I hear tell,
That some will turn thee to some leaves therein
    So void of sin,
That they in merit shall excel.

But I resolve, when thou shalt call for mine,
    That to decline,
And thrust a Testament into thy hand :
    Let that be scann'd.
There thou shalt find my faults are thine.

## HEAVEN.

O who will show me those delights on high?
    Echo.     *I.*
Thou Echo, thou art mortal, all men know.
    Echo.     *No.*
Wert thou not born among the trees and leaves?
    Echo.     *Leaves.*
And are there any leaves, that still abide?
    Echo.     *Bide.*
What leaves are they? impart the matter wholly.
    Echo.     *Holy.*
Are holy leaves the Echo then of bliss?
    Echo.     *Yes.*
Then tell me, what is that supreme delight?
    Echo.     *Light.*
Light to the mind : what shall the will enjoy?
    Echo.     *Joy.*
But are there cares and business with the pleasure?
    Echo.     *Leisure.*
Light, joy, and leisure; but shall they persever?
    Echo.     *Ever.*

## LOVE.

Love bade me welcome ; yet my soul drew back,
    Guilty of dust and sin.
But quick-eyed Love, observing me grow slack
    From my first entrance in,
Drew nearer to me, sweetly questioning,
    If I lack'd any thing.

A guest, I answer'd, worthy to be here :
    Love said, You shall be he.
I the unkind, ungrateful ? Ah, my dear,
    I cannot look on thee.
Love took my hand, and smiling did reply,
    Who made the eyes but I ?

Truth, Lord, but I have marr'd them : let my shame
    Go where it doth deserve.
And know you not, says Love, who bore the blame ?
    My dear, then I will serve.
You must sit down, says Love, and taste my meat :
    So I did sit and eat.

FINIS.

*Glory be to God on high, and on earth peace,*
*    good-will towards men.*

# THE CHURCH MILITANT.

ALMIGHTY Lord, who from thy glorious throne
Seest and rulest all things even as one:
The smallest Ant or Atom knows thy power,
Known also to each minute of an hour:
Much more do Commonweals acknowledge thee,
And wrap their policies in thy decree,
Complying with thy counsels, doing nought
Which doth not meet with an eternal thought.
But above all, thy Church and Spouse doth prove
Not the decrees of power, but bands of love.
Early didst thou arise to plant this Vine,
Which might the more endear it to be thine.
Spices come from the East; so did thy Spouse,
Trim as the light, sweet as the laden boughs
Of *Noah's* shady vine, chaste as the dove,
Prepared and fitted to receive thy love.
The course was westward, that the sun might light
As well our understanding as our sight.
Where th' Ark did rest, there *Abraham* began
To bring the other Ark from *Canaan*.
*Moses* pursued this: but King *Solomon*
Finish'd and fix'd the old religion.

When it grew loose, the Jews did hope in vain
By nailing Christ to fasten it again.
But to the Gentiles he bore cross and all,
Rending with earthquakes the partition-wall.
Only whereas the Ark in glory shone,
Now with the cross, as with a staff, alone,
Religion, like a pilgrim, westward bent,
Knocking at all doors, ever as she went.
Yet as the Sun, though forward be his flight,
Listens behind him, and allows some light,
Till all depart : so went the Church her way,
Letting, while one foot stepp'd, the other stay
Among the eastern nations for a time,
Till both removed to the western clime.
To *Egypt* first she came, where they did prove
Wonders of anger once, but now of love.
The ten Commandments there did flourish more
Than the ten bitter plagues had done before.
Holy *Macarius* and great *Anthony*
Made *Pharaoh Moses*, changing the history.
*Goshen* was darkness, *Egypt* full of lights,
Nilus for monsters brought forth Israelites.
Such power hath mighty Baptism to produce,
For things misshapen, things of highest use.
*How dear to me, O God, thy counsels are!*
    *Who may with thee compare?*
Religion thence fled into *Greece*, where Arts
Gave her the highest place in all men's hearts.
Learning was posed, Philosophy was set,
Sophisters taken in a Fisher's net.
*Plato* and *Aristotle* were at a loss,
And wheel'd about again to spell *Christ's-Cross*.
Prayers chased syllogisms into their den,
And *Ergo* was transform'd into *Amen*.

Though *Greece* took horse as soon as *Egypt* did,
And *Rome* as both ; yet *Egypt* faster rid,
And spent her period and prefixed time
Before the other.  *Greece* being past her prime,
Religion went to *Rome*, subduing those,
Who, that they might subdue, made all their foes.
The Warrior his dear scars no more resounds,
But seems to yield Christ hath the greater wounds ;
Wounds willingly endured to work his bliss,
Who by an ambush lost his Paradise.
The great heart stoops, and taketh from the dust
A sad repentance, not the spoils of lust :
Quitting his spear, lest it should pierce again
Him in his members, who for him was slain.
The Shepherd's hook grew to a Sceptre here,
Giving new names and numbers to the year.
But th' Empire dwelt in *Greece*, to comfort them,
Who were cut short in *Alexander's* stem.
In both of these Prowess and Arts did tame
And tune men's hearts against the Gospel came :
Which using, and not fearing skill in the one,
Or strength in th' other, did erect her throne,
Many a rent and struggling th' Empire knew
(As dying things are wont), until it flew
At length to *Germany*, still westward bending,
And there the Church's festival attending :
That as before Empire and Arts made way
(For no less harbingers would serve than they),
So they might still, and point us out the place,
Where first the Church should raise her downcast face.
Strength levels grounds, Art makes a garden there ;
Then showers Religion, and makes all to bear.
Spain in the Empire shared with *Germany*,
But *England* in the higher victory ;

Giving the Church a crown to keep her state,
And not go less than she had done of late.
*Constantine's* British line meant this of old,
And did this mystery wrap up and fold
Within a sheet of paper, which was rent
From Time's great Chronicle, and hither sent.
Thus both the Church and Sun together ran
Unto the farthest old meridian.
*How dear to me, O God, thy counsels are!*
     *Who may with thee compare?*
Much about one and the same time and place,
Both where and when the Church began her race,
Sin did set out of Eastern *Babylon,*
And travell'd westward also: journeying on
He chid the Church away, where'er he came,
Breaking her peace, and tainting her good name.
At first he got to *Egypt,* and did sow
Gardens of gods, which every year did grow,
Fresh and fine deities. They were at great cost,
Who for a god clearly a sallet lost.
Ah, what a thing is man devoid of grace,
Adoring Garlic with an humble face,
Begging his food of that which he may eat,
Starving the while he worshippeth his meat!
Who makes a root his god, how low is he,
If God and man be sever'd infinitely!
What wretchedness can give him any room,
Whose house is foul, while he adores his broom?
None will believe this now, though money be
In us the same transplanted foolery.
Thus Sin in *Egypt* sneaked for a while;
His highest was an ox or crocodile,
And such poor game. Thence he to *Greece* doth pass,
And being craftier much than Goodness was,

He left behind him garrisons of sins,
To make good that which every day he wins.
Here Sin took heart, and for a garden-bed
Rich shrines and oracles he purchased:
He grew a gallant, and would needs foretell
As well what should befall, as what befell.
Nay, he became a Poet, and would serve
His pills of sublimate in that conserve.
The world came both with hands and purses full
To this great lottery, and all would pull.
But all was glorious cheating, brave deceit,
Where some poor truths were shuffled for a bait
To credit him, and to discredit those,
Who after him should braver truths disclose.
From *Greece* he went to *Rome:* and as before
He was a God, now he's an Emperor.
*Nero* and others lodged him bravely there,
Put him in trust to rule the Roman sphere
Glory was his chief instrument of old:
Pleasure succeeded straight, when that grew cold:
Which soon was blown to such a mighty flame,
That though our Saviour did destroy the game,
Disparking oracles, and all their treasure,
Setting affliction to encounter pleasure;
Yet did a rogue with hope of carnal joy,
Cheat the most subtle nations. Who so coy,
So trim, as *Greece* and *Egypt?* yet their hearts
Are given over, for their curious arts,
To such Mahometan stupidities,
As the old Heathen would deem prodigies.
*How dear to me, O God, thy counsels are!*
   *Who may with thee compare?*
Only the West and *Rome* do keep them free
From this contagious infidelity.

And this is all the Rock, whereof they boast,
As *Rome* will one day find unto her cost.
Sin being not able to extirpate quite
The Churches here, bravely resolved one night
To be a Churchman too, and wear a Mitre:
The old debauched Ruffian would turn writer.
I saw him in his study, where he sate
Busy in controversies sprung of late.
A gown and pen became him wondrous well:
His grave aspect had more of heaven than hell:
Only there was a handsome picture by,
To which he lent a corner of his eye.
As Sin in *Greece* a Prophet was before,
And in old *Rome* a mighty Emperor;
So now being Priest, he plainly did profess
To make a jest of Christ's three Offices:
The rather since his scatter'd jugglings were
United now in one both time and sphere.
From *Egypt* he took petty deities,
From *Greece* oracular infallibilities,
And from old *Rome* the liberty of pleasure,
By free dispensings of the Church's treasure.
Then in memorial of his ancient throne,
He did surname his palace, *Babylon*.
Yet that he might the better gain all nations,
And make that name good by their transmigrations;
From all these places, but at divers times,
He took fine vizards to conceal his crimes:
From *Egypt* Anchorism and retiredness,
Learning from *Greece*, from old *Rome* stateliness;
And blending these, he carried all men's eyes,
While Truth sat by, counting his victories:
Whereby he grew apace and scorn'd to use
Such force as once did captivate the Jews;

But did bewitch, and finally work each nation
Into a voluntary transmigration.
All post to *Rome:* Princes submit their necks
Either to his public foot or private tricks.
It did not fit his gravity to stir,
Nor his long journey, nor his gout and fur:
Therefore he sent out able Ministers,
Statesmen within, without doors Cloisterers;
Who without spear, or sword, or other drum
Than what was in their tongue, did overcome;
And having conquer'd, did so strangely rule,
That the whole world did seem but the Pope's *mule*.
As new and old *Rome* did one empire twist;
So both together are one Antichrist;
Yet with two faces, as their *Janus* was,
Being in this their old crack'd looking-glass.
*How dear to me, O God, thy counsels are!*
    *Who may with thee compare?*
Thus Sin triumphs in Western *Babylon;*
Yet not as Sin, but as Religion.
Of his two thrones he made the latter best,
And to defray his journey from the East.
Old and new *Babylon* are to hell and night,
As is the Moon and Sun to Heaven and light.
When the one did set, the other did take place,
Confronting equally the Law and Grace.
They are hell's landmarks, Satan's double crest:
They are Sin's nipples, feeding th' east and west.
But as in vice the Copy still exceeds
The pattern, but not so in virtuous deeds;
So though Sin made his latter seat the better,
The latter Church is to the first a debtor.
The second Temple could not reach the first:
And the late reformation never durst

## THE CHURCH MILITANT.

Compare with ancient times and purer years;
But in the Jews and us deserveth tears;
Nay, it shall every year decrease and fade;
Till such a darkness do the world invade
At Christ's last coming, as his first did find:
Yet must there such proportions be assign'd
To these diminishings, as is between
The spacious world and *Jewry* to be seen.
Religion stands on tiptoe in our land,
Ready to pass to the *American* strand.
When height of malice, and prodigious lusts,
Impudent sinning, witchcrafts, and distrusts,
(The marks of future bane), shall fill our cup
Unto the brim, and make our measure up;
When *Seine* shall swallow *Tiber*, and the *Thames*,
By letting in them both, pollutes her streams:
When Italy of us shall have her will,
And all her Calendar of sins fulfil;
Whereby one may foretell, what sins next year
Shall both in *France* and *England* domineer:
Then shall Religion to *America* flee:
They have their times of Gospel, even as we.
My God, thou dost prepare for them a way,
By carrying first their gold from them away:
For gold and grace did never yet agree:
Religion always sides with poverty.
We think we rob them, but we think amiss:
We are more poor, and they more rich, by this.
Thou wilt revenge their quarrel, making grace
To pay our debts, and leave our ancient place
To go to them, while that, which now their nation
But lends to us, shall be our desolation.
Yet as the Church shall thither westward fly,
So Sin shall trace and dog her instantly:

They have their period also and set times
Both for their virtuous actions and their crimes.
And where of old the Empire and the Arts
Usher'd the Gospel ever in men's hearts,
*Spain* hath done one; when Arts perform the other,
The Church shall come, and Sin the Church shall smother:
That when they have accomplished the round,
And met in th' East their first and ancient sound,
Judgment may meet them both, and search them round.
Thus do both lights, as well in Church as Sun,
Light one another, and together run.
Thus also Sin and Darkness follow still
The Church and Sun with all their power and skill.
But as the Sun still goes both West and East:
So also did the Church by going West
Still Eastward go; because it drew more near
To time and place, where judgment shall appear.
*How dear to me, O God, thy counsels are!*
   *Who may with thee compare?*


## L'ENVOY.

*King of glory, King of peace,*
With the one make war to cease;
With the other bless thy sheep,
Thee to love, in thee to sleep.
Let not Sin devour thy fold,
Bragging that thy blood is cold;
That thy death is also dead,
While his conquests daily spread;
That thy flesh hath lost his food,
And thy Cross is common wood.

Choke him, let him say no more,
But reserve his breath in store,
Till thy conquest and his fall
Make his sighs to use it all;
And then bargain with the wind
To discharge what is behind.

*Blessed be God alone,*
*Thrice blessed Three in One.*

# MISCELLANEOUS POEMS.

### A SONNET,

SENT BY GEORGE HERBERT TO HIS MOTHER AS A NEW
YEAR'S GIFT FROM CAMBRIDGE.

My God, where is that ancient heat towards thee,
    Wherewith whole shoals of Martyrs once did burn,
Besides their other flames?    Doth poetry
    Wear Venus' livery? only serve her turn?
Why are not sonnets made of thee? and lays
    Upon thine altar burnt?    Cannot thy love
Heighten a spirit to sound out thy praise
    As well as any she?    Cannot thy Dove
Outstrip their *Cupid* easily in flight?
    Or, since thy ways are deep, and still the same,
    Will not a verse run smooth that bears thy name?
Why doth that fire, which by thy power and might
    Each breast does feel, no braver fuel choose
    Than that which, one day, worms may chance refuse?
Sure, Lord, there is enough in thee to dry
    Oceans of ink; for, as the Deluge did
Cover the earth, so doth thy Majesty:
    Each cloud distils thy praise, and doth forbid

Poets to turn it to another use.
  Roses and lilies speak thee; and to make
A pair of cheeks of them, is thy abuse.
  Why should I women's eyes for crystal take?
Such poor invention burns in their low mind
  Whose fire is wild, and doth not upward go
    To praise, and on thee, Lord, some ink bestow.
Open the bones, and you shall nothing find
  In the best face but filth; when, Lord, in thee
  The beauty lies, in the discovery.

---

## A PARADOX.

(FROM A MS. COLLECTION FORMERLY DR RAWLINSON'S, IN THE BODLEIAN LIBRARY, OXFORD)

THAT THE SICK ARE IN A BETTER CASE THAN THE WHOLE.

    You who admire yourselves because
      You neither groan nor weep,
  And think it contrary to Nature's laws
      To want one ounce of sleep,
        Your strong belief
Acquits yourselves, and gives the sick all grief.

    Your state to ours is contrary,
      That makes you think us poor,
So Black-moors think us foul, and we
      Are quit with them, and more:
        Nothing can see,
And judge of things but mediocrity.

The sick are in themselves a state
    Which health hath nought to do.
How know you that our tears proceed from woe,
    And not from better fate?
        Since that mirth hath
Her waters also and desired bath.

How know you that the sighs we send
    From want of breath proceed,
Not from excess? and therefore we do spend
    That which we do not need;
        So trembling may
As well show inward warbling, as decay.

Cease then to judge calamities
    By outward form and show,
But view yourselves, and inward turn your eyes,
    Then you shall fully know
        That your estate
Is, of the two, the far more desperate.

You always fear to feel those smarts
    Which we but sometimes prove,
Each little comfort much affects our hearts,
    None but gross joys you move:
        Why then confess
Your fears in number more, your joys are less

Then for yourselves not us embrace
    Plaints to bad fortune due,
For though you visit us, and plaint or case,
    We doubt much whether you
        Come to our bed
To comfort us, or to be comforted.

## INSCRIPTION.

IN THE PARSONAGE, BEMERTON.   TO MY SUCCESSOR.

If thou chance for to find
A new House to thy mind
And built without thy cost:
   Be good to the poor,
   As God gives thee store,
And then my labour's not lost.

---

## ON LORD DANVERS.

Sacred marble, safely keep
His dust, who under thee must sleep,
Until the years again restore
Their dead, and time shall be no more.
Meanwhile, if he (which all things wears)
Does ruin thee, or if thy tears
Are shed for him; dissolve thy frame,
Thou art requited: for his fame,
His virtue, and his worth shall be
Another monument to thee.

# THE SYNAGOGUE;

OR, THE SHADOW OF THE TEMPLE:
SACRED POEMS AND PRIVATE EJACULATIONS
IN IMITATION OF MR GEORGE HERBERT.

[BY CHRISTOPHER HARVEY, M.A.]

Stultissimum credo ad imitandum non optima quæque proponere.
PLIN. *Sec. Lib* i. *Ep* 5.

I do esteem 't a folly not the least
To imitate examples not the best.

OF Christopher Harvey or Harvie, the author of the "Synagogue," all that is known is, that he was a clergyman's son in Cheshire, was educated at Brazen-Nose College, and became Vicar of Clifton, Warwickshire. He published the "Synagogue" in 1640, without his name. Walton commended the book, and ascribed it to Harvie. He wrote another book called "Schola Cordis," sometimes ascribed to Quarles. His "Synagogue" has less poetic merit than the "Temple," but is very pious and instructive.

# THE SYNAGOGUE.

## SUBTERLIMINARE.

*Dic, cujus Templum? Christi. Quis condidit? Ede.*
   *Condidit* Herbertus. *Dic, quibus auxiliis?*
*Auxiliis multis: quibus, haud mihi dicere fas est.*
   *Tanta est ex dictis lis oriunda meis.*
*Gratia, si dicam, dedit omnia; protinus obstat*
   *Ingenium, dicens, cuncta fuisse sua.*
*Ars negat, et nihil est non nostrum dicit in illo;*
   *Nec facile est litem composuisse mihi.*
*Divide: materiam det gratia, materiæque*
   *Ingenium cultus induat, arsque modos.*
*Non: ne displiceat pariter res omnibus ista,*
   *Nec sortita velint jura vocare sua.*
*Nempe pari sibi jure petunt, cultusque, modosque,*
   *Materiamque, ars, et gratia, et ingenium.*
*Ergo, velit si quis dubitantem tollere elenchum,*
   *De Templo* Herberti *talia dicta dabit.*
*In Templo* Herbertus *condendo est gratia totus,*
   *Ars pariter totus, totus et ingenium.*
*Cedite Romanæ, Graiiæ quoque cedite Musæ;*
   *Unum par cunctis Anglia jactat opus.*

## A STEPPING-STONE

TO THE THRESHOLD OF MR HERBERT'S "CHURCH-PORCH."

WHAT Church is this?   Christ's Church.   Who builded it?
Master *George Herbert*.   Who assisted it?
Many assisted: who I may not say,
So much contention might arise that way.
If I say Grace gave all; Wit straight doth thwart,
And says, All that is there is mine : but Art
Denies, and says, There's nothing there but's mine :
Nor can I easily the right define.
Divide : say, Grace the matter gave, and Wit
Did polish it : Art measured, and made fit,
Each several piece, and framed it altogether.
No, by no means : this may not please them neither.
None's well contented with a part alone,
When each doth challenge all to be his own.
The matter, the expressions, and the measures,
Are equally Art's, Wit's, and Grace's treasures.
Then he, that would impartially discuss
This doubtful question, must answer thus :
In building of his Temple, Master *Herbert*
Is equally all grace, all wit, all art.
   Roman and Grecian Muses all give way :
   One English Poem darkens all your day.

## THE DEDICATION.

  LORD, my first fruits should have been sent to thee;
        For thou the tree,
  That bare them, only lentest unto me.

But while I had the use, the fruit was mine:
        Not so divine
As that I dare presume to call it thine.

Before 'twas ripe it fell unto the ground:
        And since I found
It bruised in the dirt, nor clean, nor sound.

Some I have pick'd, and wiped, and bring thee now,
        Lord, thou know'st how:
Gladly I would, but dare not it avow.

Such as it is, 'tis here. Pardon the best,
        Accept the rest.
Thy pardon and acceptance maketh blest.


## THE CHURCH-YARD.

Thou that intendest to the Church to-day,
Come, take a turn, or two, before thou go'st,
In the Church-yard; the walk is in thy way.
Who takes best heed in going, hasteth most:
  But he that unprepared rashly ventures,
  Hastens perhaps to seal his death's indentures.


## THE CHURCH-STILE.

Seest thou that stile? Observe then how it rises,
Step after step, and equally descends:
Such is the way to win Celestial prizes:
Humility the course begins, and ends.
  Wouldst thou in grace to high perfections grow?
  Shoot thy roots deep, ground thy foundations low.

Humble thyself, and God will lift thee up :
Those that exalt themselves he casteth down :
The hungry he invites with him to sup ;
And clothes the naked with his robe and crown.
    Think not thou hast, what thou from him wouldst have :
    His labour's lost, if thou thyself canst save.

Pride is the prodigality of grace,
Which casteth all away by griping all :
Humility is thrift, both keeps its place,
And gains by giving, riseth by its fall.
    To get by giving, and to lose by keeping,
    Is to be sad in mirth, and glad in weeping.

## THE CHURCH-GATE.

Next to the stile, see where the gate doth stand,
Which, turning upon hooks and hinges may
Easily be shut, or open'd with a hand :
Yet constant to its centre still doth stay ;
    And fetching a wide compass round about,
    Keeps the same course, and distance, never out.

Such must the course be that to heaven tends ;
He that the gates of righteousness would enter,
Must still continue constant to his ends,
And fix himself in God, as in his centre.
    Cleave close to him by faith, then move which way
    Discretion leads thee, and thou shalt not stray.

We never wander, till we loose our hold
Of him that is our way, our light, our guide :
But, when we grow of our own strength too bold,

Unhook'd from him, we quickly turn aside.
   He holds us up, whilst in him we are found :
   If once we fall from him, we go to ground.


## THE CHURCH-WALLS.

Now view the walls : the Church is compass'd round,
As much for safety, as for ornament :
'Tis an inclosure, and no common ground ;
'Tis God's freehold, and but our tenement.
   Tenants at will, and yet in tail, we be :
   Our children have the same right to 't as we.

Remember there must be no gaps left ope,
Where God hath fenced, for fear of false illusions.
God will have all, or none : allows no scope
For sin's encroachments, or men's own intrusions.
   Close binding locks his Laws together fast :
   He that plucks out the first, pulls down the last.

Either resolve for all, or else for none ;
Obedience universal he doth claim.
Either be wholly his, or all thine own :
At what thou canst not reach, at least take aim :
   He that of purpose looks beside the mark,
   Might as well hood-wink'd shoot, or in the dark.


## THE CHURCH.

LASTLY, consider where the Church doth stand,
As near unto the middle as may be ;
God in his service chiefly doth command

Above all other things sincerity.
   Lines drawn from side to side within a round,
   Not meeting in the centre, short are found.

Religion must not side with any thing
That swerves from God, or else withdraws from him;
He that a welcome sacrifice would bring,
Must fetch it from the bottom, not the brim.
   A sacred Temple of the Holy Ghost
   Each part of man must be, but his heart most.

Hypocrisy in Church is Alchemy,
That casts a golden tincture upon brass:
There is no essence in it: 'tis a lie,
Though, fairly stamp'd, for truth it often pass:
   Only the Spirit's *aqua regia* doth
   Discover it to be but painted froth.

## THE CHURCH-PORCH.

Now, ere thou passest further, sit thee down
In the Church-porch, and think what thou hast seen;
Let due consideration either crown,
Or crush, thy former purposes. Between
   Rash undertakings, and firm resolutions,
   Depends the strength, or weakness, of conclusions.

Trace thy steps backward in thy memory:
And first resolve of, what thou heardest last,
Sincerity; It blots the history
Of all religious actions, and doth blast
   The comfort of them, when in them God sees
   Nothing but outsides of formalities.

In earnest be religious, trifle not ;
And rather for God's sake, than for thine own :
Thou hast robb'd him, unless that he have got
By giving, if his glory be not grown
   Together with thy good : who seeketh more
   Himself than God, would make his roof his floor.

Next to sincerity, remember still,
Thou must resolve upon integrity.
God will have all thou hast, thy mind, thy will,
Thy thoughts, thy words, thy works. A nullity
   It proves, when God, that should have all, doth find
   That there is any one thing left behind.

And having given him all, thou must receive
All that he gives. Meet his Commandment :
Resolve that thine obedience must not leave,
Until it reach unto the same extent.
   For all his Precepts are of equal strength,
   And measure thy performance to the length :

Then call to mind that constancy must knit
Thine undertakings and thine actions fast :
He that sets forth towards heaven, and doth sit
Down by the way, will be found short at last.
   Be constant to the end, and thou shalt have
   A heavenly garland, though an earthly grave.

But he that would be constant, must not take
Religion up by fits and starts alone ;
But his continual practice must it make :
His course must be from end to end but one.
   Bones often broken, and knit up again,
   Lose of their length, though in their strength they gain.

Lastly, remember that Humility
Must solidate, and keep all close together.
What Pride puffs up with vain futility,
Lies open and exposed to all ill weather.
   An empty bubble may fair colours carry ;
   But blow upon it, and it will not tarry.

Prize not thine own too high, nor under-rate
Another's worth ; but deal indifferently :
View the defects of thy spiritual state,
And others' graces, with impartial eye.
   The more thou deemest of thyself, the less
   Esteem of thee will all men else express.

Contract thy lesson now, and this is just
The sum of all. He that desires to see
The face of God, in his Religion must
Sincere, entire, constant, and humble be.
   If thus resolved, fear not to proceed :
   Else the more haste thou makest, the worse thou'lt speed.


## CHURCH-UTENSILS.

BETWIXT two dangerous rocks, Profaneness on
The one side, on the other Superstition,
      How shall I sail secure ?
   Lord, be my steersman, hold my helm,
   And then though winds with waves o'erwhelm
      My sails, I will endure
It patiently. The bottom of the sea
Is safe enough, if thou direct the way.

I'll tug my tacklings then, I'll ply mine oars,
And cry, A fig for fear.  He that adores
  The giddy multitude
So much, as to despise my rhymes,
Because they tune not to the times,
  I wish may not intrude
His presence here.  But they (and that's enough)
Who love God's house, will like his household stuff.


## THE FONT.

The Font, I say.  Why not?  And why not near
    To the Church door?  Why not of stone?
Is not that blessed fountain open'd here,
    From whence that water flows alone,
Which from sin and uncleanness washeth clear?

And may not beggars well contented be
    Their first alms at the door to take?
Though, when acquainted better, they may see
    Others within that bolder make.
Low places will serve guests of low degree.

What?  Is he not the rock, out of whose side
    Those streams of water-blood run forth?
The elect and precious corner-stone well tried?
    Though the odds be great between their worth,
Rock-water and stone vessels are allied.

But call it what, and place it where you will:
    Let it be made indifferently
Of any form, or matter; yet, until
    The blessed Sacrament thereby
Impaired be, my hopes you shall not kill.

To want a complement of comeliness
    Some of my comfort may abate,
And for the present make my joy go less :
    Yet I will hug mine homely state,
And poverty with patience richly dress.

Regeneration is all in all ;
    Washing, or sprinkling, but the sign,
The seal, and instrument thereof ; I call
    The one, as well as the other, mine,
And my posterity's, as federal.

If temporal estates may be convey'd,
    By covenants on condition,
To men, and to their heirs ; be not afraid,
    My soul, to rest upon
The covenant of grace by mercy made.

Do but thy duty, and rely upon't,
    Repentance, faith, obedience,
Whenever practised truly, will amount
    To an authentic evidence,
Though the deed were antedated at the Font.


## THE READING-PEW.

Here my new enter'd soul doth first break fast,
    Here seasoneth her infant taste,
And at her mother-nurse the Church's dugs
    With labouring lips and tongue she tugs,
For that sincere milk, which alone doth feed
    Babes new-born of immortal seed :

Who, that they may unto perfection grow,
Must be content to creep before they go.


They, that would reading out of Church exclude,
    Sure have a purpose to obtrude
Some dictates of their own, instead of God's
    Revealed Will, his Word.   'Tis odds,
They do not mean to pay men current coin,
    Who seek the standard to purloin,
And would reduce all trials to their own,
But touch-stones, balances, and weights, alone.


What reasonable man would not misdoubt
    Those Comments, that the text leave out?
And that their main intent is alteration,
    Who dote so much on variation,
That no set Forms at all they can endure
    To be prescribed, or put in ure?
Rejecting bounds and limits is the way,
If not all waste, yet common all to lay.


But why should he, that thinks himself well grown,
    Be discontent that such a one,
As knows himself an infant yet, should be
    Dandled upon his mother's knee,
And babe-like fed with milk, till he have got
    More strength and stomach?   Why should not
Nurslings in Church, as well as weanlings, find
Their food fit for them in their proper kind?


Let them that would build castles in the air,
    Vault thither, without step or stair;
Instead of feet to climb, take wings to fly,
    And think their turrets top the sky.

But let me lay all my foundations deep,
    And learn, before I run, to creep.
Who digs through Rocks to lay his ground-works low,
May in good time build high, and sure, though slow.

To take degrees, *per saltum*, though of quick
    Dispatch, is but a truant's trick.
Let us learn first to know our letters well,
    Then syllables, then words to spell ;
Then to read plainly, ere we take the pen
    In hand to write to other men.
I doubt their preaching is not always true,
Whose way to the Pulpit's not the Reading-pew.


## THE BOOK OF COMMON PRAYER.

WHAT ! Prayer by the book ? and Common ?
                  Yes.   Why not ?
        The spirit of grace,
      And supplication,
    Is not left free alone
      For time and place ;
But manner too.  To read, or speak by rote
    Is all alike to him that prays
      With 's heart, that with his mouth he says.

They that in private by themselves alone
          Do pray, may take
      What liberty they please,
      In choosing of the ways,
        Wherein to make

Their soul's most intimate affections known
 To him that sees in secret, when
 They are most conceal'd from other men.

But he, that unto others leads the way
 In public prayer,
 Should choose to do it so,
 As all, that hear, may know
 They need not fear
To tune their hearts unto his tongue, and say
 Amen ; nor doubt they were betray'd
 To blaspheme, when they should have pray'd.

Devotion will add life unto the letter.
 And why should not
 That, which Authority
 Prescribes, esteemed be
 Advantage got ?
If the Prayer be good, the commoner, the better.
 Prayer in the Church's words, as well
 As sense, of all prayers bears the bell.


## THE BIBLE.


THE Bible ? That's the Book. The Book indeed,
 The Book of Books ;
 On which who looks,
As he should do, aright, shall never need
 Wish for a better light
 To guide him in the night :

Or, when he hungry is, for better food
    To feed upon,
    Than this alone,
If he bring stomach and digestion good:
    And if he be amiss,
    This the best Physic is.

The true Panchreston 'tis for every sore
    And sickness, which
    The poor, and rich
With equal ease may come by.   Yea, 'tis more,
    An antidote, as well
    As remedy 'gainst Hell.

'Tis Heaven in perspective, and the bliss
    Of glory here,
    If any where,
By Saints on Earth anticipated is,
    Whilst faith to every word
    A being doth afford.

It is the Looking-glass of souls, wherein
    All men may see,
    Whether they be
Still, as by nature they are, deform'd with sin;
    Or in a better case,
    As new adorn'd with grace.

'Tis the great Magazine of spiritual arms,
    Wherein doth lie
    The artillery
Of Heaven, ready charged against all harms,
    That might come by the blows
    Of our infernal foes.

God's Cabinet of revealed counsel 'tis:
      Where weal and woe
      Are order'd so,
That every man may know which shall be his;
      Unless his own mistake
      False application make.

It is the Index to Eternity.
      He cannot miss
      Of endless bliss,
That takes this chart to steer his voyage by.
      Nor can he be mistook,
      That speaketh by this Book.

A Book, to which no Book may be compared
      For excellence;
      Pre-eminence
Is proper to it, and cannot be shared.
      Divinity alone
      Belongs to it, or none.

It is the Book of God.  What if I should
      Say, God of Books?
      Let him that looks
Angry at that expression, as too bold,
      His thoughts in silence smother,
      Till he find such another.

## THE PULPIT.

'Tis dinner time: and now I look
For a full meal.  God send me a good Cook:
    This is the dresser-board, and here
I wait in expectation of good cheer.

I'm sure the Master of the house
Enough to entertain his guests allows:
And not enough of some one sort alone,
But choice of what best fitteth every one.

God grant me taste and stomach good:
My feeding will diversify my food;
    'Tis a good appetite to eat,
And good digestion, that makes good meat.
    The best food in itself will be,
Not fed on well, poison, not food, to me.
Let him that speaks look to his words; my ear
Must careful be, both what and how I hear.

    'Tis *Manna* that I look for here,
The bread of Heaven, Angels' food. I fear
    No want of plenty, where I know
The loaves by eating, more, and greater, grow;
    Where nothing but forbearance makes
A famine; where he only wants, that takes
Not what he will; provided that he would
Take nothing to himself, but what he should.

    Here the same fountain poureth forth
Water, Wine, Milk, Oil, Honey, and the worth
    Of all transcendent, infinite
In excellence, and to each appetite
    In fitness answerable; so
That none needs hence unsatisfied go,
Whose stomach serves him unto any thing,
That health, strength, comfort, or content can bring.

    Yea, dead men here invited are
Unto the bread of life, and whilst they spare

To come and take it, they must blame
Themselves, if they continue still the same.
    The body's fed by food, which it
Assimilates, and to itself doth fit:
But, that the soul may feed, itself must be
Transformed to the Word, with it agree.

    To milk the strongest men must be
As new-born babes, whenever they it see,
    Desiring, not despising it.
For strong meat babes must stay, and strive to fit
    Themselves in time, until they can
Get by degrees (which best beseem a man)
Experience-exercised senses, able
Good to discern from evil, truth from fable.

    Here I will wait then; till I see
The steward reaching out a mess for me:
    Resolve I'll take it thankfully,
Whate'er it be, and feed on't heartily.
    Although no *Benjamin's* choice mess,
Five times as much as others, but far less;
Yea, if it be but a basket full of crumbs,
I'll bless the hand, from which, by which, it comes.

    Like an invited guest, I will
Be bold, but mannerly withal, sit still
    And see what the Master of the feast
Will carve unto me, and account that best
    Which he doth choose for me, not I
Myself desire: yea, though I should espy
Some fault in the dressing, in the dishing, or
The placing, yet I will not it abhor.

So that the meat be wholesome, though
The sauce shall not be toothsome, I'll not go
    Empty away, and starve my soul,
To feed my foolish fancy; but control
    My appetite to dainty things,
Which oft instead of strength diseases brings:
But, if my Pulpit-hopes shall all prove vain,
I'll back unto the Reading-pew again.


## THE COMMUNION TABLE.

Here stands my banquet ready, the last course,
    And best provision,
    That I must feed upon,
Till death my soul and body shall divorce,
    And that I am
Call'd to the marriage-supper of the Lamb.

Some call 't the Altar, some the holy Table.
    The name I stick not at,
    Whether 't be this, or that,
I care not much, so that I may be able
    Truly to know
Both why it is, and may be called so.

And for the matter whereof it is made,
    The matter is not much,
    Although it be of tuch,[1]
Or wood, or metal, what will last, or fade;
    So vanity
And superstition avoided be.

---

[1] 'Tuch:' old word for cloth.

Nor would it trouble me to see it found
    Of any fashion,
   That can be thought upon,
Square, oval, many-angled, long, or round :
    If close it be,
Fix'd, open, moveable, all's one to me.

And yet, methinks, at a Communion
    In uniformity
   There's greatest decency,
And that which maketh most for union :
    But needlessly
To vary, tends to the breach of charity.

Yet, rather than I'll give, I will not take
    Offence, if it be given,
   So that I be not driven
To thwart authority, a party make
    For faction,
Or side, but seemingly, in the action.

At a Communion I wish I might
    Have no cause to suspect
   Any, the least, defect
Of unity and peace, either in sight
    Apparently,
Or in men's hearts concealed secretly.

That, which ordained is to make men one,
    More than before they were,
   Should not itself appear,
Though but appear, distinctly diverse. None
    Too much can see
Of what, when most, yet but enough can be.

If others will dissent, and vary, who
    Can help it ?  If I may,
    As hath been done alway,
By the best, and most ; I will myself do so.
     Of one accord
The servants should be of one God, one Lord.


## COMMUNION PLATE.

Never was gold, or silver, graced thus
      Before.
To bring this body, and this blood, to us
     Is more
    Than to crown Kings,
    Or be made rings,
For star-like diamonds to glitter in.

No precious stones are meet to match this bread
      Divine.
Spirits of pearls dissolved would but dead
     This wine.
    This heavenly food
    Is too too good
To be compared to any earthly thing.

For such inestimable treasure can
      There be
Vessels too costly made by any man ?
     Sure he
    That knows the meat
    So good to eat,
Would wish to see it richly served in.

Although 'tis true, that sanctity's not tied
                    To state,
Yet sure Religion should not be envied
                    The fate
                    Of meaner worth,
                    To be set forth
As best becomes the service of a King.

A King unto whose cross all Kings must vail
                    Their crowns,
And at his beck in their full course strike sail:
                    Whose frowns
                    And smiles give date
                    Unto their fate,
And doom them, either unto weal, or woe.

A King, whose will is justice: and whose word
                    Is power,
And wisdom both.   A King, whom to afford
                    An hour
                    Of service truly
                    Perform'd, and duly,
Is to bespeak eternity of bliss.

When such a King offers to come to me
                    As food,
Shall I suppose his carriages can be
                    Too good?
                    No: Stars to gold
                    Turn'd, never could
Be rich enough to be employ'd so.

If I might wish then, I would have this bread,
                    This wine,

Vessell'd in what the Sun might blush to shed
                His shine.
    When he should see :
    But, till that be,
I'll rest contented with it, as it is.


## CHURCH-OFFICERS.

Stay. Officers in Church ? Take heed : it is
    A tender matter to be touch'd.
If I chance to say any thing amiss,
    Which is not fit to be avouch'd,
I must expect whole swarms of wasps to sting me,
Few, or no bees, honey or wax, to bring me.

Some would have none in Church do any thing
    As Officers, but gifted men ;
Others into the number more would bring,
    Than I see warrant for : So then,
All that I say, 'tis like, will censured be,
Through prejudice, or partiality.

But 'tis no matter ; If men censure me,
    They but my fellow-servants are :
Our Lord allows us all like liberty.
    I write, mine own thoughts to declare,
Not to please men : and, if I displease any,
I will not care, so they be of the Many.

## THE SEXTON.

The Church's key-keeper opens the door,
   And shuts it, sweeps the floor,
Rings bells, digs graves, and fills them up again ;
   All Emblems unto men,
Openly owning Christianity,
To mark, and learn many good lessons by.

O thou that hast the key of *David*, who
   Open'st and shuttest so,
That none can shut or open after thee,
   Vouchsafe thyself to be
Our soul's door-keeper, by thy blessed Spirit :
The lock and key 's thy mercy, not our merit.

Cleanse thou our sin-soil'd souls from the dirt and dust
   Of every noisome lust,
Brought in by the foul feet of our affections :
   The besom of afflictions,
With the blessing of thy Spirit added to it,
If thou be pleased to say it shall, will do it.

Lord, ringing changes all our bells hath marr'd,
   Jangled they have, and jarr'd
So long, they're out of tune, and out of frame,
   They seem not now the same.
Put them in frame anew, and once begin
To tune them so, that they may chime all in.

Let all our sins be buried in thy grave,
   No longer rant and rave,

As they have done, to our eternal shame,
        And the scandal of thy name.
Let's as door-keepers in thine house attend,
Rather than the throne of wickedness ascend.


## THE CLERK.

The Church's Bible-Clerk attends
    Her Utensils, and ends
    Her Prayers with Amen ;
Tunes Psalms, and to the Sacraments
    Brings in the Elements,
    And takes them out again ;
Is humble-minded, and industrious handed,
Doth nothing of himself, but as commanded.

All that the Vessels of the Lord
    Do bear with one accord
    Must study to be pure,
As they are : if his holy eye
    Do any spot espy,
    He cannot it endure ;
But most expecteth to be sanctified
In those come nearest him, and glorified.

Psalms then are always tuned best,
    When there is most exprest
    The holy Penman's heart :
All Music is but discord where
    That wants, or doth not bear
    The first and chiefest part.
Voices, without affections answerable,
When best, to God are most abominable.

Though in the blessed Sacraments
    The outward Elements
    Are but as husks and shells;
Yet he that knows the kernel's worth,
    If even those send forth
    Some Aromatic smells,
Will not esteem it waste, lest, Judas-like,
Through *Mary's* side he Christ himself should strike.

Lord, without whom we cannot tell
    How to speak or think, well,
    Lend us thy helping hand,
That what we do may pleasing be,
    Not to ourselves but thee,
    And answer thy command:
So that, not we alone, but thou may'st say
Amen to all our prayers, pray'd the right way.


## THE OVERSEER OF THE POOR.

THE Church's Almoner takes care, that none
    In their necessity
    Shall unprovided be
Of maintenance, or employment; those alone,
    Whom careless Idleness,
    Or riotous excess,
Condemns to needless want, he leaves to be
Chasten'd a while by their own poverty.

Thou gracious Lord, rich in thyself, dost give
    To all men liberally,
    Upbraiding none. Thine eye
Is open upon all. In thee we live,

We move, and have our being:
But there is more than seeing.
For the poor with thee: they are thy special charge;
To them thou dost thine heart and hand enlarge.

Four sorts of poor there are, with whom thou deal'st.
　　　　Though always differently,
　　　　With such indifferency,
That none hath reason to complain: thou heal'st
　　　　All those whom thou dost wound:
　　　　If there be any found
Hurt by themselves, thou leavest them to endure
The pain, till the pain render them fit for cure.

Some in the world are poor, but rich in faith:
　　　　Their outward poverty
　　　　A plentiful supply
Of inward comforts and contentments hath.
　　　　And their estate is blest,
　　　　In this above the rest,
It was thy choice, whilst thou on earth didst stay,
And hadst not whereupon thy head to lay.

Some poor in spirit in the world are rich,
　　　　Although not many such:
　　　　And no man needs to grutch
Their happiness, who to maintain that pitch,
　　　　Have a hard task in hand,
　　　　Nor easily can withstand
The strong temptations that attend on riches:
Mountains are more exposed to storms than ditches.

　Some rich in the world are spiritually poor,
　　　　And destitute of grace,

Who may perchance have place
In the Church upon earth; but Heaven's door
    Too narrow is to admit
    Such camels in at it,
Till they sell all they have, that field to buy,
Wherein the true treasure doth hidden lie.

Some spiritually poor, and destitute
    Of grace in the world are poor,
    Begging from door to door,
Accursed both in God's and man's repute,
    Till by their miseries
    Tutor'd they learn to prize
Hungering and thirsting after righteousness,
Whilst they're on earth, their greatest happiness.

Lord, make me poor in spirit, and relieve
    Me how thou wilt thyself,
    No want of worldly pelf
Shall make me discontented, fret and grieve.
    I know thine alms are best :
    But, above all the rest,
Condemn me not unto the hell of riches,
Without thy grace to countercharm the witches.


## THE CHURCH-WARDEN.

The Church's guardian takes care to keep
    Her buildings always in repair,
Unwilling that any decay should creep
    On them, before he is aware.

> Nothing defaced,
> Nothing displaced
> He likes; but most doth long and love to see
> The living stones order'd as they should be.
>
> Lord, thou not only supervisor art
> Of all our works, but in all those,
> Which we dare own, thine is the chiefest part;
> For there is none of us, that knows
> How to do well;
> Nor can we tell
> What we should do, unless by thee directed:
> It prospers not that's by ourselves projected.
>
> That which we think ourselves to mend, we mar,
> And often make it ten times worse:
> Reforming of Religion by war
> Is the chymic blessing of a curse.
> Great odds it is
> That we shall miss
> Of what we looked for: Thine ends cannot
> By any but by thine own means be got.
>
> 'Tis strange we so much dote upon our own
> Deformity, and others scorn;
> As if ourselves were beautiful alone;
> When that which did us most adorn
> We purposely
> Choose to lay by,
> Such decency and order, as did place us
> In highest esteem, and guard as well as grace us.
>
> Is not thy daughter glorious within,
> When clothed in needle-work without?

Or is't not rather both their shame and sin,
  That change her robe into a clout,
    Too narrow, and
    Too thin, to stand
Her need in any stead, much less to be
An ornament fit for her high degree?

Take pity on her, Lord, and heal her breaches;
  Clothe all her enemies with shame:
All the despite that's done unto her reaches
  To the dishonour of thy name.
    Make all her sons
    Rich precious stones,
To shine each of them in his proper place,
Receiving of thy fulness grace for grace.


## THE DEACON.

The Deacon! That's the Minister.
    True, taken generally;
  And without any sinister
    Intent, used specially,
He's purposely ordain'd to minister,
In sacred things, to another officer.

  At whose appointment, in whose stead,
    He doth what he should do,
  In some things, not in all: is led
    By Law, and custom too.
Where that doth neither bid, nor forbid, he
Thinks this sufficient authority:

Loves not to vary, when he sees
    No great necessity;
To what's commanded he agrees,
    With all humility;
Knowing how highly God submission prizes,
Pleased with obedience more than sacrifices.

Lord, thou didst of thyself profess
    Thou wast as one that served,
And freely choosest to go less,
    Though none so much deserved.
With what face can we then refuse to be
Enter'd thy servants in a low degree?

Thy way to exaltation
    Was by humility;
But we, proud generation,
    No difference of degree
In holy orders will allow, nay, more,
All holy orders would turn out of door.

But, if thy precept cannot do 't,
    To make us humbly serve,
Nor thy example added to 't,
    If still from both we swerve,
Let none of us proceed, till he can tell,
How to use the office of a Deacon well.

Which by the blessing of thy Spirit,
    Whom thou hast left to be
Thy Vicar here, we may inherit,
    And minister to thee,
Though not so well as thou may'st well expect,
Yet so, as thou wilt pleased be to accept.

## THE PRIEST.

The Priest, I say, the Presbyter, I mean,
        As now-a-days he's call'd
By many men : but I choose to retain
        The name wherewith install'd
He was at first in our own mother tongue :
And doing so, I hope, I do no wrong.

The Priest, I say, 's a middle Officer,
        Between the Bishop and
The Deacon ; as a middle offerer,
        Which in the Church doth stand
Between God and the people, ready press'd
In the behalf of both to do his best.

From him to them offers the promises
        Of mercy which he makes ;
For them to him doth all their faults confess,
        Their prayers and praises takes ;
And offers for them, at the throne of grace,
Contentedly attending his own place.

The Word and Sacraments, the means of grace,
        He duly doth dispense,
The flourishes of falsehood to deface,
        With truth's clear evidence ;
And sin's usurped tyranny suppress,
By advancing righteousness, and holiness.

The public censures of the Church he sees
        To execution brought:
But nothing rashly of himself decrees,
        Nor covets to be thought
Wiser than his superiors; whom always
He actively, or passively, obeys.

Lord Jesus, thou the Mediator art
        Of the new Testament,
And fully didst perform thy double part
        Of God and man, when sent
To reconcile the world, and to atone
'Twixt it and heaven, of two making one.

Yea, after the order of Melchisedeck,
        Thou art a Priest for ever.
With perfect righteousness thyself dost deck,
        Such as decayeth never.
Like to thyself make all thy Priests on earth,
Bless'd fathers to thy sons of the second birth.

Thou camest to do the will of him that sent thee,
        And didst his honour seek
More than thine own: well may it then repent thee,
        Being thyself so meek,
To have admitted them into the place
Of sons, that seek their fathers to disgrace.

Lord, grant that the abuse may be reform'd,
        Before it ruin bring
Upon thy poor despised Church, transform'd
        As if 'twere no such thing:
Thou that the God of order art, and peace,
Make cursed confusion and contention cease.

## THE BISHOP.

The Bishop? Yes, why not? What doth that name
Import that is unlawful, or unfit?
To say the Overseer is the same
In substance, and no hurt, I hope, in it:
 But sure if men did not despise the thing,
 Such scorn upon the name they would not fling.

Some Priests, some Presbyters, I mean, would be
Each Overseer of his several cure;
But one Superior, to oversee
Them altogether, they will not endure:
 This the main difference is, that I can see,
 Bishops they would not have, but they would be.

But who can show of old that ever any
Presbyteries without their Bishops were:
Though Bishops without Presbyteries many,
At first must needs be, almost every where?
 That Presbyters from Bishops first arose,
 To assist them, 's probable, not these from those.

However, a true Bishop I esteem
The highest Officer the Church on earth
Can have, as proper to itself, and deem
A Church without one an imperfect birth,
 If constituted so at first, and maim'd,
 If whom it had, it afterwards disclaim'd.

All order first from unity ariseth,
And th' essence of it is subordination:
Whoever this contemns, and that despiseth,
 May talk of, but intends not, reformation.

'Tis not of God, of Nature, or of Art,
To ascribe to all what's proper to one part.

To rule and to be ruled are distinct,
And several duties, severally belong
To several persons, can no more be link'd
In altogether, than amidst the throng
   Of rude unruly passions, in the heart,
   Reason can see to act her sovereign part.

But a good Bishop, as a tender father,
Doth teach and rule the Church, and is obey'd ;
And reverenced by it, so much the rather,
By how much he delighted more to lead
   All by his own example in the way,
   Than punish any, when they go astray.

Lord, thou the Bishop, and chief Shepherd, art
Of all that flock, which thou hast purchased
With thine own blood : to them thou dost impart
The benefits which thou hast merited,
   Teaching, and ruling, by thy blessed Spirit,
   Their souls in grace, till glory they inherit :

The stars which thou dost hold in thy right hand,
The Angels of the Churches, Lord, direct
Clearly thy holy will to understand,
And do accordingly : Let no defect
   Nor fault, no not in our new politics,
   Provoke thee to remove our candlesticks ;

But let thy Urim and thy Thummim be
Garments of praise to adorn thine holy ones :
Light and perfection let all men see
Brightly shine forth in those rich precious stones ;

Of whom thou wilt make a foundation,
To raise thy new Hierusalem upon.

And, at the brightness of its rising, let
All nations with thy people shout for joy :
Salvation for walls and bulwarks set
About it, that nothing may it annoy.
    Then the whole world thy Diocess shall be,
    And Bishops all but Suffragans to Thee.


## CHURCH FESTIVALS.

Marrow of time, Eternity in brief
Compendiums Epitomized, the chief
Contents, the Indices, the Title-pages
Of all past, present, and succeeding ages,
Sublimate graces, antedated glories,
    The cream of holiness,
      The inventories
    Of future blessedness,
The Florilegia of celestial stories,
Spirits of joys, the relishes and closes
Of Angels' music, pearls dissolved, roses
Perfumed, sugar'd honey-combs, delights
    Never too highly prized,
    The marriage rites,
    Which duly solemnized
Usher espoused souls to bridal nights,
Gilded sunbeams, refined Elixirs,
And quintessential extracts of stars :
Who loves not you, doth but in vain profess
That he loves God, or heaven, or happiness.

## THE SABBATH, OR LORD'S DAY.

Hail  
Holy  
King of days,  
The Emperor,  
Or Universal  
Monarch of time, the week's  
Perpetual Dictator.  
Thy  
Beauty  
Far exceeds  
The reach of art,  
To blazon fully;  
And I thy light eclipse,  
When I most strive to raise  
                [thee.  
What  
Nothing  
Else can be,  
Thou only art;  
Th' extracted spirit  
Of all Eternity,  
By favour antedated.

Vail  
Wholly  
To thy praise,  
For evermore  
Must the rehearsal  
Of all, that honour seeks,  
Under the world's Creator.  
My  
Duty  
Yet must needs  
Yield thee mine heart,  
And that not dully:  
Spirits of souls, not lips  
Alone, are fit to praise  
                [thee.  
That  
Slow thing  
Time by thee  
Hath got the start,  
And doth inherit  
That immortality  
Which sin anticipated.

    O  
    That I  
    Could lay by  
    This body so,  
    That my soul might be  
    Incorporate with thee,  
    And no more to six days owe.

## THE ANNUNCIATION, OR LADY-DAY.

Unto the music of the spheres
Let men, and Angels, join in concert theirs.
  So great a messenger
   From heaven to earth
   Is seldom seen,
  Attired in so much glory ;
  A message welcomer,
   Fraught with more mirth,
   Hath never been
  Subject of any story :
This by a double right, if any, may
  Be truly styled the world's birth-day.

  The making of the world ne'er cost
So dear, by much, as to redeem it lost.
   God said but, *Let it be*,
    And every thing
    Was made straightway,
   So as he saw it good :
   But ere that he could see
    A course to bring
    Man gone astray
   To the place where he stood,
His wisdom with his mercy, for man's sake,
  Against his justice part did take.

  And the result was this day's news
Able the messenger himself to amuse,
   As well as her, to whom
    By him 'twas told,
    That though she were

A Virgin pure, and knew
No man, yet in her womb
A son she should
Conceive and bear,
As sure as God was true.
Such high place in his favour she possess'd,
Being among all women bless'd.

But bless'd especially in this,
That she believed, and for eternal bliss
Relied on him, whom she
Herself should bear,
And her own son
Took for her Saviour.
And if there any be,
That when they hear,
As she had done,
Suit their behaviour,
They may be blessed, as she was, and say,
'Tis their Annunciation-day.

## THE NATIVITY, OR CHRISTMAS-DAY.

UNFOLD thy face, unmask thy ray,
Shine forth bright sun, double the day.
Let no malignant misty fume,
Nor foggy vapour, once presume
To interpose thy perfect sight
This day, which makes us love thy light
For ever better, that we could
That blessed object once behold,
Which is both the circumference,
And centre of all excellence .

Or rather neither, but a treasure
Unconfined without measure,
Whose centre, and circumference,
Including all pre-eminence,
Excluding nothing but defect,
And infinite in each respect,
Is equally both here and there,
And now, and then, and every where,
And always, one, himself, the same,
A being far above a name.
Draw nearer then, and freely pour
Forth all thy light into that hour,
Which was crowned with his birth,
And made heaven envy earth.
 Let not his birth-day clouded be,
 By whom thou shinest, and we see.


## THE CIRCUMCISION, OR NEW-YEAR'S DAY.

Sorrow betide my sins! Must smart so soon
Seize on my Saviour's tender flesh scarce grown
  Unto an eighth day's age?
  Can nothing else assuage
The wrath of heaven, but his infant-blood?
Innocent Infant, infinitely good!

Is this thy welcome to the world, great God!
No sooner born, but subject to the rod
  Of sin-incensed wrath?
  Alas! what pleasure hath
Thy Father's justice to begin thy passion,
Almost together with thine incarnation?

Is it to antedate thy death? to indite
Thy condemnation himself, and write
   The copy with thy blood,
   Since nothing is so good?
Or, is't by this experiment to try,
Whether thou beest born mortal, and canst die?

If man must needs draw blood of God, yet why
Stays he not till thy time be come to die?
   Didst thou thus early bleed
   For us to show what need
We have to hasten unto thee as fast;
And learn that all the time is lost that's pass'd?

'Tis true, we should do so: Yet in this blood
There's something else, that must be understood;
   It seals thy covenant,
   That so we may not want
Witness enough against thee, that thou art
Made subject to the Law, to act our part.

The sacrament of thy regeneration
It cannot be; it gives no intimation
   Of what thou wert, but we:
   Native impurity;
Original corruption, was not thine,
But only as thy righteousness is mine.

In holy Baptism this is brought to me,
As that in Circumcision was to thee:
   So that thy loss and pain
   Do prove my joy and gain.
Thy Circumcision writ thy death in blood:
Baptism in water seals my livelihood.

O blessed change! Yet, rightly understood,
That blood was water, and this water's blood.
  What shall I give again,
   To recompense thy pain?
Lord, take revenge upon me for this smart:
To quit thy fore-skin, circumcise my heart.


## THE EPIPHANY, OR TWELFTH-DAY.

Great, without controversy great,
  They that do know it will confess
  The mystery of godliness;
Whereof the Gospel doth intreat.

God in the flesh is manifest,
  And that which hath for ever been
  Invisible, may now be seen,
The eternal Deity new drest.

Angels to shepherds brought the news:
  And Wise men, guided by a Star,
  To seek the Sun, are come from far:
Gentiles have got the start of Jews.

The stable and the manger hide
  His glory from his own; but these
  Though strangers, his resplendent rays
Of Majesty divine have spied.

Gold, frankincense, and myrrh, they give;
  And worshipping him plainly show,
  That unto him they all things owe,
By whose free gift it is they live.

Though clouded in a veil of flesh,
   The Sun of Righteousness appears,
   Melting cold cares, and frosty fears,
And making joys spring up afresh.

O that his light and influence,
   Would work effectually in me
   Another new Epiphany,
Exhale, and elevate me hence:

That, as my calling doth require,
   Star-like I may to others shine;
   And guide them to that Sun divine,
Whose day-light never shall expire!


## THE PASSION, OR GOOD FRIDAY.

This day my Saviour died: and do I live?
   What, hath not sorrow slain me yet?
Did the immortal God vouchsafe to give
   His life for mine, and do I set
More by my wretched life, than he by his,
   So full of glory, and of bliss?

Did his free mercy, and mere love to me,
   Make him forsake his glorious throne,
And mount a cross, the stage of infamy,
   That so he might not die alone;
But dying suffer more through grief and shame,
   Than mortal men have power to name?

And can ingratitude so far prevail,
  To keep me living still? Alas!
Methinks some thorn out of his crown, some nail,
  At least his spear, might pierce, and pass
Thorough, and thorough, till it rived mine heart,
  As the right death-deserving part.

And doth he not expect it should be so?
  Would he lay down a price so great,
And not look that his purchases should grow
  Accordingly? Shall I defeat
His just desire? O no, it cannot be:
  His death must needs be death to me.

My life's not mine, but his: for he did die
  That I might live: yet died so,
That being dead he was alive; and I
  Thorough the gates of death must go
To live with him: yea, to live by him here
  Is a part in his death to bear.

Die then, dull soul, and if thou canst not die,
  Dissolve thyself into a Sea
Of living tears, whose streams may ne'er go dry,
  Nor turned be another way,
Till they have drown'd all joys, but those alone,
  Which sorrow claimeth for its own.

For sorrow hath its joys: and I am glad
  That I would grieve, if I do not:
But, if I neither could, nor would, be sad
  And sorrowful, this day, my lot
Would be to grieve for ever, with a grief
  Uncapable of all relief.

No grief was like that, which he grieved for me,
    A greater grief than can be told :
And like my grief for him no grief should be,
    If I could grieve so, as I would :
But what I would, and cannot, he doth see,
    And will accept, that died for me.

Lord, as thy grief and death for me are mine,
    For thou hast given them unto me ;
So my desires to grieve and die are thine,
    For they are wrought only by thee.
Not for my sake then, but thine own, be pleased
    With that, which thou thyself hast raised.

## THE RESURRECTION, OR EASTER-DAY.

Up, and away,
    Thy Saviour's gone before.
Why dost thou stay,
    Dull soul ? Behold, the door
Is open, and his Precept bids thee rise,
Whose power hath vanquish'd all thine enemies.

Say not, I live,
    Whilst in the grave thou liest :
He that doth give
    Thee life would have thee prize 't
More highly than to keep it buried, where
Thou canst not make the fruits of it appear.

Is rottenness,
    And dust so pleasant to thee,
That happiness,
    And heaven, cannot woo thee,
To shake thy shackles off, and leave behind thee
Those fetters, which to death and hell do bind thee?

In vain thou say'st,
    Thou art buried with thy Saviour,
If thou delay'st,
    To show, by thy behaviour,
That thou art risen with him; Till thou shine
Like him, how canst thou say his light is thine?

Early he rose,
    And with him brought the day,
Which all thy foes
    Frighted out of the way:
And wilt thou sluggard-like turn in thy bed,
Till noon-sun beams draw up thy drowsy head?

Open thine eyes,
    Sin-seized soul, and see
What cobweb-ties
    They are, that trammel thee;
Not profits, pleasures, honours, as thou thinkest;
But loss, pain, shame, at which thou vainly winkest.

All that is good
    Thy Saviour dearly bought
With his heart's blood;
    And it must there be sought,
Where he keeps residence, who rose this day:
Linger no longer then; up, and away.

## THE ASCENSION, OR HOLY THURSDAY.

Mount, mount, my soul, and climb, or rather fly
      With all thy force on high,
Thy Saviour rose not only, but ascended;
      And he must be attended
Both in his conquest and his triumph too.
      His glories strongly woo
His graces to them, and will not appear
In their full lustre, until both be there,

Where he now sits, not for himself alone,
      But that upon his throne
All his redeemed may attendants be
      Robed, and crown'd as he.
Kings without Courtiers are lone men, they say;
      And dost thou think to stay
Behind on earth, whilst thy King reigns in heaven,
Yet not be of thy happiness bereaven?

Nothing that thou canst think worth having's here.
      Nothing is wanting there,
That thou canst wish, to make thee truly blest.
      And, above all the rest,
Thy life is hid with God in Jesus Christ,
      Higher than what is high'st.
O grovel then no longer here on earth,
Where misery every moment drowns thy mirth.

But tower, my soul, and soar above the skies,
      Where thy true treasure lies.

Though with corruption and mortality
    Thou clogg'd and pinion'd be;
Yet thy fleet thoughts, and sprightly wishes, may
    Speedily glide away.
To what thou canst not reach, at least aspire,
Ascend, if not in deed, yet in desire.

## WHIT-SUNDAY.

NAY, startle not to hear that rushing wind,
    Wherewith this place is shaken:
Attend a while, and thou shalt quickly find,
    How much thou art mistaken;
      If thou think here
      Is any cause of fear.

Seest thou not how on those twelve reverend heads
    Sit cloven tongues of fire?
And as the rumour of that wonder spreads,
    The multitude admire
      To see it: and
      Yet more amazed stand

To hear at once so great variety
    Of language from them come,
Of whom they dare be bold to say they be
    Bred no where but at home,
      And never were
      In place such words to hear.

Mock not, profane despisers of the Spirit,
    At what's to you unknown:
This earnest he hath sent, who must inherit

All nations as his own :
That they may know
How much to him they owe.

Now that he is ascended up on high
To his celestial throne,
And hath led captive all captivity,
He'll not receive alone,
But likewise give
Gifts unto all that live ;

To all that live by him, that they may be,
In his due time, each one,
Partakers with him in his victory,
Nor he triumph alone ;
But take all his
Unto him where he is.

To fit them for which blessed state of glory,
This is his agent here :
To publish to the World that happy story,
Always, and every where,
This resident
Embassador is sent.

Heaven's lieger upon earth to counter-work
The mines that Satan made,
And bring to light those enemies, that lurk
Under sin's gloomy shade :
That hell may not
Still boast what it hath got.

Thus Babel's curse, confusion, is retrieved ;
Diversity of tongues
By this division of the Spirit relieved :

And to prevent all wrongs,
    One faith unites
    People of different rites.

O let his entertainment then be such
    As doth him best befit :
Whatever he requireth think not much
    Freely to yield him it :
      For who doth this
    Reaps the first-fruits of bliss.

## TRINITY SUNDAY.

GRACE, Wit, and Art, assist me ; for I see
The subject of this day's solemnity
    So far excels in worth,
      That sooner may
      I drain the sea,
      Or drive the day
      With light away,
    Than fully set it forth,
Except you join all three to take my part,
And chiefly Grace fill both my head and heart.

Stay, busy soul, presume not to enquire
Too much of what Angels can but admire,
    And never comprehend :
      The Trinity
      In Unity,
      And Unity
      In Trinity,
    All reason doth transcend.
God Father, Son God, and God Holy Ghost,
Who most admireth, magnifieth most.

And who most magnifies best understands,
And best expresseth what the heads, and hands,
   And hearts, of all men living,
      When most they try
      To glorify,
      And raise on high,
      Fall short, and lie,
   Grovelling below : Man's giving
Is but restoring by retail, with loss,
What from his God he first received in gross.

Faith must perform the office of invention,
And Elocution, struck with apprehension
   Of wonder, silence keep.
      Not tongues, but eyes
      Lift to the skies
      In reverend wise,
      Best solemnize
   This day : whereof the deep
Mysterious subject lies out of the reach
Of wit to learn, much more of Art to teach.

Then write *non Ultra* here ; Look not for leave
To speak of what thou never canst conceive
   Worthily, as thou shouldst :
      And it shall be
      Enough for thee,
      If none but he
      Himself doth see,
   Though thou canst not, thou wouldst
Make his praise glorious, who is alone
Thrice blessed one in three, and three in one.

## INVITATION.

Turn in, my Lord, turn in to me ;
    Mine heart's a homely place ;
But thou canst make corruption flee,
    And fill it with thy grace :
So furnished it will be brave,
And a rich dwelling thou shalt have.

It was thy lodging once before,
    It builded was by thee :
But I to sin set ope the door,
    It render'd was by me.
And so thy building was defaced,
And in thy room another placed.

But he usurps, the right is thine :
    O dispossess him, Lord.
Do thou but say, This heart is mine,
    He's gone at the first word.
Thy word's thy will, thy will's thy power,
Thy time is always ; now's mine hour.

    Now say to sin, depart :
    And, *Son, give me thine heart.*
Thou, that by saying, *Let it be,* didst make it,
Canst, if thou wilt, by saying, *Give 't me,* take it.

## COMFORT IN EXTREMITY.

Alas! my Lord is going,
        Oh my woe!
It will be mine undoing;
        If he go,
I'll run and overtake him:
        If he stay,
I'll cry aloud, and make him
        Look this way.
O stay, my Lord, my Love, 'tis I;
Comfort me quickly, or I die.

*Cheer up thy drooping spirits,*
        *I am here.*
*Mine all-sufficient merits*
        *Shall appear*
*Before the throne of glory*
        *In thy stead:*
*I'll put into thy story*
        *What I did.*
*Lift up thine eyes, sad soul, and see*
*Thy Saviour here. Lo, I am he.*

Alas! shall I present
        My sinfulness
To thee? thou wilt resent
        The loathsomeness.
*Be not afraid, I'll take*
        *Thy Sins on me,*
*And all my favour make*
        *To shine on thee.*

Lord, what thou'lt have me, thou must make me.
*As I have made thee now, I take thee.*


## RESOLUTION AND ASSURANCE.

Lord, thou wilt love me. Wilt thou not?
   Beshrew that not:
  It was my sin begot
That Question first: Yes, Lord, thou wilt:
   Thy blood was spilt
  To wash away my guilt,
Lord, I will love thee. Shall I not?
   Beshrew that not.
  'Twas death's accursed plot
To put that question; Yes, I will,
   Lord, love thee still,
  In spite of all my ill.
Then life, and love continue still
   We shall, and will,
  My Lord and I, until,
  In his celestial hill,
   We love our fill,
When he hath purged all mine ill.


## VOWS BROKEN AND RENEWED.

Said I not so, that I would sin no more?
  Witness my God, I did;
Yet I am run again upon the score:
  My faults cannot be hid.

What shall I do? Make vows, and break them still?
    'Twill be but labour lost?
My good cannot prevail against mine ill:
    The business will be crost.

O, say not so: thou canst not tell what strength
    Thy God may give thee at the length:
Renew thy vows, and if thou keep the last,
    Thy God will pardon all that's past.
Vow, whilst thou canst; while thou canst vow, thou may'st
Perhaps perform it, when thou thinkest least.

    Thy God hath not denied thee all,
    Whilst he permits thee but to call:
    Call to thy God for grace to keep
    Thy vows; and if thou break them, weep.
Weep for thy broken vows, and vow again:
Vows made with tears cannot be still in vain.
        Then once again
      I vow to mend my ways;
        Lord, say Amen,
      And thine be all the praise.

## CONFUSION.

O how my mind
    Is gravell'd!
        Not a thought,
That I can find,
    But's ravell'd
        All to nought.
Short ends of threads,
    And narrow shreds

Of lists,[1]
Knot snarled ruffs,
    Loose broken tufts
    Of twists,
Are my torn meditation's ragged clothing,
Which, wound and woven shape a suit for nothing:
One while I think, and then I am in pain
To think how to unthink that thought again.

How can my soul
    But famish
        With this food?
Pleasure's full bowl
    Tastes ramish,[2]
        Taints the blood.
Profit picks bones,
    And chews on stones
        That choke:
Honour climbs hills,
    Fats not, but fills
        With smoke.
And whilst my thoughts are greedy upon these,
They pass by pearls, and stoop to pick up pease.
Such wash and draff is fit for none but swine:
And such I am not, Lord, if I am thine.
    Clothe me anew, and feed me then afresh;
    Else my soul dies famish'd, and starved with flesh.

---

[1] 'Lists,' 'snarled ruffs,' &c.: old pieces of dress.—[2] 'Ramish:' what is called in Scotland 'wersh,' *i. e.*, tasteless.

## A PARADOX.

### THE WORSE THE BETTER.

WELCOME mine health : this sickness makes me well.
    Medicines adieu :
When with diseases I have list to dwell,
    I'll wish for you.

Welcome my strength : this weakness makes me able.
    Powers adieu :
When I am weary grown of standing stable,
    I'll wish for you.

Welcome my wealth : this loss hath gain'd me more.
    Riches adieu :
When I again grow greedy to be poor,
    I'll wish for you.

Welcome my credit : this disgrace is glory.
    Honours adieu :
When for renown and fame I shall be sorry,
    I'll wish for you.

Welcome content : this sorrow is my joy.
    Pleasures adieu :
When I desire such griefs as may annoy,
    I'll wish for you.

Health, strength, and riches, credit, and content,
Are spared best, sometimes, when they are spent :
Sickness and weakness, loss, disgrace, and sorrow,
Lend most sometimes, when they seem most to borrow.

Blest be that hand, that helps by hurting, gives
By taking, by forsaking me relieves.
If in my fall my rising be thy will,
Lord, I will say, *The worse the better still.*
I'll speak the Paradox, maintain thou it,
And let thy grace supply my want of wit.
    Leave me no learning that a man may see,
    So I may be a scholar unto thee.


## INMATES.

A HOUSE I had (a heart, I mean), so wide,
And full of spacious rooms on every side,
    That viewing it I thought I might do well,
Rather than keep it void, and make no gain,
Of what I could not use, to entertain
    Such guests as came : I did ; But what befell
    Me quickly in that course, I sigh to tell.

A guest I had (alas ! I have her still),
A great big bellied guest, enough to fill
    The vast content of hell, Corruption.
By entertaining her, I lost my right
To more than all the world hath now in sight.
    Each day, each hour, almost, she brought forth one,
    Or other base begot Transgression.

The charge grew great. I, that had lost before
All that I had, was forced now to score
    For all the charges of their maintenance
In dooms-day book : Whoever knew 't would say
The least sum there was more than I could pay,
    When first 'twas due, besides continuance,
    Which could not choose but much the debt enhance.

To ease me first I wish'd her to remove :
But she would not.  I sued her then above,
   And begg'd the Court of heaven but in vain
To cast her out.  No, I could not evade
The bargain, which she pleaded I had made,
   That, whilst both lived, I should entertain,
   At mine own charge, both her and all her train.

No help then, but or I must die or she ;
And yet my death of no avail would be :
   For one death I had died already then,
When first she lived in me : and now to die
Another death again were but to tie,
   And twist them both into a third, which when
   It once hath seized on, never looseth men.

Her death might be my life ; but her to kill
I, of myself, had neither power nor will.
   So desperate was my case.  Whilst I delay'd,
My guest still teem'd, my debts still greater grew ;
The less I had to pay, the more was due.
   The more I knew, the more I was afraid :
   The more I mused, the more I was dismay'd.

At last I learn'd, there was no way but one :
A friend must do it for me.  He alone,
   That is the Lord of life, by dying can
Save men from death, and kill Corruption :
And many years ago the deed was done,
   His heart was pierced ; out of his side there ran
   Sins' corrosives, restoratives for man.

This precious balm I begg'd, for pity's sake,
At Mercy's gate : where Faith alone may take

What Grace and Truth do offer liberally.
Bounty said, Come. I heard it, and believed;
None ever there complain'd but was relieved.
    Hope waiting upon Faith said instantly,
    That thenceforth I should live, Corruption die.

And so she died, I live. But yet, alas!
We are not parted: She is where she was,
    Cleaves fast unto me still, looks through mine eyes,
Speaks in my tongue, and museth in my mind,
Works with mine hands: her body's left behind,
    Although her soul be gone. My miseries
    All flow from hence; from hence my woes arise.

I loathe myself, because I leave her not;
Yet cannot leave her. No, she is my lot,
    Now being dead, that living was my choice;
And still, though dead, she both conceives and bears,
Many faults daily, and as many fears:
    All which for vengeance call with a loud voice,
    And drown my comforts with their deadly noise.

Dead bodies kept unburied quickly stink
And putrefy. How can I then but think
    Corruption noisome, even mortified?
Though such she were before, yet such to me
She seemed not. Kind fools can never see,
    Or will not credit, until they have tried,
    That friendly looks oft false intents do hide.

But mortified Corruption lies unmask'd,
Blabs her own secret filthiness unask'd,
    To all that understand her. That do none

In whom she lives embraced with delight :
She first of all deprives them of their sight ;
   Then dote they on her, as upon their own,
And she to them seems beautiful alone.

But woe is me! One part of me is dead ;
The other lives : Yet that which lives is led,
   Or rather carried captive unto sin,
By the dead part. I am a living grave,
And a dead body I within me have.
   The worse part of the better, oft doth win :
   And, when I should have ended, I begin.

The scent would choke me, were it not that grace
Sometimes vouchsafeth to perfume the place
   With odours of the Spirit, which do ease me,
And counterpoise Corruption. Blessed Spirit,
Although eternal torments be my merit,
   And of myself Transgressions only please me,
   Add grace enough being revived to raise me.

Challenge thine own. Let not intruders hold
Against thy right, what to my wrong I sold.
   Having no state myself, but tenancy,
And tenancy at will, what could I grant
That is not voided, if thou say, Avaunt!
   O speak the word, and make these inmates flee :
   Or, which is one, take me to dwell with thee.

## THE CURB.

Peace, rebel thought : dost thou not know thy King,
    My God, is here ?
Cannot his presence, if no other thing,
    Make thee forbear ?
Or were he absent, all the standers by
    Are but his spies :
And well he knows, if thou shouldst it deny,
    Thy words were lies.
If others will not, yet I must, and will,
    Myself complain.

My God, even now a base rebellious thought
    Began to move,
And subt'ly twining with me would have wrought
    Me from thy love :
Fain he would have me to believe, that Sin
    And thou might both
Take up my heart together for your Inn,
    And neither loathe
The other's company : a while sit still,
    And part again.

Tell me, my God, how this may be redrest :
    The fault is great,
And I the guilty party have confest,
    I must be beat.
And I refuse not punishment for this,
    Though to my pain ;
So I may learn to do no more amiss,
    Nor sin again :

Correct me, if thou wilt; but teach me then,
   What I shall do.

Lord of my life, methinks I heard thee say,
   That labour's eased:
The fault, that is confess'd, is done away,
   And thou art pleased.
How can I sin again, and wrong thee then,
   That dost relent,
And cease thine anger straight, as soon as men
   Do but repent?
No, rebel thought; for if thou move again,
   I'll tell that too.


### THE LOSS.

The match is made
      Between my Love and me:
And therefore glad
      And merry now I'll be.
Come, glory, crown
      My head;
         And, pleasures, drown
      My bed
         Of thorns in down.
Sorrow, be gone;
      Delight
         And joy alone
      Befit
         My honey-moon.
Be packing now,
      You cumb'rous cares, and fears:

Mirth will allow
        No room to sighs and tears.
Whilst thus I lay,
        As ravish'd with delight,
I heard one say,
        So fools their friends requite.
I knew the voice,
    My Lord's,
        And at the noise
    His words
        Did make, arose.
I look'd, and spied
    Each where,
        And loudly cried,
    My dear;
        But none replied:
Then to my grief
        I found my Love was gone,
Without relief,
        Leaving me all alone.


## THE SEARCH.

WHITHER, oh! whither is my Lord departed?
What can my Love, that is so tender-hearted,
Forsake the soul, which once he thorough darted,
        As if it never smarted?

No, sure my Love is here, if I could find him:
He that fills all can leave no place behind him.
But oh! my senses are too weak to wind him:
        Or else I do not mind him

O no, I mind him not so as I ought;
Nor seek him so as I by him was sought,
When I had lost myself: he dearly bought
      Me, that was sold for nought.

But I have wounded him, that made me sound;
Lost him again, by whom I first was found:
Him, that exalted me, have cast to the ground;
      My sins his blood have drown'd.

Tell me, oh! tell me (thou alone canst tell),
Lord of my life, where thou art gone to dwell:
For, in thy absence heaven itself is hell:
      Without thee none is well.

Or, if thou beest not gone, but only hidest
Thy presence in the place where thou abidest,
Teach me the sacred art, which thou providest
      For all them, whom thou guidest,

To seek and find thee by. Else here I'll lie,
Until thou find me. If thou let me die,
That only unto thee for life do cry,
      Thou diest as well as I.

For, if thou live in me, and I in thee,
Then either both alive, or dead must be:
At least I'll lay my death on thee, and see
      If thou wilt not agree.

For, though thou be the Judge thyself, I have
Thy promise for it, which thou canst not wave,
That who salvation at thine hands do crave,
      Thou wilt not fail to save.

Oh! seek, and find me then ; or else deny
Thy truth, thyself.  Oh! thou that canst not lie,
Show thyself constant to thy word, draw nigh.
    Find me Lo, here I lie.


## THE RETURN.

  Lo, now my Love appears ;
   My tears
  Have clear'd mine eyes : I see
   'Tis he.
Thanks, blessed Lord, thine absence was my hell ;
And, now thou art returned, I am well.

  By this I see I must
   Not trust
  My joys unto myself :
   This shelf,
Of too secure, and too presumptuous pleasure,
Had almost sunk my ship, and drown'd my treasure.

  Who would have thought a joy
   So coy
  To be offended so,
   And go
So suddenly away ?  As if enjoying
Full pleasure and contentment, were annoying.

  Hereafter I had need
   Take heed.
  Joys, amongst other things,
   Have wings,

And watch their opportunities of flight,
Converting in a moment day to night.

   But, is 't enough for me
    To be
   Instructed to be wise ?
    I'll rise,
And read a lecture unto them that are
Willing to learn, how comfort dwells with care.

   He that his joys would keep
    Must weep ;
   And in the brine of tears
    And fears
Must pickle them. That powder will preserve :
Faith with repentance is the soul's conserve.

   Learn to make much of care ·
    A rare
   And precious balsam 'tis
    For bliss ;
Which oft resides, where mirth with sorrow meets :
Heavenly joys on earth are bitter-sweets.

## INUNDATIONS.

  We talk of *Noah's* flood, as of a wonder ;
    And well we may ;
    The Scriptures say,
The water did prevail, the hills were under,
  And nothing could be seen but sea.

And yet there are two other floods surpass
        That flood, as far,
        As heaven one star,
Which many men regard, as little, as
        The ordinariest things that are.

The one is Sin, the other is Salvation :
        And we must need
        Confess indeed,
That either of them is an inundation,
        Which doth the deluge far exceed.

In Noah's flood he and his household lived :
        And there abode
        A whole Ark-load
Of other creatures, that were then reprieved :
        All safely on the waters rode.

But when Sin came, it overflowed all,
        And left none free :
        Nay, even he,
That knew no sin, could not release my thrall,
        But that he was made sin for me ;

And, when Salvation came, my Saviour's blood
        Drown'd Sin again,
        With all its train
Of evils, overflowing them with good,
        With good that ever shall remain.

O, let there be one other inundation,
        Let Grace o'erflow
        In my soul so,
That thankfulness may level with Salvation,
        And sorrow Sin may overgrow.

Then will I praise my Lord and Saviour so,
    That Angels shall
    Admire man's fall,
When they shall see God's greatest glory grow,
    Where Satan thought to root out all.


## SIN.

Sin, I would fain define thee; but thou art
    An uncouth thing:
    All that I bring
To show thee fully, shows thee but in part.

I call thee the transgression of the Law,
    And yet I read
    That Sin is dead
Without the Law; and thence its strength doth draw.

I say thou art the sting of death. 'Tis true:
    And yet I find
    Death comes behind:
The work is done before the pay be due.

I say thou art the devil's work; Yet he
    Should much rather
    Call thee father;
For he had been no devil but for thee.

What shall I call thee then? If death and devil,
    Right understood,
    Be names too good,
I'll say thou art the quintessence of evil.

## TRAVELS AT HOME.

OFT have I wish'd a traveller to be:
Mine eyes did even itch the sights to see,
That I had heard and read of. Oft I have
Been greedy of occasion, as the grave,
That never says, enough; yet still was crost,
When opportunities had promised most.
At last I said, What mean'st thou, wandering elf,
To straggle thus? Go travel first thyself.
Thy little world can show thee wonders great:
The greater may have more, but not more neat
And curious pieces. Search, and thou shalt find
Enough to talk of. If thou wilt, thy mind
Europe supplies, and Asia thy will,
And Afric thine affections. And if still
Thou list to travel further, put thy senses
For both the Indies. Make no more pretences
Of new discoveries, whilst yet thine own,
And nearest, little world is still unknown.
Away then with thy quadrants, compasses,
Globes, tables, cards, and maps, and minute glasses:
Lay by thy journals, and thy diaries,
Close up thine annals, and thine histories.
Study thyself, and read what thou hast writ
In thine own book, thy conscience. Is it fit
To labour after other knowledge so,
And thine own nearest, dearest, self not know?
Travels abroad both dear and dangerous are,
Whilst oft the soul pays for the body's fare:
Travels at home are cheap, and safe. Salvation
Comes mounted on the wings of meditation.
*He that doth live at home, and learns to know*
*God and himself, needeth no further go.*

## THE JOURNEY.

LIFE is a journey.  From our mothers' wombs,
As houses, we set out : and in our tombs,
As inns, we rest, till it be time to rise.
'Twixt rocks and gulfs our narrow foot-path lies .
Haughty presumption and hell-deep despair
Make our way dangerous, though seeming fair.
The world, with its enticements sleek and sly,
Slabbers our steps, and makes them slippery.
The flesh, with its corruptions, clogs our feet,
And burdens us with loads of lusts unmeet.
The devil, where we tread, doth spread his snares,
And with temptations takes us unawares.
Our footsteps are our thoughts, our words, our works :
These carry us along ; in these there lurks
Envy, lust, avarice, ambition,
The crooked turnings to perdition.
One while we creep amongst the thorny brakes
Of worldly profits ; and the devil takes
Delight to see us pierce ourselves with sorrow
To-day, by thinking what may be to-morrow.
Another while we wade, and wallow in
Puddles of pleasure : and we never lin[1]
Daubing ourselves, with dirty damn'd delights,
Till self-begotten pain our pleasure frights.
Sometimes we scramble to get up the banks
Of icy honour ; and we break our ranks
To step before our fellows ; though, they say,
He soonest tireth, that still leads the way.

[1] 'Lin' cease

Sometimes, when others justle and provoke us,
We stir that dust ourselves, that serves to choke us;
And raise those tempests of contention, which
Blow us beside the way into the ditch.
Our minds should be our guides; but they are blind:
Our wills outrun our wits, or lag behind.
Our furious passions, like unbridled jades,
Hurry us headlong to the infernal shades.
    If God be not our guide, our guard, our friend,
    Eternal death will be our journey's end.


## ENGINES.

MEN often find, when Nature's at a stand,
And hath in vain tried all her utmost strength,
That Art, her Ape, can reach her out a hand,
To piece her powers with to a full length.
    And may not Grace have means enough in store
    Wherewith to do as much as that, and more?

She may: she hath engines of every kind,
To work, what Art and Nature, when they view,
Stupendous miracles of wonder find,
And yet must needs acknowledge to be true;
    So far transcending all their power and might,
    That they amazed stand even at the sight.

Take but three instances; Faith, Hope, and Love.
Souls help'd by the perspective glass of Faith
Are able to perceive what is above
The reach of Reason: yea, the Scripture saith,
    Even him that is invisible behold,
    And future things, as if they'd been of old.

Faith looks into the secret Cabinet
Of God's eternal Counsels, and doth see
Such mysteries of glory there, as set
Believing hearts on longing, till they be
   Transform'd to the same image, and appear
   So altered, as if themselves were there.

Faith can raise earth to heaven, or draw down
Heaven to earth, make both extremes to meet,
Felicity and misery, can crown
Reproach with honour, season sour with sweet.
   Nothing's impossible to Faith : a man
   May do all things that he believes he can.

Hope founded upon Faith can raise the heart
Above itself in expectation
Of what the soul desireth for its part :
Then, when its time of transmigration
   Is delay'd longest, yet as patiently
   To wait, as if 'twere answer'd by and by.

When grief unwieldy grows, Hope can abate
The bulk to what proportion it will :
So that a large circumference of late
A little centre shall not reach to fill.
   Nor that, which giant-like before did strout,[1]
   Be able with a pigmy's pace to hold out.

Hope can disperse the thickest clouds of night,
That fear hath overspread the soul withal ;
And make the darkest shadows shine as bright
As the Sunbeams spread on a silver wall.
   Sin-shaken souls Hope anchor-like holds steady,
   When storm and tempests make them more than giddy.

[1] 'Strout' strut

Love led by Faith, and fed with Hope, is able
To travel through the world's wide wilderness;
And burdens seeming most intolerable
Both to take up, and bear with cheerfulness.
  To do, or suffer, what appears in sight
  Extremely heavy, Love will make most light.

Yea, what by men is done, or suffered,
Either for God, or else for one another,
Though in itself it be much blemished
With many imperfections, which smother,
  And drown, the worth, and weight of it; yet, fall
  What will, or can, Love makes amends for all.

Love doth unite, and knit, both make, and keep
Things one together, which were otherwise,
Or would be both diverse, and distant. Deep,
High, long, and broad, or whatsoever size
  Eternity is of, or happiness,
  Love comprehends it all, be 't more or less.

Give me this threefold cord of graces then,
Faith, Hope, and Love, let them possess mine heart,
And gladly I'll resign to other men
All I can claim by Nature or by Art.
  To mount a soul, and make it still stand stable,
  These are alone Engines incomparable.

# JACULA PRUDENTUM;

OR, OUTLANDISH PROVERBS, SENTENCES, ETC.

SELECTED BY MR GEORGE HERBERT, LATE
ORATOR OF THE UNIVERSITY
OF CAMBRIDGE.

# JACULA PRUDENTUM.

OLD men go to Death, Death comes to young men.
Man proposeth, God disposeth.
He begins to die, that quits his desires.
A handful of good life is better than a bushel of Learning.
He that studies his content, wants it.
Every day brings its bread with it.
Humble hearts have humble desires.
He that stumbles and falls not, mends his pace.
The house shows the owner.
He that gets out of debt, grows rich.
All is well with him who is beloved of his neighbours.
Building and marrying of Children are great wasters.
A good bargain is a pick-purse.
The scalded dog fears cold water.
Pleasing ware is half sold.
Light burdens, long borne, grow heavy.
The Wolf knows what the ill beast thinks.
Who hath none to still him, may weep out his eyes.
When all sins grow old, covetousness is young.
If ye would know a knave, give him a staff.
You cannot know wine by the barrel.
A cool mouth, and warm feet, live long.
A horse made, and a man to make.
Look not for musk in a dog's kennel.

Not a long day, but a good heart, rids work.
He pulls with a long rope, that waits for another's death.
Great strokes make not sweet music.
A cask and an ill custom must be broken.
A fat housekeeper makes lean executors.
Empty chambers make foolish maids.
The gentle Hawk half mans herself.
The Devil is not always at one door.
When a friend asks, there is no to-morrow.
God sends cold according to clothes.
One sound blow will serve to undo us all.
He loseth nothing, that loseth not God.
The German's wit is in his fingers.
At dinner my man appears.
Who gives to all, denies all.
Quick believers need broad shoulders.
Who remove stones, bruise their fingers.
Benefits please like flowers while they are fresh.
Between the business of life and the day of death, a space ought to be interposed.
All came from and will go to others.
He that will take the bird, must not scare it.
He lives unsafely that looks too near on things.
A gentle housewife mars the household.
A crooked log makes a straight fire.
He hath great need of a fool that plays the fool himself.
A Merchant that gains not, loseth.
Let not him that fears feathers come among wild-fowl.
Love, and a Cough, cannot be hid.
A Dwarf on a Giant's shoulder sees further of the two.
He that sends a fool, means to follow him.
Brabbling Curs never want sore ears.
Better the feet slip than the tongue.
For washing his hands, none sells his lands.

A Lion's skin is never cheap.
The goat must browse where she is tied.
Nothing is to be presumed on, or despaired of.
Who hath a Wolf for his mate, needs a Dog for his man.
In a good house all is quickly ready.
A bad dog never sees the Wolf.
God oft hath a great share in a little house.
Ill ware is never cheap.
A cheerful look makes a dish a feast.
If all fools had baubles, we should want fuel.
Virtue never grows old.
Evening words are not like to morning.
Were there no fools, bad ware would not pass.
Never had ill workman good tools.
He stands not surely that never slips.
Were there no hearers, there would be no backbiters.
Every thing is of use to a housekeeper.
When prayers are done, my Lady is ready.
Cities seldom change Religion only.
At length the Fox turns Monk.
Flies are busiest about lean horses.
Hearken to reason, or she will be heard.
The bird loves her nest.
Every thing new is fine.
When a dog is a drowning, every one offers him drink.
Better a bare foot than none.
Who is so deaf as he that will not hear?
He that is warm thinks all so.
At length the Fox is brought to the Furrier.
He that goes bare-foot must not plant thorns.
They that are booted are not always ready.
He that will learn to pray, let him go to Sea.
In spending lies the advantage.
He that lives well, is learned enough.

Ill vessels seldom miscarry.
A full belly neither fights nor flies well.
All truths are not to be told.
An old wise man's shadow is better than a young buzzard's
Noble housekeepers need no doors.                   [sword.
Every ill man hath his ill day.
Sleep without supping, and wake without owing.
I gave the mouse a hole, and she is become my heir.
Assail who will, the valiant attends.
Whither goest, grief? where I am wont.
Praise day at night, and life at the end.
Whither shall the Ox go where he shall not labour?
Where you think there is bacon, there is no chimney.
Mend your clothes, and you may hold out this year.
Press a stick, and it seems a youth.
The tongue walks where the teeth speed not.
A fair wife and a frontier Castle breed quarrels.
Leave jesting whiles it pleaseth, lest it turn to earnest.
Deceive not thy Physician, Confessor, nor Lawyer.
Ill natures, the more you ask them, the more they stick.
Virtue and a Trade are the best portion for children.
The Chicken is the Country's, but the City eats it.
He that gives thee a Capon, give him the leg and the wing.
He that lives ill, fear follows him.
Give a clown your finger, and he will take your hand.
Good is to be sought out, and evil attended.
A good paymaster starts not at assurances.
No Alchymy to saving.
To a grateful man give money when he asks.
Who would do ill ne'er wants occasion.
To fine folks a little ill finely wrapt.
To a fair day, open the window, but make you ready as to
A child correct behind, and not before.            [a foul.
Keep good men company, and you shall be of the number.

No love to a Father's.
The Mill gets by going.
To a boiling pot flies come not.
Make haste to an ill way, that you may get out of it.
A snow year, a rich year.
Better to be blind than to see ill.
Learn weeping, and thou shalt laugh gaining.
Who hath no more bread than need, must not keep a dog.
A garden must be looked unto, and dressed as the body.
The Fox, when he cannot reach the grapes, says, They are
Water trotted is as good as oats. [not ripe.
Though the Mastiff be gentle, yet bite him not by the lip.
Though a lie be well drest, it is ever overcome.
Though old and wise, yet still advise.
Three helping one another, bear the burthen of six.
Slander is a shipwreck by a dry Tempest.
Old wine and an old friend are good provisions.
Happy is he that chastens himself.
Well may he smell fire, whose gown burns.
The wrongs of a Husband or Master are not reproached.
Welcome evil, if thou comest alone.
Love your neighbour, yet pull not down your hedge.
The bit that one eats, no friend makes.
A drunkard's purse is a bottle.
She spins well that breeds her children.
Play with a fool at home, and he will play with you in the
Good is the *mora* that makes all sure. [market.
Every one stretcheth his legs according to his coverlet.
Autumnal Agues are long or mortal.
Marry your son when you will; your daughter when you can.
Dally not with money or women.
Men speak of the Fair as things went with them there.
The best remedy against an ill man, is much ground between
The mill cannot grind with water that's past. [both

Corn is cleaned with wind, and the soul with chastenings.
Good words are worth much, and cost little.
To buy dear is not bounty.
Jest not with the eye, or with Religion.
The eye and Religion can bear no jesting.
Without favour none will know you, and with it you will not
Buy at a fair, but sell at home.           [know yourself.
Cover yourself with your shield, and care not for cries.
A wicked man's gift hath a touch of his master.
None is a fool always, every one sometimes.
From a choleric man, withdraw a little; from him that says
Debtors are liars.                         [nothing, for ever.
Of all smells, bread: of all tastes, salt.
In a great River great fish are found: but take heed lest
  you be drowned.
Ever since we wear clothes, we know not one another.
God heals, and the Physician hath the thanks.
Hell is full of good meanings and wishings.
Take heed of still waters, the quick pass away.
After the house is finished, leave it.
Our own actions are our security, not others' judgments.
Think of ease, but work on.
He that lies long abed, his estate feels it.
Whether you boil snow or pound it, you can have but water
One stroke fells not an oak.                     [of it.
God complains not, but doth what is fitting.
A diligent Scholar, and the Master's paid.
Milk says to wine, Welcome, friend.
They that know one another, salute afar off.
Where there is no honour, there is no grief.
Where the drink goes in, there the wit goes out.
He that stays, does the business.
Alms never make poor. Or thus,
  Great alms-giving lessens no man's living.

Giving much to the poor, doth enrich a man's store.
It takes much from the account, to which his sin doth amount.
It adds to the glory both of soul and body.
Ill comes in by ells, and goes out by inches.
The smith and his penny both are black.
Whose house is of glass, must not throw stones at another.
If the old dog bark, he gives counsel.
The tree that grows slowly, keeps itself for another.
I wept when I was born, and every day shows why.
He that looks not before, finds himself behind.
He that plays his money, ought not to value it.
He that riseth first, is first drest.
Diseases of the eye are to be cured with the elbow.
A gentleman's greyhound and a salt-box, seek them at the
The hole calls the thief.                                    [fire.
A child's service is little, yet he is no little fool that de-
The river past, and God forgotten.                [spiseth it.
Evils have their comfort; good none can support (to wit)
    with a moderate and contented heart.
Who must account for himself and others, must know both.
He that eats the hard, shall eat the ripe.
The miserable man maketh a penny of a farthing, and the
    liberal of a farthing sixpence.
The honey is sweet, but the Bee stings.
Weight and measure take away strife.
The son full and tattered, the daughter empty and fine.
Every path hath a puddle.
In good years corn is hay, in ill years straw is corn.
Send a wise man on an errand, and say nothing unto him.
In life you loved me not, in death you bewail me.
Into a mouth shut flies fly not.
The heart's letter is read in the eyes.
The ill that comes out of our mouth falls into our bosom.
In great pedigrees there are Governors and Chandlers.

In the house of a fiddler, all fiddle.
Sometimes the best gain is to lose.
Working and making a fire doth discretion require.
One grain fills not a sack, but helps his fellows.
It is a great victory that comes without blood
In war, hunting, and love, men for one pleasure a thousand
Truth and oil are ever above. [griefs prove.
Reckon right, and February hath one-and-thirty days.
Honour without profit is a ring on the finger.
Estate in two Parishes is bread in two wallets.
Honour and profit lie not in one sack.
A naughty child is better sick than whole.
He that riseth betimes, hath something in his head.
Advise none to Marry or go to war.
To steal the Hog, and give the feet for alms.
The thorn comes forth with the point forwards.
One hand washeth another, and both the face.
The fault of the horse is put on the saddle.
The corn hides itself in the snow as an old man in furs.
The Jews spend at Easter, the Moors at marriages, the
Punishment is lame, but it comes. [Christians in suits.
Fine dressing is a foul house swept before the doors.
A woman and a glass are ever in danger.
An ill wound is cured, not an ill name.
The wise hand doth not all that the foolish mouth speaks.
On painting and fighting look aloof.
Knowledge is folly, except grace guide it.
The more women look in their glass, the less they look to
A long tongue is a sign of a short hand. [their house.
Marry a widow before she leave mourning.
The worst of law is, that one suit breeds twenty.
Providence is better than a rent.
What your glass tells you, will not be told by Counsel.
There are more men threatened than stricken.

A fool knows more in his house, than a wise man in another's.
I had rather ride on an ass that carries me, than a horse that throws me.
The hard gives more than he that hath nothing.
The beast that goes always, never wants blows.
Good cheap is dear.
It costs more to do ill than to do well.
Good words quench more than a bucket of water.
An ill agreement is better than a good judgment.
There is more talk than trouble.
Better spare to have of thine own, than ask of other men.
Better good afar off, than evil at hand.
Fear keeps the garden better than the gardener.
I had rather ask of my fire brown bread, than borrow of my neighbour white.
Your pot broken seems better than my whole one.
Let an ill man lie in thy straw, and he looks to be thy heir.
By suppers more have been killed than *Galen* ever cured.
While the discreet advise, the fool doth his business.
A mountain and a river are good neighbours.
Gossips are frogs, they drink and talk.
Much spends the traveller more than the abider.
Prayers and provender hinder no journey.
A well-bred youth neither speaks of himself, nor, being spoken to, is silent.
A journeying woman speaks much of all, and all of her.
The Fox knows much, but more he that catcheth him.
Many friends in general, one in special.
The fool asks much, but he is more fool that grants it.
Many kiss the hand they wish cut off.
Neither bribe, nor lose thy right.
In the world who knows not to swim, goes to the bottom.
Choose not a house near an Inn (viz for noise); or in a corner (for filth).

He is a fool that thinks not that another thinks.
Neither eyes on letters, nor hands in coffers.
The lion is not so fierce as they paint him.
Go not for every grief to the Physician, nor for every quarrel to the Lawyer, nor for every thirst to the pot.
Good service is a great enchantment.
There would be no great ones, if there were no little ones.
It is no sure rule to fish with a cross-bow.
There were no ill language, if it were not ill taken.
The groundsel speaks not, save what it heard at the hinges.
The best mirror is an old friend.
Say no ill of the year till it be past.
A man's discontent is his worst evil.
Fear nothing but sin.
The child says nothing, but what it heard by the fire.
Call me not an olive, till thou see me gathered.
That is not good language which all understand not.
He that burns his house, warms himself for once.
He will burn his house to warm his hands.
He will spend a whole year's rent at one meal's meat.
All is not gold that glisters.
A blustering night, a fair day.
Be not idle, and you shall not be longing.
He is not poor that hath little, but he that desireth much.
Let none say, I will not drink water.
He wrongs not an old man that steals his supper from him.
The tongue talks at the head's cost.
He that strikes with his tongue, must ward with his head.
Keep not ill men company, lest you increase the number.
God strikes not with both hands, for to the sea he made heavens, and to rivers fords.
A rugged stone grows smooth from hand to hand.
No lock will hold against the power of gold.
The absent party is still faulty.

Peace and patience, and death with repentance.
If you lose your time, you cannot get money nor gain.
Be not a Baker, if your head be of butter.
Ask much to have a little.
Little sticks kindle the fire; great ones put it out.
Another's bread costs dear.
Although it rain, throw not away thy watering pot.
Although the sun shine, leave not thy cloak at home.
A little with quiet is the only diet.
In vain is the mill-clack, if the Miller his hearing lack.
By the needle you shall draw the thread, and by that which is past, see how that which is to come will be drawn on.
Stay a little, and news will find you.
Stay till the lame messenger come, if you will know the truth of the thing.
When God will, no wind but brings rain.
Though you rise early, yet the day comes at his time, and [not till then.
Pull down your hat on the wind's side.
As the year is, your pot must seethe.
Since you know all, and I nothing, tell me what I dreamed [last night.
When the Fox preacheth, beware geese.
When you are an Anvil, hold you still; when you are a [hammer, strike your fill.
He that sows, trusts in God.
He that makes his bed ill, lies there.
He that labours and thrives, spins gold.
Poor and liberal, rich and covetous.
He that lies with the dogs, riseth with fleas.
He that repairs not a part, builds all.
A discontented man knows not where to sit easy.
Who spits against heaven, it falls in his face.
He that dines and leaves, lays the cloth twice.
Who eats his cock alone, must saddle his horse alone.
He that doth what he will, doth not what he ought.
He that will deceive the Fox must rise betimes.

He that is not handsome at twenty, nor strong at thirty, nor rich at forty, nor wise at fifty, will never be handsome, strong, rich, or wise.
He that lives well, sees afar off.
He that hath a mouth of his own, must not say to another,
He that will be served, must be patient. [Blow.
He that gives thee a bone, would not have thee die.
He that chastens one, chastens twenty.
He that hath lost his credit, is dead to the world.
He that hath no ill fortune, is troubled with good.
He that demands, misseth not, unless his demands be foolish.
He that hath no honey in his pot, let him have it in his
He that takes not up a pin, slights his wife. [mouth
He that owes nothing, if he makes not mouths at us, is
He that loseth his due, gets not thanks. [courteous.
He that believes all, misseth; he that believeth nothing, hits
A married man turns his staff into a stake. [not.
Pardons and pleasantness are great revenges of slanders.
If you would know secrets, look them in grief or pleasure.
Serve a noble disposition; though poor, the time comes that he will repay thee.
The fault is as great as he that is faulty.
If folly were grief, every house would weep.
He that would be well old, must be old betimes.
Sit in your place, and none can make you rise.
If you could run as you drink, you might catch a hare.
Would you know what money is, Go borrow some.
The morning Sun never lasts a day.
Thou hast death in thy house, and dost bewail another's.
All griefs with bread are less.
All things require skill but an appetite.
All things have their place, knew we how to place them.
Little pitchers have wide ears.
We are fools one to another.

This world is nothing except it tend to another.
There are three ways, the Universities, the Sea, the Court.
God comes to see without a bell.
Life without a friend, is death without a witness.
Clothe thee in war, arm thee in peace.
The horse thinks one thing, and he that saddles him another.
Mills and wives ever want.
The dog that licks ashes, trust not with meal.
The buyer needs a hundred eyes, the seller not one.
He carries well, to whom it weighs not.
The comforter's head never aches.
Step after step the ladder is ascended.
Who likes not the drink, God deprives him of bread.
To a crazy ship all winds are contrary.
Justice pleaseth few in their own house.
In time comes he, whom God sends.
Water afar off quencheth not fire.
In sports and journeys men are known.
An old friend is a new house.
Love is not found in the market.
Dry feet, warm head, bring safe to bed.
He is rich enough that wants nothing.
One father is enough to govern one hundred sons, but not a hundred sons one father.
Far shooting never killed bird.
An upbraided morsel never choked any.
Dearths foreseen come not.
An ill labourer quarrels with his tools.
He that falls into the dirt, the longer he stays there the fouler he is.
He that blames, would buy.
He that sings on Friday, will weep on Sunday.
The charges of building, and making of gardens are unknown.
My house, my house, though thou art small, thou art to me the Escurial.

A hundred load of thought will not pay one of debts.
He that comes of a hen must scrape.
He that seeks trouble never misses.
Being on sea, sail; being on land, settle.
Who doth his own business, fouls not his hands.
He that makes a good war, makes a good peace.
He that works after his own manner, his head aches not at
He that once deceives, is ever suspected.    [the matter.
Who hath bitter in his mouth, spits not all sweet.
He that hath children, all his morsels are not his own.
He that hath the spice, may season as he list.
He that hath a head of wax, must not walk in the sun.
He that hath love in his breast, hath spurs in his sides.
He that hath a fox for his mate, hath need of a net at his
He that respects not, is not respected.    [girdle.
He that hath right, fears; he that hath wrong, hopes.
He that hath patience, hath fat thrushes for a farthing.
Never was strumpet fair.
He that measures not himself is measured.
He that hath one hog, makes him fat; and he that hath one son, makes him a fool.
Who lets his Wife go to every feast, and his horse drink at every water, shall neither have good wife nor good horse.
He that speaks sows, and he that holds his peace gathers.
He that hath little is the less dirty.
He that lives most dies most.
He that hath one foot in the straw hath another in the spittle.
He that is fed at another's hand, may stay long ere he be
He that makes a thing too fine, breaks it.    [full.
He that bewails himself hath the cure in his hands.
He that would be well, needs not go from his own house.
Counsel breaks not the head.
Fly the pleasure that bites to-morrow.
He that knows what may be gained in a day, never steals.

Money refused loseth its brightness.
Health and money go far.
Where your will is ready, your feet are light.
A great ship asks deep waters.
Woe to the house where there is no chiding.
Take heed of the vinegar of sweet wine.
Fools bite one another, but wise men agree together.
Trust not one night's ice.
Good is good, but better carries it.
To gain teacheth how to spend.
Good finds good.
The dog gnaws the bone because he cannot swallow it.
The crow bewails the sheep, and then eats it.
Building is a sweet impoverishing.
The first degree of folly is to hold one's self wise, the second to profess it, the third to despise counsel.
The greatest step is that out of doors.
To weep for joy is a kind of Manna.
The first service a child doth his father is to make him foolish.
The resolved mind hath no cares.
In the kingdom of a cheater, the wallet is carried before.
The eye will have his part.
The good mother says not, Will you? but gives.
A house and a woman suit excellently.
In the kingdom of blind men, the one eyed is king.
A little Kitchen makes a large house.
War makes thieves, and peace hangs them.
Poverty is the mother of health.
In the morning mountains, in the evening fountains.
The back door robs the house.
Wealth is like rheum, it falls on the weakest parts.
The gown is his that wears it, and the world his that enjoys [it.
Hope is the poor man's bread.
Virtue now is in herbs, and stones, and words only.

Fine words dress ill deeds.
Labour as long-lived, pray as even dying.
A poor beauty finds more lovers than husbands.
Discreet women have neither eyes nor ears.
Things well fitted abide.
Prettiness dies first.
Talking pays no toll.
The master's eye fattens the horse, and his foot the ground.
Disgraces are like cherries, one draws another.
Praise a hill, but keep below.
Praise the sea, but keep on land.
In choosing a wife, and buying a sword, we ought not to
The wearer knows where the shoe wrings.     [trust another.
Fair is not fair, but that which pleaseth.
There is no jollity but hath a smack of folly.
He that's long a giving knows not how to give.
The filth under the white snow the sun discovers.
Every one fastens where there is gain.
All feet tread not in one shoe.
Patience, time, and money accommodate all things.
For want of a nail the shoe is lost, for want of a shoe the
  horse is lost, for want of a horse the rider is lost.
Weight justly and sell dearly.
Little wealth little care.
Little journeys and good cost bring safe home.
Gluttony kills more than the sword.
When children stand quiet, they have done some ill.
A little and good fills the trencher.
A penny spared is twice got.
When a knave is in a plum-tree, he hath neither friend nor
Short boughs, long vintage.                    [kin.
Health without money is half an ague.
If the wise erred not, it would go hard with fools.
Bear with evil, and expect good.

He that tells a secret, is another's servant.
If all fools wore white Caps, we should seem a flock of geese.
Water, fire, and soldiers, quickly make room.
Pension never enriched a young man.
Under water, famine; under snow, bread.
The Lame goes as far as your staggerer.
He that loseth is Merchant, as well as he that gains.
A jade eats as much as a good horse.
All things in their being are good for something.
One flower makes no garland.
A fair death honours the whole life.
One enemy is too much.
Living well is the best revenge.
One fool makes a hundred.
One pair of ears draws dry a hundred tongues.
A fool may throw a stone into a well, which a hundred wise men cannot pull out.
One slumber finds another.
On a good bargain think twice.
To a good spender God is the Treasurer.
A curst Cow hath short horns.
Music helps not the tooth-ache.
We cannot come to Honour under Coverlet.
Great pains quickly find ease.
To the counsel of fools a wooden bell.
The choleric man never wants woe.
Help thyself, and God will help thee.
At the game's end we shall see who gains.
There are many ways to fame.
Love is the true price of love.
Love rules his kingdom without a sword.
Love makes all hard hearts gentle.
Love makes a good eye squint.
Love asks faith, and faith firmness.
A sceptre is one thing, and a ladle another.

Great trees are good for nothing but shade.
He commands enough that obeys a wise man.
Fair words make me look to my purse.
Though the fox run, the chicken hath wings.
He plays well that wins.
You must strike in measure, when there are many to strike [on one anvil.
The shortest answer is doing.
It is a poor stake that cannot stand one year in the ground.
He that commits a fault, thinks every one speaks of it.
He that is foolish in the fault, let him be wise in the punish- [ment.
The blind eats many a fly.
He that can make a fire well, can end a quarrel.
The tooth-ache is more ease than to deal with ill people.
He that would have what he hath not, should do what he [doth not.
He that hath no good trade, it is to his loss.
The offender never pardons.
He that lives not well one year, sorrows seven after.
He that hopes not for good, fears not evil.
He that is angry at a feast, is rude.
He that mocks a cripple, ought to be whole.
When the tree is fallen, all go with their hatchet.
He that hath horns in his bosom, let him not put them on [his head.
He that burns most, shines most.
He that trusts in a lie, shall perish in truth.
He that blows in the dust, fills his eyes with it.
Bells call others, but themselves enter not into the Church.
Of fair things, the Autumn is fair.
Giving is dead, restoring very sick.
A gift much expected is paid, not given.
Two ill meals make the third a glutton.
The Royal Crown cures not the head-ache.
'Tis hard to be wretched, but worse to be known so.
It is better to be the head of a Lizard than the tail of a [Lion.
A feather in hand is better than a bird in the air.

Good and quickly seldom meet.
Happier are the hands compassed with iron, than a heart
Folly grows without watering.         [with thoughts.
If the staff be crooked, the shadow cannot be straight.
To take the nuts from the fire with the dog's foot.
He is a fool that makes a wedge of his fist.
Valour that parleys, is near yielding.
Thursday come, and the week is gone.
A flatterer's throat is an open sepulchre.
There is great force hidden in a sweet command.
The command of custom is great.
To have money is a fear, not to have it a grief.
The Cat sees not the mouse ever.
Little dogs start the hare, the great get her.
Willows are weak, yet they bind other wood.
A good payer is master of another's purse.
The thread breaks where it is weakest.
Old men, when they scorn young, make much of death.
God is at the end, when we think he is furthest off it.
A good Judge conceives quickly, judges slowly.
Rivers need a spring.
He that contemplates, hath a day without night.
Give losers leave to talk.
Gaming, Women, and Wine, while they laugh, they make
Loss embraceth shame.         [men pine.
The fat man knoweth not what the lean thinketh.
Wood half burnt is easily kindled.
The fish adores the bait.
He that goeth far hath many encounters.
Every bee's honey is sweet.
The slothful is the servant of the counters.
Wisdom hath one foot on land, and another on Sea.
The thought hath good legs, and the quill a good tongue.
A wise man needs not blush for changing his purpose.

The March sun raises, but dissolves not.
Time is the Rider that breaks youth.
The wine in the bottle doth not quench thirst.
The sight of a Man hath the force of a Lion.
An examined enterprise goes on boldly.
In every art it is good to have a master.
In every Country dogs bite.
In every Country the sun rises in the morning.
A noble plant suits not with a stubborn ground.
You may bring a horse to the river, but he will drink when and what he pleaseth.
Before you make a friend, eat a bushel of salt with him.
Speak fitly, or be silent wisely.
Skill and confidence are an unconquered army.
I was taken by a morsel, says the fish.
A disarmed peace is weak.
The balance distinguisheth not between gold and lead.
The persuasion of the fortunate sways the doubtful.
To be beloved is above all bargains.
To deceive one's self is very easy.
The reasons of the poor weigh not.
Perverseness makes one squint-eyed.
The evening praises the day, and the morning a frost.
The table robs more than a thief.
When age is jocund, it makes sport for death.
True praise roots and spreads.
Fears are divided in the midst.
The soul needs few things, the body many.
Astrology is true, but the Astrologers cannot find it.
Tie it well, and let it go.
Empty vessels sound most.
Send not a Cat for Lard.
Foolish tongues talk by the dozen.
Love makes one fit for any work.

A pitiful mother makes a scald head.
An old Physician, and a young Lawyer.
Talk much, and err much, says the Spaniard.
Some make a conscience of spitting in the Church, yet rob
An idle head is a box for the wind.       [the Altar.
Show me a liar, and I will show thee a thief.
A bean in liberty is better than a comfit in prison.
Show a good man his error, and he turns it to a virtue;
None is born Master.     [but an ill, it doubles his fault.
None is offended but by himself.
None says his Garner is full.
In the husband wisdom, in the wife gentleness.
Nothing dries sooner than a tear.
In a leopard the spots are not observed.
Nothing lasts but the Church.
A wise man cares not for what he cannot have.
It is not good fishing before the net.
He cannot be virtuous that is not rigorous.
That which will not be spun, let it not come between the
    spindle and the distaff.
When my house burns, it is not good playing at Chess.
No barber shaves so close but another finds work.
There is no great banquet, but some fares ill.
A holy habit cleanseth not a foul soul.
Forbear not sowing because of birds.
Mention not a halter in the house of him that was hanged.
Speak not of a dead man at the table.
A hat is not made for one shower.
No sooner is a Temple built to God, but the Devil builds
Every one puts his fault on the Times.   [a Chapel hard by.
You cannot make a windmill go with a pair of bellows.
Every one is weary, the poor in seeking, the rich in keeping,
Pardon all but thyself.       [the good in learning.
The escaped mouse ever feels the taste of the bait.

A little wind kindles, much puts out the fire.
Dry bread at home is better than roast meat abroad.
More have repented speech than silence.
The covetous spends more than the liberal.
Divine ashes are better than earthly meal.
Beauty draws more than oxen.
One father is more than a hundred Schoolmasters.
One eye of the master's sees more than ten of the servant's.
When God will punish, he will first take away the under-
A little labour, much health. [standing.
When it thunders, the thief becomes honest.
The tree that God plants, no wind hurts it.
Knowledge is no burthen.
It is a bold mouse that nestles in the cat's ear.
If a good man thrive, all thrive with him.
If the mother had not been in the oven, she had never sought her daughter there.
If great men would have care of little ones, both would last
Long jesting was never good. [long.
Though you see a Church-man ill, yet continue in the Church
Old praise dies, unless you feed it. [still.
If things were to be done twice, all would be wise.
Had you the world on your Chess-board, you could not fill
Suffer and expect. [all to your mind.
If fools should not fool it, they shall lose their season.
Love and business teach eloquence.
That which two will, takes effect.
He complains wrongfully on the sea, that twice suffers ship-
He is only bright that shines by himself. [wreck.
A valiant man's look is more than a coward's sword.
The effect speaks, the tongue needs not.
Divine grace was never slow.
Reason lies between the spur and the bridle.
It is a proud horse that will not carry his own provender.

Three women make a market.
Three can hold their peace if two be away.
It is an ill counsel that hath no escape.
All our pomp the earth covers.
To whirl the eyes too much, shows a kite's brain.
Comparisons are odious.
All keys hang not on one girdle.
Great businesses turn on a little pin.
The wind in one's face makes one wise.
All the arms of England will not arm fear.
One sword keeps another in the sheath.
Be what thou wouldst seem to be.
Let all live as they would die.
A gentle heart is tied with an easy thread.
Sweet discourse makes short days and nights.
God provides for him that trusteth.
He that will not have peace, God gives him war.
To him that will, ways are not wanting.
To a great night, a great Lanthorn.
To a child all weather is cold.
Where there is peace, God is.
None is so wise, but the fool overtakes him.
Fools give to please all but their own.
Prosperity lets go the bridle.
The Friar preached against stealing, and had a goose in his
To be too busy gets contempt.                [sleeve.
February makes a bridge, and March breaks it.
The best smell is bread, the best savour salt, the best love
A horse stumbles that hath four legs.    [that of children.
That is the best gown that goes up and down the house.
The Market is the best Garden.
The first dish pleaseth all.
The higher the Ape goes, the more he shows his tail.
Night is the mother of Councils.

God's Mill grinds slow, but sure.
Every one thinks his sack heaviest.
Drought never brought dearth.
All complain.
Gamesters and race-horses never last long.
It is a poor sport that is not worth the candle.
He that is fallen cannot help him that is down.
Every one is witty for his own purpose.
A little let lets an ill workman.
Good workmen are seldom rich.
By doing nothing we learn to do ill.
A great dowry is a bed full of brambles.
No profit to honour, no honour to Religion.
Every sin brings its punishment with it.
Of him that speaks ill, consider the life more than the word.
You cannot hide an eel in a sack.
Give not Saint *Peter* so much, to leave Saint *Paul* nothing.
You cannot flay a stone.
The chief disease that reigns this year is folly.
A sleepy master makes his servant a Lout.
Better speak truth rudely, than lie covertly.
He that fears leaves, let him not go into the wood.
One foot is better than two crutches.
Neither praise nor dispraise thyself, thy actions serve the
Better suffer ill, than do ill. [turn.
The constancy of the benefit of the year in their seasons
Soft and fair goes far. [argues a Deity.
Praise none too much, for all are fickle.
It is absurd to warm one in his armour.
Lawsuits consume time, and money, and rest, and friends.
Nature draws more than ten teams.
He that hath a wife and children, wants not business.
A ship and a woman are ever repairing.
He that fears death, lives not.

He that pities another, remembers himself.
He that doth what he should not, shall feel what he would not.
He that marries for wealth, sells his liberty.
He that once hits, is ever bending.
He that serves, must serve.
He that lends, gives.
He that preacheth, giveth alms.
He that cockers his child, provides for his enemy.
A pitiful look asks enough.
Who will sell the cow, must say the word.
Service is no inheritance.
The faulty stands on his guard.
A kinsman, a friend, or whom you entreat, take not to serve you, if you will be served neatly.
At Court, every one for himself.
To a crafty man, a crafty and a half.
He that is thrown, would ever wrestle.
He that serves well, needs not ask his wages.
Fair language grates not the tongue.
A good heart cannot lie.
Good swimmers at length are drowned.
Good land, evil way.
In doing we learn.
It is good walking with a horse in one's hand.
God, and Parents, and our Master, can never be requited.
An ill deed cannot bring honour.
A small heart hath small desires.
All are not merry that dance lightly.
Courtesy on one side only, lasts not long.
Wine-Counsels seldom prosper.
Weening is not measure.
The best of the sport is to do the deed, and say nothing.
If thou thyself canst do it, attend no other's help or hand.
Of a little thing, a little displeaseth.

God keep me from four houses, a Usurer's, a Tavern, a
He warms too near that burns.    [Spital, and a Prison.
In a hundred ells of contention, there is not an inch of love.
Do what thou oughtest, and come what come can.
Hunger makes dinners, pastime suppers.
In a long journey straw weighs.
Women laugh when they can, and weep when they will.
War is death's feast.
Set good against evil.
He that brings good news knocks hard.
Beat the Dog before the Lion.
Haste comes not alone.
You must lose a fly to catch a trout.
Better a snotty child than his nose wiped off.
He is not free that draws his chain.
He goes not out of his way that goes to a good inn.
There comes nought out of the sack, but what was there.
A little given seasonably, excuses a great gift.
He looks not well to himself that looks not ever.
He thinks not well, that thinks not again.
Religion, Credit, and the Eye are not to be touched.
The tongue is not steel, yet it cuts.
A white wall is the paper of a fool.
They talk of Christmas so long, that it comes.
That is gold which is worth gold.
It is good tying the sack before it be full.
Words are women, deeds are men.
Poverty is no sin.
A stone in a well is not lost.
He can give little to his servant that licks his knife.
Promising is the eve of giving.
He that keeps his own, makes war.
The wolf must die in his own skin.
Goods are theirs that enjoy them.

He that sends a fool, expects one.
He that can stay, obtains.
He that gains well and spends well, needs no account book.
He that endures, is not overcome.
He that gives all before he dies, provides to suffer.
He that talks much of his happiness, summons grief.
He that loves the tree, loves the branch.
Who hastens a glutton, chokes him.
Who praiseth Saint *Peter*, doth not blame Saint *Paul*.
He that hath not the craft, let him shut up shop.
He that knows nothing, doubts nothing.
Green wood makes a hot fire.
He that marries late, marries ill.
He that passeth a winter's day, escapes an enemy.
The rich knows not who is his friend.
A morning Sun, and a Wine-bred child, and a Latin-bred woman, seldom end well.
To a close shorn sheep, God gives wind by measure.
A pleasure long expected, is dear enough sold.
A poor man's cow dies, a rich man's child.
The cow knows not what her tail is worth till she have lost it.
Choose a horse made, and a wife to make.
It is an ill air where we gain nothing.
He hath not lived, that lives not after death.
So many men in court, and so many strangers.
He quits his place well, that leaves his friend here.
That which sufficeth is not little.
Good news may be told at any time, but ill in the morning.
He that would be a Gentleman, let him go to an assault.
Who pays the Physician, does the cure.
None knows the weight of another's burthen.
Every one hath a fool in his sleeve.
One hour's sleep before midnight is worth three after.
In a retreat the lame are foremost.

It is more pain to do nothing than something.
Amongst good men two men suffice.
There needs a long time to know the world's pulse.
The offspring of those that are very young, or very old, lasts
A tyrant is most tyrant to himself. [not.
Too much taking heed is loss.
Craft against craft, makes no living.
The Reverend are ever before.
*France* is a meadow that cuts thrice a year.
It is easier to build two chimneys, than to maintain one.
The Court hath no Almanack.
He that will enter into Paradise, must have a good key.
When you enter into a house, leave the anger ever at the
He hath no leisure who useth it not. [door.
It is a wicked thing to make a dearth one's garner.
He that deals in the world needs four sieves.
Take heed of an ox before, of a horse behind, of a monk on
The year doth nothing else but open and shut. [all sides.
The ignorant hath an Eagle's wings and an Owl's eyes.
There are more Physicians in health than drunkards.
The wife is the key of the house.
The Law is not the same at morning and at night.
War and Physic are governed by the eye.
Half the world knows not how the other half lies.
Death keeps no Calendar.
Ships fear fire more than water.
The least foolish is wise.
The chief box of health is time.
Silks and Satins put out the fire in the chimney.
The first blow is as much as two.
The life of man is a winter way.
The way is an ill neighbour.
An old man's staff is the rapper of death's door.
Life is half spent, before we know what it is.

The singing man keeps his shop in his throat.
The body is more dressed than the soul.
The body is sooner dressed than the soul.
The Physician owes all to the patient, but the patient owes nothing to him but a little money.
The little cannot be great, unless he devour many.
The Choleric drinks, the Melancholic eats, the Phlegmatic Time undermines us. [sleeps.
The Apothecary's mortar spoils the luter's music.
Conversation makes one what he is.
The deaf gains the injury.
Years know more than books.
Wine is a turn-coat (first a friend, then an enemy).
Wine ever pays for his lodging.
Wine makes all sorts of creatures at table.
Wine that cost nothing is digested before it be drunk.
Trees eat but once.
Armour is light at table.
Good horses make short miles.
Castles are Forests of stones.
The dainties of the great are the tears of the poor.
Parsons are souls' waggoners.
Children when they are little make parents fools, when they are great they make them mad.
The Master absent, and the house dead.
Dogs are fine in the field.
Sins are not known till they be acted.
Thorns whiten, yet do nothing.
All are presumed good till they are found in a fault.
The great put the little on the hook.
The great would have none great, and the little all little.
The Italians are wise before the deed, the Germans in the deed, the French after the deed.
Every mile is two in winter.

Spectacles are death's Arquebuse.
Lawyers' houses are built on the heads of fools.
The house is a fine house when good folks are within.
The best bred have the best portion.
The first and last frosts are the worst.
Gifts enter every where without a wimble.
Princes have no way.
Knowledge makes one laugh, but wealth makes one dance.
The Citizen is at his business before he rise.
The eyes have one language every where.
It is better to have wings than horns.
Better be a fool than a knave.
Count not four, except you have them in a wallet.
To live peaceably with all, breeds good blood.
You may be on land, yet not in a garden.
You cannot make the fire so low, but it will get out.
We know not who lives or dies.
An ox is taken by the horns, and a man by the tongue.
Many things are lost for want of asking.
No Church-yard is so handsome, that a man would desire straight to be buried there.
Cities are taken by the ears.
Once a year a man may say, On his conscience.
We leave more to do when we die, than we have done.
With customs we live well, but laws undo us.
To speak of a Usurer at the table, mars the wine.
Pains to get, care to keep, fear to lose.
For a morning rain, leave not your journey.
One fair day in winter makes not birds merry.
He that learns a trade, hath a purchase made.
When all men have what belongs to them, it cannot be much.
Though God take the sun out of the heaven, yet we must have patience.
When a man sleeps, his head is in his stomach.

When God is made the master of a family, he orders the disorderly.
When one is on horseback, he knows all things.
When a Lackey comes to hell's door, the Devils lock the gates.
He that is at ease, seeks dainties.
He that hath charge of souls, transports them not in bundles.
He that tells his wife news, is but newly married.
He that is in a town in May loseth his Spring.
He that is in a Tavern, thinks he is in a vine-garden.
He that praiseth himself, spattereth himself.
He that is surprised with the first frost, feels it all the winter after.
He that is a master, must serve (another).
He a beast doth die, that hath done no good to his country.
He that follows the Lord, hopes to go before.
He that dies without the company of good men, puts not himself into a good way.
Who hath no haste in his business, mountains to him seem valleys.
Who hath no head, needs no heart.
Speak not of my debts, unless you mean to pay them.
He that is not in the wars, is not out of danger.
He that gives me small gifts, would have me live.
He that is his own Counsellor, knows nothing sure but what he hath laid out.
He that hath lands, hath quarrels.
He that goes to bed thirsty, riseth healthy.
Who will make a door of gold, must knock a nail every day.
A trade is better than service.
He that lives in hope, danceth without music.
To review one's store is to mow twice.
Saint *Luke* was a Saint and a Physician, yet is dead.
Without business, debauchery.
Without danger we cannot get beyond danger.
Health and sickness surely are men's double enemies.
If gold knew what gold is, gold would get gold, I wis.
Little losses amaze, great tame.
Choose none for thy servant who hath served thy betters.

Service without reward is punishment.
If the husband be not at home, there is nobody.
An oath that is not to be made, is not to be kept.
The eye is bigger than the belly.
If you would be at ease, all the world is not.
Were it not for the bone in the leg, all the world would turn Carpenters (to make them crutches).
If you must fly, fly well.
All that shakes falls not.
All beasts of prey are strong, or treacherous.
If the brain sows not corn, it plants thistles.
A man well mounted is ever Choleric.
Every one is a master and servant.
A piece of a Church-yard fits every body.
One mouth doth nothing without another.
A master of straw eats a servant of steel.
An old cat sports not with her prey.
A woman conceals what she knows not.
He that wipes the child's nose, kisseth the mother's cheek.[1]
Gentility is nothing but Ancient Riches.
To go where the King goes afoot; *i. e.*, to the stool.
To go upon the Franciscans' Hackney; *i. e.*, on foot.
*Amiens* was taken by the Fox, and retaken by the Lion.
After Death the Doctor.
Ready money is a ready Medicine.
It is the Philosophy of the Distaff.
It is a sheep of *Beery*, it is marked on the nose: applied to those that have a blow.
To build castles in Spain.
An Idle youth, a needy Age.
Silk doth quench the fire in the Kitchen.
The words ending in *ique*, do mock the Physician; as Hectique, Paralytique, Apoplectique, Lethargique.

---

[1] The proverbs which follow were added to the second edition.

He that trusts much Obliges much, says the Spaniard.
He that thinks amiss, concludes worse.
A man would live in Italy (a place of pleasure), but he would choose to die in Spain, where they say the Catholic Religion is professed with greatest strictness.
Whatsoever was the father of a disease, an ill diet was the Frenzy, Heresy, and Jealousy, seldom cured.     [mother.
There is no heat of affection but is joined with some idleness of brain, says the Spaniard.
The War is not done so long as my Enemy lives.
Some evils are cured by contempt.
Power seldom grows old at Court.
Danger itself the best remedy for danger.
Favour will as surely perish as life.
Fear the Beadle of the Law.
For the same man to be a heretic and a good subject, is in-
Heresy is the school of pride.     [compossible.
Heresy may be easier kept out than shook off.
Infants' manners are moulded more by the example of Parents, than by stars at their nativities.
They favour learning whose actions are worthy of a learned
Modesty sets off one newly come to honour.     [pen.
No naked man is sought after to be rifled.
There is no such conquering weapon as the necessity of con-
Nothing secure unless suspected.     [quering.
No tie can oblige the perfidious.
Spies are the ears and eyes of Princes.
The life of spies is to know, not be known.
Religion a stalking-horse to shoot other fowl.
It is a dangerous fire begins in the bed straw.
Covetousness breaks the bag.
Fear keeps and looks to the vineyard, and not the owner.
The noise is greater than the nuts.
Two sparrows on one Ear of Corn make an ill agreement.

The world is now-a-days, God save the Conqueror.
Unsound minds, like unsound Bodies, if you feed, you poison.
Not only ought fortune to be pictured on a wheel, but every thing else in this world.
All covet, all lose.
Better is one *Accipe*, than twice to say, *Dabo tibi*.
An Ass endures his burden, but not more than his burden.
Threatened men eat bread, says the Spaniard.
The beads in the Hand, and the Devil in Capuch; or, cape of the cloak.
He that will do thee a good turn, either he will be gone or [die.
I escaped the Thunder, and fell into the Lightning.
A man of a great memory without learning, hath a rock and a spindle, and no staff to spin.
The death of wolves is the safety of the sheep.
He that is once born, once must die.
He that hath but one eye, must be afraid to lose it.
He that makes himself a sheep, shall be eat by the wolf.
He that steals an egg, will steal an ox.
He that will be surety, shall pay.
He that is afraid of leaves, goes not to the wood.
In the mouth of a bad dog falls often a good bone.
Those that God loves, do not live long.
Still fisheth he that catcheth one.
All flesh is not venison.
A City that parleys is half gotten.
A dead bee maketh no honey.
An old dog barks not in vain.
They that hold the greatest farms, pay the least rent: applied to rich men that are unthankful to God.
Old Camels carry young Camels' skins to the market.
He that hath time and looks for better time, time comes that he repents himself of time.
Words and feathers the wind carries away.

Of a pig's tail you can never make a good shaft.
The Bath of the Blackamoor hath sworn not to whiten.
To a greedy eating horse a short halter.
The Devil divides the world between Atheism and Supersti-
Such a Saint, such an offering. [tion.
We do it soon enough, if that we do be well.
Cruelty is more cruel, if we defer the pain.
What one day gives us, another takes away from us.
To seek in a Sheep five feet when there are but four.
A scabbed horse cannot abide the comb.
God strikes with his finger, and not with all his arm.
God gives his wrath by weight, and without weight his mercy.
Of a new Prince, new bondage.
Fortune to one is Mother, to another is Step-mother.
There is no man, though never so little, but sometimes he
New things are fair. [can hurt.
The horse that draws after him his halter, is not altogether
No love is foul, nor prison fair. [escaped.
We must recoil a little, to the end we may leap the better.
No day so clear, but hath dark clouds.
No hair so small, but hath his shadow.
A wolf will never make war against another wolf.
We must love, as looking one day to hate.
It is good to have some friends both in heaven and hell.
It is very hard to shave an egg.
It is good to hold the ass by the bridle.
The healthful man can give counsel to the sick.
The death of a young wolf doth never come too soon.
The rage of a wild boar is able to spoil more than one wood.
Virtue flies from the heart of a Mercenary man.
The wolf eats oft of the sheep that hath been warned.
The mouse that hath but one hole is quickly taken.
To play at Chess when the house is on fire.
The itch of disputing is the scab of the Church.

Follow not truth too near the heels, lest it dash out thy teeth.
Either wealth is much increased, or moderation is much
When war begins, then hell openeth. [decayed.
Say to pleasure, Gentle *Eve*, I will none of your apple.
There is a remedy for every thing, could men find it.
There is an hour wherein a man might be happy all his life,
 could he find it.
Great Fortune brings with it Great misfortune.
A fair day in winter is the mother of a storm.
Woe be to him that reads but one book.
Tithe, and be rich.

Take heed of
{
The wrath of a mighty man, and the tumult of the
Mad folks in a narrow place. [people.
Credit decayed, and people that have nothing.
A young wench, a prophetess, and a Latin-bred woman.
A person marked, and a Widow thrice married.
Foul dirty ways, and long sickness.
Wind that comes in at a hole, and a reconciled Enemy.
A Step-mother; the very name of her sufficeth.
}

Critics are like brushers of Noblemen's clothes.
He is a great Necromancer, for he asks counsel of the
 Dead: *i. e.*, books.
A man is known to be mortal by two things, Sleep and
Princes are venison in Heaven. [Lust.
Love without end, hath no end, says the Spaniard: meaning,
 if it were not begun on particular ends, it would last.
Stay a while, that we may make an end the sooner.
Presents of love fear not to be ill taken of strangers.
To seek these things is lost labour: Geese in an oil pot,
 fat Hogs among Jews, and Wine in a fishing net.
Some men plant an opinion they seem to eradicate.
The Philosophy of Princes is to dive into the Secrets of
 men, leaving the secrets of nature to those that have
 spare time.

States have their conversions and periods as well as natural
Great deservers grow Intolerable presumers.     [bodies.
The love of money and the love of learning rarely meet.
Trust no friend with that you need, fear him if he were your enemy.
Some had rather lose their friend than their Jest.
Marry your daughters betimes, less they marry themselves.
Soldiers in peace are like chimneys in summer.
Here is a talk of the Turk and the Pope, but my next neighbour doth me more harm than either of them both.
Civil Wars of *France* made a million of Atheists, and thirty thousand Witches.
We Bachelors laugh and show our teeth, but you married men laugh till your hearts ache.
The Devil never assails a man except he find him either void of knowledge, or of the fear of God.
There is nobody will go to hell for company.
Much money makes a Country poor, for it sets a dearer price upon every thing.
The virtue of a coward is suspicion.
A man's destiny is always dark.
Every man's censure is first moulded in his own nature.
Money wants no followers.
Your thoughts close, and your countenance loose.
Whatever is made by the hand of man, by the hand of man may be overturned.

THE END.

www.ingramcontent.com/pod-product-compliance
Lightning Source LLC
Chambersburg PA
CBHW071227230426
43668CB00011B/1339